I0869060

The Torah Commentary of
Rabbi Shlomo Carlebach

אבן שלמה

THE TORAH COMMENTARY OF

RABBI SHLOMO CARLEBACH

Edited by

RABBI SHLOMO KATZ

שמות

Exodus

THE RABBI SHLOMO CARLEBACH FOUNDATION

URIM PUBLICATIONS

Jerusalem · New York

The Torah Commentary of Rabbi Shlomo Carlebach: Exodus

Edited by Shlomo Katz

Copyright © 2020 by The Rabbi Shlomo Carlebach Foundation

All rights reserved. No part of this work may be used or reproduced in any manner whatsoever without written permission from the copyright owner, except in the case of brief quotations embodied in reviews and articles.

Typeset by Ariel Walden

Printed in Israel
First Edition

ISBN 978-1-60280-397-8
The Torah Commentary of Rabbi Shlomo Carlebach:
Genesis – Part I: ISBN 978-965-524-074-0
Genesis – Part II: ISBN 978-965-524-121-1

Library of Congress Control Number: 2012426265

The Rabbi Shlomo Carlebach Foundation

Urim Publications
P.O. Box 52287, Jerusalem 91521 Israel

www.ShlomoCarlebachFoundation.org

www.UrimPublications.com

CONTENTS

FOREWORD TO SEFER SH'MOS

In honor of Rabbi Shlomo Carlebach *zt"l* and in perpetuation of his life's work, we give thanks to everyone who contributed to the publication of this volume of Sh'mos in the Even Shlomo Chumash series.

Sefer Sh'mos has a special connection to Reb Shlomo.

As his first commentary in this volume tells us,

> "And these are the names of the children of Israel who were coming down to Egypt." (Sh'mos 1:1) The story of our exile in the book of Exodus is called *Sh'mos,* "names." In order to go into exile and come out alive, you have to hold on to your name.

Rabbi Shlomo Carlebach was personally responsible for helping generations of young Jews hold on to their names in the exile of the diaspora from the early-60s through the mid-90s. His stirring melodies and deep Torah insights brought tens of thousands back to their spiritual roots.

A number of years ago an ambitious project was launched by Nachman Futterman, Rabbi Shlomo Katz and Shema Yisrael Witt, together with Rabbi Shlomo Carlebach's daughters, Neshama and Nedara, to acquire, preserve, archive and disseminate Reb Shlomo's teachings.

Many privately recorded collections of Reb Shlomo's teachings, spanning four decades, have been contributed by *chevre* from all over the globe.

The selection of teachings in this book was compiled by Rabbi Shlomo

Katz using only a small part of the more than 16,000 audio and 1,000 video hours that have been digitized to date.

The fire that destroyed the Rabbi Shlomo Carlebach Moshav – Meor Modiim – bears testament to the wisdom of this project as thousands of hours of Shlomo's irreplaceable and transformative teachings were consumed in the fire and would – G-d forbid - have been lost forever.

Additionally, we take this opportunity to appeal to anyone who has recordings, or any other materials, to please share their content with the Rabbi Shlomo Carlebach Foundation so that we we can add to the material being collected for the archive.

Through the eyes of a new generation, the older generation is rediscovering the deep and joyous approach to Judaism that Reb Shlomo brought to the world.

More than anything, the central message that Reb Shlomo brought to the world was the responsibility we have to value ourselves and to improve the world by showering it with the light of joy and love.

www.shlomocarlebachfoundation.org

שמות

SH'MOS

שמות

לעילוי נשמות הורינו:

אבינו מורנו ר׳ צבי הירש בן ר׳ יחזקאל ומרת אסתר
אמנו מורתנו מרת פראדל רחל בת ר׳ מרדכי יוסף ומרת בילה

Whose love and devotion for us was constant,
allowing us to be proud and thankful Jews,
filled with "Simchat HaChaim,"
an inner, deeper joy of life.

Their loving and grateful
children, grandchildren
and great grandchildren

לכבוד מורי ורבי ר׳ שלמה

For my dear Rebbe Shlomo

לעילוי נשמת
הרב הגאון החסיד והצדיק
ר׳ שלמה בן הרב נפתלי

Who opened doors for me and tens of thousands of others
to come closer to Hashem and His Torah.
I will always be grateful for all that he did for me.

SHARIE YASGUR SOFAIR

AN ISHBITZER ACCOMPANIMENT INTO *GALUS*

And these are the names of the children of Israel who were coming down to Egypt. (Sh'mos 1:1)

THE STORY OF OUR EXILE IN THE BOOK OF EXODUS is called *Sh'mos,* "Names." This isn't just a sweet concept. It's so much deeper than that. In order to go into exile and come out alive, you have to hold on to your name.

The Beis Ya'akov of Ishbitz says that there are two kinds of holiness in the world. One kind depends on what I do and, if I can build this holiness, I can also destroy it. But then there is another kind of holiness which has nothing to do with my actions. It's something I have in me but it's a holiness that is hidden.

Each time I do something good, I reconnect myself to that holiness and make it shine with more strength. But each time I do something wrong, I cover it up a little more so it doesn't shine.

You know something? We each have so many questions.

What is our story as *Am Yisrael*? What's going on in the world today? What makes me part of the Jewish people? And most of all, why am I still in exile?

None of these things have much to do with any of my actions. Yes, I am responsible for my actions, but what really connects me – and what connects one *Yid* to another? It is not what I'm doing or what you're doing in the world; it's this holiness which we all have . . . this second type of holiness.

You see, I was born with the same inner holiness as the Baal Shem Tov. Basically, the lowest *Yiddele* has the same fire inside him as Moshe Rabbeinu. So how is it that Moshe Rabbeinu and the Baal Shem were so much higher?

It's because they worked so hard on their own to make their inner holiness shine more and more. So when it comes to my personal story, it really all depends both on what I don't do . . . and on what I do.

A title is something I get later in life and it depends on what I do. Doctor, psychiatrist, or *shlepper* – these are all names I get later on. But let's say that when I was born I received the name Miriam or Chaim. This has nothing to do with my actions. It's much deeper than that. The name I am given when I am born comes from a totally different place.

Someone once came to the Kotzker Rebbe and asked him, "Rebbe, tell me . . . what name should I give to my son?" And the Kotzker said to him, "Once in your life G-d gives you prophecy. Why should I take it away from you?"

You see what it is, to give somebody a name borders on prophecy because my name is what connects me to my roots. I don't receive a name just so people will know what to call me. That's what the world thinks. The fact is if G-d forbid, somebody is fainting and you call him by his name, you might be able to revive him.

One of the great Rebbes once said that if a person is about to die, G-d forbid, the most important thing is for someone to keep calling his name. Then he will live because calling out his name brings together his soul and his body. So my name can't just be a mechanical thing, something just for identification. My name really is the connection between my body and my soul.

When someone is ill, G-d forbid, and a name is added on, it connects that person to a new root. He must have used up all his old batteries. As far as his old roots are concerned, obviously his time is up. So you connect his soul to new roots by giving him a new name.

Maybe, maybe that will help. But again, it borders on prophecy to know what name to add for him. You can't just pick any name. You can't just look in the phone book and find something new to call him. It doesn't work that way. You have to ask someone very holy what name will connect him to his new roots.

Let me explain this on another level.

Imagine I'm walking on the street and I feel a bit low. Suddenly someone comes and says, "Hey, Shlomo! How are you?" Suddenly I feel very happy. At that moment this person really filled my needs. I needed someone to talk to me. I needed someone to smile at me . . . and it's very beautiful. Then I say goodbye and I do something else.

Now imagine that somebody calls my name and it reaches me in the deepest depths. It's not because I needed that person at that moment. It has nothing to do with that moment or with any other one. It's that the way this person said my name was *mamesh* touching eternity.

*

"And these are the names of the children of Israel who came down to Egypt." The Beis Ya'akov says (*Beis Ya'akov,* Sh'mos 6): When the *Yidden* went down to Egypt, suddenly G-d gave them a strong name.

What does it mean that G-d gave them a strong name? It means that G-d gave them this great holiness, but not because of their actions. G-d gave them such powerful holiness that they simply weren't able to tear themselves away from being *Yidden.*

The craziest thing in the world is that when we were in Egypt, we never did anything wrong. But right after we stood on Mount Sinai we did wrong all the time. Isn't that crazy? Before Mount Sinai we didn't know anything and yet we never went against G-d's will, without even knowing it.

Even after G-d told us what we were supposed to do, we kept making mistakes. But the reason for this is very simple. After Mount Sinai we were operating on the level of our own actions. Maybe we had this holiness inside of us, but it was up to us to bring it out. While we were in Egypt, the holiness was completely beyond.

It was as if we were high on holiness.

How could we exist in exile? Take the Russian Jews. In America there is complete free choice, in Israel we have free choice . . . and yet our *Yiddishkeit* is not so strong.

The lowest *Yiddele* in Russia didn't even know what *Eretz Yisrael* means. He didn't know anything about Yerushalayim. And yet he was willing to sit in Siberia because he wanted so much to go to Jerusalem. This comes from a higher level because G-d is filling him with this inside holiness.

There are times when I really want to do wrong, but I can't. I know it's not my own doing. It's not because I don't want to. I really want to, but I just can't. This doesn't come from my head. So where is it coming from? It comes from the roots of my soul.

*

Everyone knows that there were two covenants: There was the covenant of our forefathers, and then there was the covenant on Mount Sinai. What's the difference between them? It's really very simple.

Do you know what a covenant means?

It means to be tied together. When I take two things and I tie them together like mad so that they can't be separated anymore, that is a covenant. So the Beis Ya'akov says that the first thing about the covenant of our fathers, Avraham, Yitzchak, and Ya'akov, is that a *Yiddele* has a holiness which comes from a deeper place than the level of learning and knowing.

Mount Sinai was about learning and knowledge. We stood before G-d and Moshe Rabbeinu told us everything. But the covenant of Avraham, Yitzchak, and Ya'akov was much higher and much deeper than this.

Therefore, the Beis Ya'akov says that when we were in Egypt, the roots of our holiness became so strong because the exile was so strong.

In other words, if the exile had reached only as deep as our minds, then our own holiness would have been enough to get us through it. But in Egypt we had no Torah. We had nothing mind-wise. We hadn't learned anything yet. So our survival had to come from a higher place than our minds. It had to come from the roots of our souls.

Now listen to this.

What is a name? My name is the root of my life. Everything is included in my name. It's who I really am. I may be a person who is split in ten thousand directions, but when someone calls my name, it hits that one spot inside me which is one . . . which is all of me.

The Beis Ya'akov says that a person has so many different needs. I need a house. I need food – apples, coffee. I need clothes and boots when it's raining. But then I need something which is deeper than all that. I need to be connected to the core of my life. And this need is beyond everything else.

It's the same thing when it comes to learning Torah. There are all kinds of *divrei* Torah. Every day, every split second there is new Torah coming down. Sometimes I learn something and I like it. It turns me on.

This is the level of when I'm hungry and someone gives me food. I take the food and it satisfies my need. But then there is Torah that I learn and something happens to me deep inside. This is on the level of someone calling my name and all of me turns around.

When I learn this kind of Torah, all of me is *mamesh* turning around. Do you know how deep this is? G-d forbid, a person can live his or her whole life without ever tasting this level of Torah.

What is my vessel for receiving these *divrei* Torah, these holy words of Torah which touch me so deeply and which I need beyond needing? This is the covenant of Avraham, Yitzchak, and Ya'akov. This is the holy kind of *Yiddishkeit* where I am completely tied to G-d. This is not just about my needs. This is about life itself.

You see, even when I am trying to serve G-d, I'm not praying all the time. I don't learn all the time. I don't have Shabbos all the time. What is it that is always with me? It's my name. And this is what the Ishbitzer is saying.

There is *Yiddishkeit* that I need in the same way I need food or a house or a shirt. And then there is Torah on the level of my name. It is with me all the time. It is with me when I eat and it is with me when I sleep. I can't move without it. I can't exist without it.

My very life is a vessel for this kind of *divrei* Torah. This is the covenant, and this is my name.

*

Why is it that Avraham Avinu's name was shining all over? This is because he did something with his name. The Baal Shem Tov's name was Yisrael. How many people are called Yisrael and their names aren't shining?

The Beis Ya'akov says that you still have your name when you sleep. But when you're awake it's a different thing. People call you by your name and you respond. In this way you can make your name bigger.

Now imagine that I'm learning. And what I am learning turns me on for a little while. But then I forget it. What happened? It turned off.

Sometimes you meet kids and you tell them some Torah. If you tell them Torah on the level of food, they eat it, digest it and maybe lose it. But sometimes you tell them something holy and it's with them all their lives. This means you've told them Torah on the level of their real name. It stays with them forever.

What happens to you in exile? In exile your name gets deeper . . . shining to the utmost. Everyone has their own little exiles. And when that happens to me, what is it that gets deeper? Not my actions and not that part of me where I am the master. It's the core of my being that gets deeper.

How did we keep going while we were in exile for two thousand years?

We couldn't fulfill all the *mitzvos* because we weren't in Israel. We couldn't learn so much either. But do you know what got so strong? Our names got strong, which is another way of saying that the *divrei* Torah which are on the level of our names got stronger. These stay with us all our lives . . . these holy words of Torah, which we cannot live without.

The most heartbreaking thing is if, G-d forbid, we get cut off from G-d for even one split second – it's the end. That's the thing about exile, the whole world wants to tear us away from G-d.

Why is our land called *Eretz Yisrael* – the Land of Israel? Because that is *mamesh* our name . . . Israel. Our connection with the Land is not like our connection with Shabbos. Shabbos is only once a week but our name is forever.

Our name is deeper than Rosh Hashanah or Yom Kippur. It's even deeper than our connection with the Torah, because sometimes we're learning and sometimes we're not.

The holiness of *Eretz Yisrael* is that it's so connected to our name. And the problem is that the whole world wants to tear us away from that holy name.

There is tremendous evil going on in the world today. Tremendous evil. Right now, evil is concentrating its forces for the last battle, once and forever, before the coming of *Mashiach*.

First, they want to destroy us physically. And then the new thing is that people don't talk against Jews, they talk against Zionists.

Covering it up, they say, "Listen, you can be a Jew. You can go to India. You can belong to any religion and you can be anything you want and just send money to Israel. Really, we have nothing against your religion. But there's just one thing – don't live in Israel!"

What are people like that really doing? They want to tear out our name . . . to tear out those *divrei* Torah on the level of our name.

So how do we fight this?

Everybody has to get themselves a weapon. My weapon is *divrei Torah* on the level of my name. We have to dig so deep and find the holy words which are on the level of our name.

*

What is Shabbos all about?

On Shabbos I'm not doing anything on a physical level. And that means that I also don't do much of anything on a spiritual level either.

You might say, "What are you talking about? I *daven* on Shabbos. I learn on Shabbos." But *mitzvohs* and learning Torah on Shabbos are not on the level of doing. On Shabbos everything is on the level of receiving.

The holiness of Shabbos is receiving. Because what is Shabbos? The Zohar Hakadosh says Shabbos is *"Sh'ma d'kudsha brich hu"* – the name of G-d.

What is the difference between my relationship with G-d during the week and my relationship with Him on Shabbos? It's like the difference between my learning Torah on the level of food or on the level of my name. On Shabbos I reach G-d on the level of His Holy Name. Can you imagine how deep this is?

Now listen to this.

To be able to do something on the level of action is very strong. But even when I'm trying as hard as I can, I can only do so much. I can only learn so much because I am finite. What is the most infinite thing within me? It is the holiness that is my name. This is what connects me to the infinite . . . to life itself.

Shabbos is infinite. This means that on Shabbos I'm on the level of calling G-d by His name. During the week I call G-d by His titles. But what's the difference between calling someone "Doctor" and calling the same person by his name? It's a completely different relationship.

On Shabbos I'm ready to receive from G-d that which I never dreamed of, never even thought of. If on Shabbos I ask G-d to give me a thousand dollars, G-d will answer me, "Why just a thousand? I was thinking of giving you a million." Or imagine I say, "Listen G-d, I want to be as holy as the *Heilige* Baal Shem Tov." G-d will say, "Why only like the Baal Shem? I was thinking of making you even holier."

Because infinite is infinite.

*

Now listen to one more sweet thing.

How can a person know what level he is learning on – whether it's on the level of food and shelter or on the level of a name? The answer is very simple. How much are you running after it?

I might be very hungry, but I'm not going to run barefoot all the way to *Yerushalayim* to find some food. Maybe I'm thirsty, but I won't run ten miles in the rain just to get a little coffee.

But if my learning is on the level of a name, it's infinite. An infinite need. It's so deep that I just can't be without it. I'm running after it . . . no matter what it takes.

Now the Beis Ya'akov says something very deep. How can I ever taste the holiness of my own name? How can I ever taste the sweetness of the infinite? Every morning I put on *tefillin*, but I don't taste the holiness of my name. It might be hidden there but I don't taste it. I can do all the *mitzvos* my whole life and never taste that sweetness.

At a certain point we realize that our lives are full of really important tests, strong tests, hard tests. Imagine I have a really big test and I'm standing at the crossroads. Then suddenly, I don't know what happens to me but G-d helps me and I don't fall.

It is at that moment that I taste who I am. I taste the holiness, the sweetness, of my own name. And where did this come from? The Beis Ya'akov says it comes from the holiness deep inside me, which I inherited from Avraham, Yitzchak, and Ya'akov.

When did the exile in Egypt begin? According to Rashi, the four hundred years of *Galus Mitzrayim* (Egyptian exile) began with the birth of Yitzchak (Sh'mos 6:18 re Bereishis 15:13.) Yitzchak was the first person that was born a Jew. He was the first *Yiddele* who had a *bris* and received a name when he was eight days old. And who chose his name? G-d did. G-d said to Avraham, "Give your son the name Yitzchak." (Bereishis 17:19.)

Yitzchak was the first person in the world whose name was given to him by G-d. When Yitzchak was born he was already on the highest level, and he had to work himself down to our world. So what keeps us going in exile? It's this unconscious high level. It's this name.

Everybody knows that the exile in Egypt was a preparation to stand on Mount Sinai. What was G-d doing while we were in exile? He was strengthening our name.

We must have a name . . . that deepest depths of our souls which must always be with us and which gives us the strength to go through anything.

*

How does the Book of Exodus begin?

"V'eileh Sh'mos b'nei Yisrael" – "These are the names of the children of Israel." What is this telling us? You have to know your name. What gets you out of Egypt, out of exile, out of slavery? Your name does. A name is not just what other people call me. If I know my name, then I know who I really am.

Chassidus makes it very clear. Our Egypts don't have to be low Egypts. They might be very holy, but they're still exile . . . they're still slavery. Everybody has excuses for their own Egypt. But the truth is, you can be a very good person, but if you don't know your name, you're still not free. You simply don't know who you can be.

So the beginning of Sh'mos is *"V'eile Sh'mos"* – I know my name. I know what I can become. And that is what gets me out of Egypt.

Reb Tzadok HaKohen says that slavery begins when I lose my roots, when nothing touches my roots. Now my roots are much deeper than my mind. So how can I reach them? It's really very simple. I have to stop my mind from thinking.

The Kotzker Rebbe tells us – Imagine how deep my mind becomes when I don't think. You know, there are two kinds of depth. On the one hand, the more I think, the deeper my mind becomes. If I study a lot and think about what I study, then my mind can become more and more of a vessel for the light which can be contained in vessels. This is one level of depth.

But then there are certain depths which my mind can only reach by not thinking. This is because there is a great light which has no vessels . . . which is beyond vessels. How can my mind receive this kind of light? It can only do so if I stop thinking – not because I'm stupid, but because I am so wise that I can empty my mind of thought in a holy way. Then when that great light is shining, my mind can be a vessel for it too.

Most people will ask, "How can you have light without vessels? How can you drink coffee without a cup? What holds the coffee? What holds the light?" This is slave thinking.

A free person will ask, "Where does it say that I need a cup to drink coffee, a vessel to receive light?" Slave thinking says, "Okay, you say you know there is one G-d. But if you have stopped thinking, how do you know this in your mind?" This is only a question of a slave. A free man says, "My mind knows beyond thinking. I know beyond my mind!"

Once my mind is connected again to my roots, to who I really am, to my name, then I can do anything in the world.

*

Everyone knows that a name has two levels. People are given names so that other people can call out to them, but this is on the outside. If a person would be all alone in the world, he or she wouldn't need a name because no one would be calling them.

Now there is a name which absolutely reaches into the deepest depths of your being. What's so special about parents giving a baby a name?

You really have to be on the level of prophecy to give a name for the inside. I can call you Fritz, Max or any other name in the world, and you will turn your head when I call out to you. For this you don't have to be a father or a mother.

A father and mother are *mamesh* given this prophetic vision to know which name to give for a much higher and exalted reason.

Now the Ishbitzer says like this (*Beis Ya'akov*, Sh'mos 3):

Whatever happens in this world mirrors that which takes place above. In paradise there are no garments. Outside paradise everything is covered up. Not with one garment, but with two million garments.

Sometimes a name is a cover-up. It's a low-level name, which is outside paradise. Sometimes people call you by your name, adding hundreds of more garments onto you. The way they call your name makes you shrink away and close up even more.

Sometimes somebody calls you and you *mamesh* open your whole heart to that person. Suddenly you are back in paradise.

But there is something even deeper.

Being created in G-d's image means that inside each and every one of us, there is *mamesh* infinite holy power. But you know what it is?

Someone has to call us by our name to wake up this infinite power that exists within.

Parents have this tremendous holiness of giving their child a name, which they know will wake up the deepest depths of their child's soul.

Imagine I'm in a restaurant and I'm getting soup that tastes very good. But there is just one thing. The soup was not made just for me. I can buy it, I can get it, but it was not made for me. When I come home from *Shul* on Friday night and my wife gives me soup, this soup was *mamesh* made for me. It's a different kind of taste.

I can have a taste of life like everyone else, but you know what a name does to me? A name makes me feel that something was made just for me.

When our holy fathers and mothers gave us a name, they gave us this holiness that the whole world is meant just for me.

HOLINESS WHICH IS CONNECTED

. . . who were coming down to Egypt . . . (*Sh'mos 1:1*)

I WANT TO SHARE WITH YOU ONE OF THE DEEPEST concepts in the Zohar HaKadosh.

The Hebrew word for "holy" – *kadosh* – is sometimes written with the letter *vav,* and sometimes without a *vav.* Everyone knows that the letter *vav* is the letter of connection. In Hebrew, whenever you want to say "and," you always use a *vav.*

So you see what it is, this means there are two kinds of holiness: When *kadosh* is spelled with a *vav,* this is the holiness of connection. *Kadosh* without a *vav* is holiness without connection . . . holiness beyond connection.

What does this mean?

The Zohar says the deepest depths (Zohar 3:94b). Holiness within the framework of this world is the holiness of connection. What is a holy person to us? This is a person who is connected to holiness. You see, someone who observes all of G-d's commandments is a really good person and is close to G-d. So – they are holy.

But G-d's holiness has no *vav.* His holiness is deeper than connection. Sometimes you meet a *shlepper,* a drunkard, a thief and he seems to be the lowest of the low, *mamesh* not connected to anything. But you sense something so beautiful in this person. He has something of G-d's holiness inside him.

What is the deepest depths of this world? The deepest depths is to understand that the holiness of connection is based upon the holiness beyond connection . . . a holiness which is not clear to us.

I have seen great rabbis where everything is kosher and sweet and yet something is missing. You can love someone very much and everything connects, but something is missing. What's the problem? They don't have that deep holiness which is beyond connection.

I can walk up to my wife and say, "I love you." Then ten minutes later I tell her this again, and ten minutes after that I again say, "I love you." And this time she tells me, "Enough already! You are repeating yourself." What's the problem here? I love her on the level of connection, and on that level, it is repetition. Either we are connected or we're not.

Now listen to the other side – I'm madly in love with my wife and I tell her, "I love you." Ten minutes later I say I love her again, and she answers me, "Why did you wait ten minutes to tell me?" Ah, this means we love each other beyond connection.

If I love somebody on the level which is deeper than connection, then I can tell her how much I love her a hundred times, one after another, and it's still not enough.

Because it's *mamesh* infinite. It's G-d's level of holiness . . . holiness without a *vav.*

I want you to open your hearts.

Moshe and Aharon were the two masters of the Jewish people. Moshe was the master of Mount Sinai and Aharon was the master of the Holy Temple. Mount Sinai was about connection.

On Mount Sinai G-d told us what to do and what not to do, what to believe in and what not to believe in, so that we connect to Him in the deepest way. It was absolutely the holiness of connection.

The Holy Temple was the place where we received this holiness which is deeper than connection. In the Holy Temple nobody gave a speech.

You just came in there and prayed and poured out your heart. When you walked out maybe you would connect everything. But inside the Temple it was deeper than connection.

Now I want to you to know that there is a difference between praying and pouring out my heart. When I pray, I thank G-d for all His blessings, and I ask Him to give me this and give me that. It's all about connection.

But pouring out my heart is not about connection. It's deeper than all that. I don't ask or thank G-d for anything . . . I just pour out everything that I feel inside of me. If I am relating to G-d or if I am relating to you on the level of *kadosh* without a *vav*, then I can pour out my heart.

I can walk on the street and meet a stranger and pour out my heart and soul before him. I don't know his name and he doesn't know mine. But we share this holiness beyond connection.

Some people judge prayers according to how long they last. If you pray for one hour, that's pretty good. If you pray for half an hour, who knows? If you pray for just one minute, then for sure it means nothing. Do you think G-d bothers to listen to a one-minute prayer?

But in Kotzk, the most important thing was not how long the prayers lasted. The most important thing was how sincerely you poured out your heart. I cannot speak for other religions. I can only talk about my own and in the Synagogue today we are missing the outpouring of the heart.

I want you to know the deepest depths.

Do you know what it is to be in exile? A person in exile can be holy. A slave can be honest. So what is the problem with exile? To be in exile means that I'm missing that holiness which is deeper than connection.

Something is happening in the world today. There is suddenly an unbelievably deep awakening where people want to know the secrets of life. The first awakening is not that I am looking for the holiness of connection.

I don't want someone telling me to do this and not to do that in order to be holy or to have meaning in my life. What I am looking for doesn't have to connect to the way I eat my ice-cream. I am waiting for someone to give me this holiness which is beyond connection.

I want to experience something so deep that it will fill my heart with light. And hopefully if I find that *kadosh* without a *vav,* this will help me to find the holiness of connection as well.

FEARING I DIDN'T DO GOOD ENOUGH

. . . with Ya'akov, each man and his household came. (Sh'mos 1:1)

THERE ARE ALL KINDS OF FEARS IN THE WORLD. There is a fear where I am afraid for my life and I have no peace. Then there is another type of fear, and this is when I'm afraid I didn't do enough. But in a crazy deep way, this type of fear gives me so much strength.

Can you imagine how deep my davening is, that each time I finish davening I feel I didn't daven enough?

At one time the holy Ropshitzer came to a city of *Misnagdim*, those who opposed the *Chassidic* tradition. When they finished praying they would learn. But by the holy Ropshitzer, after you pray, you have a *le'chaim* and you might eat some cake.

So the Ropshitzer arrives at this *Beis Medrash* and after he finishes praying, he says, "*Gevalt,* I need a little bit of cake and a drink." The *Misnagdim* are looking at him, thinking he is crazy. Suddenly one of them gets up and says, "You just stood before G-d and the first thing you are doing is looking for a piece of cake? We just stood before G-d and we went straight to the learning."

"I'll tell you," Reb Naftali Ropshitzer says. "You, when you pray, you are so pleased with yourselves. You think to yourselves, 'Not only did I daven good but I also know how to learn real good.' I want you to know that when I finish praying I *mamesh* feel so broken. I feel so broken that I didn't pray properly and if I wouldn't eat something, I would *mamesh* die."

This greatest fear of all fears – that I don't feel that I did enough – this is absolutely the Holy of Holies.

You see what it is.

When I am fearful for my life, I'm paralyzed and I can't do anything. If someone holds a gun to me, there is nothing I can do. But imagine I have this utmost fear that maybe I didn't learn enough, maybe I didn't understand enough. I'm not paralyzed at all. On the contrary . . . at that moment I can do anything in the world.

I want you to know, this second type of fear doesn't exist in heaven. In heaven the angels get a clear message as to what they have to do . . . and they either do it or they don't. The holiness of this world is that there is such a thing as having a fear that maybe I didn't do enough.

What I'm capable of doing in this world is beyond. Since this world is so hidden and covered up and I never know if I did enough, there is this holiness of never knowing if I really did enough.

Now listen to this, and I want you to open your hearts like mad.

On the one hand, when G-d sends me a message that's not so clear, I walk around thinking, "I could be doing more, I should be doing more." Yet when G-d's light is shining straight into you, when things are clear to you, it's the greatest thing, but something is missing.

What is it that you are missing when something is clear to you? It's this holiness of being afraid that maybe I could have done things better.

When G-d sends me a message that's not so clear, I walk around thinking, "I could be doing more, I should be doing more."

Basically, this is the difference between being in exile and being out of exile. The holiness of being in exile is that G-d's light is not so clear to you. I have this absolute urge to do more. The Talmud was composed in exile because things were not so clear.

Our great sages were always thinking that maybe it's not deep enough, maybe it's not clear enough yet. This is one side of the coin. The danger in this is that exile really is a very heavy scene.

What happens to you when things are not so clear to you? On the one hand you have this holiness of doing more, but you also have the chance that maybe you will get completely lost. Maybe I will lose the whole thing.

Now listen to the deepest depths.

How could it be that when we were in Egypt we never did anything wrong, and yet the moment we came out of Egypt we start to sin? The Ishbitzer says (*Beis Ya'akov* Sh'mos, 6) that this is because in exile we were armed with an unbelievable shield.

What was this shield? Before we even got to exile, G-d gave us so much strength by giving us our name: "Ve'eile sh'mos b'nei Yisrael" – "These are the names of the children of Israel." G-d gives us this utmost holiness that we shouldn't get lost, so that in the deepest depths we know who we are.

My name is that vessel through which G-d gives me so much strength.

When you love somebody very much, and you call them by their name, not only do you wake up the deepest depths of their being, you give them infinite strength. You reawaken that holiness and you make it even greater.

Then it says *"es Ya'akov ish u-beiso ba'u"* – "with Ya'akov, each man with his family came." (Sh'mos 1:1) The Ishbitzer says that outside of the land, Ya'akov is called Ya'akov, but in *Eretz Yisrael* (the Land of Israel) he is called Yisrael.

The holiness of Ya'akov is *Eikev*. He always thinks that he's at the beginning . . . just at the heels. I have to do more, more and more.

You know why G-d sent us into exile?

In order for us to learn what it means that maybe I didn't do enough.

FEELING SOMEONE ELSE'S PAIN

. . . and he saw their suffering . . . (Sh'mos 2:11)

IN THE CITY OF VORKE THERE LIVED A HOLY RABBI and his name was Reb Yitzchak Vorker.

There was one crazy thing about him – he always gave everything away. Hundreds, maybe thousands of people came to be with the Vorker on the Sabbath, and he had to buy food. But he gave all his money to the poor and nobody ever paid his grocery bill. Finally, the grocer said to him, "We are not giving you food anymore because you don't pay the bills."

When the Vorker's *chassidim* heard about this, they got together and collected ten thousand rubles for the Rebbe. They walked into his private room, gave him the money and said, "Here Holy Rabbi, this is to pay all your bills."

About fifteen minutes later the Vorker's secretary came in and said, "Ah, *Heilege* Rebbe, I'm so happy that now we can pay for our food."

The Rabbi looked at him and said, "*Nu*? With what kind of money?"

"What is this? The *Chassidim* just gave you ten thousand rubles fifteen minutes ago."

"Fifteen minutes is a very long time," the Vorker said. "I've already given all the money away to ten poor brides to make their weddings."

Now the *chassidim* got very angry. They had worked so hard to raise money for the Rebbe and he immediately gave it all away! They went in to the Vorker and said, "You know we love you very much, but this is going too far!"

The Rebbe was silent for a moment. Then he answered, "Come into my room. I want to talk to you." And when they came in, he went on, "I want you to know that you are one hundred percent right. I shouldn't have given away the ten thousand rubles. But I couldn't help myself. When I see people in pain, I have to help them. When I see people crying, I have to dry their tears. Let me tell you how I learned this . . ."

"When I was seventeen years old, I came to my Holy Rebbe of Nadvorna. And one Friday morning I was praying with all my heart. I had never prayed so strong in all my life. I needed five more minutes to finish my *davening*, when the Nadvorner's secretary came up to me and said, 'The Rebbe needs you right away.' I didn't want to interrupt my prayers so I wrote on a piece of paper, 'I'll be there in five minutes,' and went back to my *davening*.

"One minute later the secretary was back: 'The Rebbe says to come now or never to come to see him again.' I thought it must be a matter of life and death, so I interrupted my prayers and went into my Rebbe's room.

"There, lying on the floor, was a drunkard. The Nadvorner said to me, 'Moishele has a wife and seven children, and they have no money. Nobody wants to give them *tzedakah* because they think Moishele will just drink it away. So I want you to go out right now to collect money for Moishele the drunkard's wife.'

"I was so angry. This couldn't wait five minutes until I finished my prayers? So I thought, 'The Nadvorner is not a good Rebbe for me. He doesn't know what is going on in my heart. And I decided that right after Shabbos I would look for another Rebbe.

"After *Havdalah* I quickly packed my suitcase and got ready to run out. But the Rebbe's secretary took me by my ear and said, 'The Rebbe wants to see you,' and he dragged me to the Nadvorner.

"When I first went in I was still very angry. But you know, the Rebbe was really very holy. He said to me, 'Do you really think I don't know what you are feeling? But let me ask you something. Do you really think G-d needs your prayers? G-d has time. G-d can always wait. But Moishele's wife and the children . . . they are so hungry. They are *mamesh* starving. They can't wait.

"Listen to me, Yitzchak – never let anything, anything in the world, make you deaf to the cries of people in need."

*

When we pray for peace we say: "Please, G-d, give us *tovah,* goodness – the real goodness of holy eyes; *bracha,* blessings – to be connected to our roots; *chaim,* life itself; *chen,* holy charm; *chesed,* unreserved love; and *rachamim,* the prophetic vision of compassion."

You can have *chaim, chen,* and *chesed* without having prophecy. But *rachamim* needs the level of prophecy. To have compassion on somebody who is in bad shape means to have a vision of how that person could be. I compare what he is now to what he could be and I say, "*Oy vey,* I have to help him get there."

Sometimes we don't make peace with someone because we have lost the vision of how that person could be. The highest peace between people is when each one knows the other's potential . . . what he could be and what he would be. We have to live in two worlds.

We have to live in a world where there is evil and we are fighting it. And at the same time we have to live in a world where there is no evil . . . like after *Mashiach* comes. The highest combination of these two worlds is *rachamim.* True compassion means that I see you the way you are, but I also know how you could be on the level of *Mashiach.*

A person who laughs at someone who is crying is very sick. Sick to the core. Someone who can see another person in pain and just walk away is *mamesh* not in the image of G-d.

When someone is in pain and I feel that pain, it means I love that person. If somebody hurts themselves and has a little bit of pain, deep down that brings back all the pain he or she ever went through. And if you feel compassion toward that person, then you feel all the pain he or she has ever felt, in this lifetime and also in other lifetimes.

This kind of compassion is a key ingredient for peace in the world.

THE DEATH OF HUMANITY

. . . the King of Egypt died . . . (Sh'mos 2:23)

DO YOU KNOW WHAT HAPPENED TO US WHEN we came out of Auschwitz?

We didn't walk out completely free. We still thought, "What's so bad about our world, about western civilization?" Now don't get me wrong. Our world is okay if you know how to take it. Medicine is good but you have to know how many pills to take.

The Rambam was a wonderful doctor. The Lubavitcher Rebbe was a great engineer. But this is not what I mean by "western civilization." I'm talking about what the world thinks about humanity.

According to the Ishbitzer, the Torah says, "*Vayamas melech Mitzrayim*" – "And the king of Egypt died." But really Pharaoh was still alive. The Ishbitzer says – and only he can say such a thing – that "*vayamas melech Mitzrayim*" means that everything human in him died. Everything human died. He was not a human being anymore.

All the Rebbes say that before we left Egypt, G-d had to show us how bad Pharaoh was. We still thought: "Okay, maybe he's harsh but he does give us Shabbos off." Or we thought: "Okay, he's cruel but at least he gives us straw to make the bricks."

So Pharaoh decreed, "For three days there will be no straw for bricks and no Shabbos." During those three days, the *Yidden* worked for Pharaoh during the day. But after the daytime work was done, any Egyptian had the right to force a *Yid* to work all night. How long can anyone function like this? It was not human!

So G-d said, "I have to take them out from the depths. I want them to know there is another way."

Please don't get me wrong. I love the world and I know there are a lot of good people. But even their own goodness in some way comes from G-d speaking to us on Mount Sinai and teaching us the right way to live. In the same way that G-d's voice is still being heard all over the world today.

When we look at the world it has to be clear to us. Which side are we on . . . which side are we on?

I want to bless you and me that G-d should take us out of the abyss, the abyss of inhumanity. What was the beginning of *Yiddishkeit*? It was with Avraham Avinu. What a human being he was. What a person! Avraham Avinu had a heart for everyone . . . even for the lowest pagans in the world.

But the other side – those on the other side – don't care if millions of people are dying. And not only the peoples of other nations. They don't even care about their own people. They don't care about anyone or anything. Nothing!

We all have to stand up for the good. We have to thank the Master of the World for choosing us from all the nations and giving us His Torah. And we have to hope and pray that one day, one day soon, all the nations of the world will join us, so that together with all the good people of the nations, we can create a world that *mamesh* cares.

SEARCHING FOR A LEADER

And Moshe was shepherding the sheep of Yisro . . . (*Sh'mos 3:1*)

IMAGINE IF TODAY WE WERE LOOKING FOR SOMEbody to save the world. What kind of person would we look for? We would want someone who looks very intelligent and who is handsome and a good speaker. A real polished personality.

But when G-d looks for a leader, this is not what He is looking for. When G-d wanted to find someone to take the Jews out of Egypt, He was looking for something else.

Do you know why Moshe was chosen?

The *Medrash* says (*Sh'mos Rabbah* 2:2) that Moshe was a shepherd. His father-in-law lived on Mount Sinai and he used to take his father-in-law's sheep out on the mountain to graze. One day a little sheep ran off. Moshe Rabbeinu started running after the sheep, calling it all kinds of sweet names and saying, "Please come back, please come back."

The sheep ran all the way up to the top of Mount Sinai. It found a tiny little lake and stopped to drink and Moshe found it there. He waited until it finished drinking. He then took the sheep, put it over his shoulders, and he said to the sheep, "You poor little thing. You must be so tired after all that running."

Then Moshe looked fondly at the sheep and said, "My sweetest sheep, I wish we could talk to each other."

At that moment G-d said to the angels, "If Moshe takes such good care of sheep, can you imagine how well he will take care of My children?"

And that was the moment that G-d appeared to Moshe Rabbeinu at the burning bush.

SECRET OF ENDURANCE

. . . *Why isn't the bush burning up? (Sh'mos 3:3)*

SOMETIMES G-D REVEALS TO YOU WHAT IS MOST important in life and when you know what's most important in life, *gevalt!* Do you hold onto it!

I want you to know something awesome.

When children are born, they hold onto their parents. When little kids give you their hand, they are holding onto you. What does it mean when you hold hands with the one you love? You are holding onto each other.

The first time G-d reveals himself to Moshe was by the burning bush. When Moshe asked *"Madua lo yiv'ar ha-sneh?"* – "Why isn't the bush burning?" (Sh'mos 3:3), what was he really asking?

The *Heilige* Avodas Yissaschar says a *gevalt* Torah. At the burning bush, Moshe Rabbeinu saw what every *Yiddele* is going through until the coming of *Mashiach*. He saw all the exiles, he saw the Inquisition, he saw Auschwitz. He saw everything.

The question he was asking was – how could it be that despite everything we go through, we Jewish people can still exist? How are we still in this world?

Do you know what level Moshe Rabbeinu's understanding was by the burning bush? It was the highest understanding of G-d, the highest understanding of life there is.

So when G-d tells Moshe Rabbeinu to take off his shoes, He was telling him, "I want to take you out of everything you understand. I want to give you something deeper than the highest knowledge. I want to reveal to you what is most important in life."

And everyone knows that the burning bush took place on Mount Sinai, where the Torah was given. You see friends, the Torah is not a higher level of knowledge. The Torah comes from a different world.

On Shavuos G-d gives me the Torah, but I'm not holding the Torah and dancing with it. I don't dance with it because knowledge doesn't make me dance. I dance with the Torah when I realize that the Torah is something to hold onto forever . . . and this happens on Simchas Torah.

Did you ever notice the way university students carry their books? Nothing special. Have you ever seen the way a *Yid* walks around with a Gemara? I hold onto the Gemara with so much love and longing because the Gemara is not just a book. "*Eitz chayim hi lamachazikim bah*" – "She is a Tree of Life to those that hold onto her." (*Mishlei* / Proverbs 3:18). I'm holding onto it.

Listen to this.

For twenty years, the holy Beis Ya'akov would teach every night from midnight until four in the morning. Two *gabba'im* would enter the Beis Midrash exactly at midnight. They would walk up and down the aisles with two candles, which was a sign that the Beis Ya'akov was about to start teaching. A student who was there said, that after three weeks everyone would *mamesh* collapse.

Every three weeks there was another shift of a few hundred different Chassidim. But he says the two highest moments were first, to see the way the Rebbe was holding the Gemara when he walked in. The second most awesome moment was the way the Rebbe kissed the Gemara when he closed it after the learning.

And this is what the burning bush was all about – revealing to Moshe Rabbeinu what is most important . . . what we have been holding onto forever.

DOUBLE REDEMPTION

. . . I remembered you twice . . . (Sh'mos, 3:16)

IMAGINE THAT I'M A SLAVE, AND I REALLY THINK that's what I am, a slave.

Then even if somebody comes and redeems me, I'm still not free. I'm still enslaved to my past.

Now imagine, that even while I'm a slave, deep in my heart I *mamesh* know, "This can't be true. It can't be. I know that I'm not really a slave."

Then when someone comes to redeem me, he not only takes me out of my present, but right away, also out of my past. But for that to happen the redeemer has to shine so deeply into me and make it clear to me that I am not, and I never was, a slave.

Before Yosef HaTzaddik left this world, he told *Am Yisrael*, "This will be your sign. Someone will come and say to you, "*Pakod pakadeti eschem*" – "I remembered you twice" in a double redemption. (Sh'mos 3:16)

Let me share with you what the Ishbitzer says.

He says that it's not enough for someone to redeem you from now on. It has to be a double redemption. It has to be clear to you that you were never a slave. You have to know that I might have been in Egypt and maybe Pharaoh hit me . . . but I was never a slave.

Listen to this unbelievable thing.

Moshe Rabbeinu came down to Egypt, and if you could just visualize it, there were thousands and thousands of slaves. Moshe probably had some *Chassidim* with him, who made him a little stage. He got up on the stage with Aharon HaKohen and said, "*Yidden,* G-d sends word to you" – "*Pakod pakadeti eschem.*"

This was double redemption. Right away one *Yiddele* looked at the man next to him and said, "I always knew someone would come and take us out." Another *Yid* answered, "I also knew we wouldn't be slaves forever." And someone else said, "Why didn't you ever tell me you felt that way?"

According to the *Medrash,* suddenly every *Yid* started talking to one another and each of them said, "I always knew we weren't really slaves."

This was the double redemption. Moshe didn't just take them out of their physical slavery in Egypt saying, "No big deal, I'll perform a few miracles and then set you free." He also took them out of the spiritual slavery of their collective past. When Moshe Rabbeinu came, he made it clear to all the *Yidden* that in the deepest depths they were not slaves . . . and they had never been slaves.

FREEDOM FRIENDS

WHATEVER YOU THINK OF YOURSELF IS WHAT you think of G-d, and whatever you think of G-d is what you think of yourself.

If you think of yourself as someone who is limited and maybe able to do just a few things, then really, who do you think you are? If you believe you can just do a few things and that's it, then that's what you think of G-d as well. We are in G-d's image and G-d is also our image.

Everybody knows that *Mitzrayim*, Egypt, comes from the word *meitzar*, narrowness. *Meitzarim* means boundaries, limits.

A slave is not a bad person. In fact, a slave can serve G-d, be married, and have children. The problem is that a slave puts limits on himself.

You know friends, if I would call up my friends and say, "Can you do me a favor?" and they would say, "Listen, it's too much for me," then they are good friends but they are slave friends.

Freedom means there are absolutely no boundaries. Not the past, not the present, not the future . . . nothing in the world.

The two greatest G-d revelations in the world are the night of the Seder and Shavuos. On Shavuos we stood at Mount Sinai and G-d gave us the Torah and G-d told us what we have to do. G-d *mamesh* gives us everything He wants us to do. But this is not the beginning. The beginning is Pesach when it's clear to me there is nothing I cannot do. There is nothing I cannot do.

FREEDOM VISION

A SLAVE IS SOMEONE WHO LOST THE VISION OF how great he or she could be, how holy he or she could be. The Gemara says that if a person could be digging for gold and he becomes a garbage collector, it is heartbreaking. What's wrong with this garbage collector? He doesn't know who he is, he doesn't know what he can do. But you know something? We all suffer from this. We don't have the faintest idea of what we are *mamesh* able to do.

A great light is shining into me on Pesach. This light lets me know once again who I am. And this knowing who I am gets me out of Egypt in a second. I'm suddenly not hung up on those little things I do. I only build little pyramids for Pharaoh until I know what I am capable of doing. The moment I know that I can go up to Mount Sinai and talk to G-d, nothing can hold me back anymore . . . not even Pharaoh himself.

Knowing what I am capable of doing means to be completely aware of the depths of my life. A dead person can't do anything. So the more I can do, the more I am alive. The question of being a slave or not being a slave is a question of what life level you are on. A slave *Yiddele* thinks I can only daven a little bit, but not too much. A free *Yiddele* knows I can knock off the davening like the Holy Baal Shem.

I'll tell you the greatest story in the world.

Reb Michel Zlotchover had seven sons. One of them was Reb Yossele. The story is that Reb Yossele was once very sick. He nearly *mamesh* died. While he was taking a turn for the worse, he began sweating. He sweated for two hours and basically sweated out all his sickness.

After two hours he opens his eyes and says, "Friends, I am okay." So what happened? He says, "I *mamesh* died and came up to heaven and they brought in all my prayers. People in heaven said, 'This is what you call praying?' So they wanted to keep me up there. Suddenly the Holy Baal Shem Tov walked in and asked, 'What's going on here?' So they said, 'This Yossele didn't daven properly.'

'You are telling me about my Yossele?' the Baal Shem says, 'Yossele, do me a favor, knock off a little *Ma'ariv* and show them what you can do.' I want you to know, I began to daven *Ma'ariv* in heaven with all my heart and soul and I was sweating like a dog." While he was sweating from this *Ma'ariv*, he sweated out his sickness.

All you need is one good friend, like the Holy Baal Shem, to tell you, "Listen brother, you can do it. Just sweat it out. You can do it."

All we need is one good friend to remind us what we are capable of.

RIDDING YOURSELF OF SCARS

EVEN AFTER YOU ARE FREED FROM SLAVERY, WHAT about all the scars you have from being a slave?

Everybody knows that some people who were in Auschwitz are still there, because of the scars. We all go through so much in life. And even after G-d helps us, how do we get rid of the scars?

Let me tell you an awesome story.

There was once a *Yid* named Yehoshua Volf who was a top Bobover *Chassid*. He was in Auschwitz for five years, and somehow he made it through. Then one day, some Russian soldiers came and freed the camp. And when they came, Yehoshua Volf collapsed. He *mamesh* fainted.

Later he explained that what had kept him going for five years in Auschwitz was that he knew *Mashiach* was the only one who could free him. But what happened? Some soldier came and took him out. And he thought, "*Gevalt,* I was here for nothing." So he *mamesh* broke down.

You see what it is, the *ikar,* the essence of our going out of Egypt, was not that Pharaoh let us go. It was that Moshe Rabbeinu was the one who took us out. This was the secret sign that Yosef gave the *Yidden* – "*Pakod pakadeti*" (Sh'mos 3:16).

Yosef was telling the Jews that when the day for them to leave Egypt finally arrives, it will not just be that somebody would come and say, "Come on, let's go. I'm taking you out of here. I'm a Zionist and I'm taking you to our own homeland."

That's cute and sweet, but it just doesn't go.

Moshe had to be the one to take us out of Egypt, because only with him could we realize that not only were we not slaves any more, but we were never really slaves. Not to anyone or anything, but only to G-d.

But that still leaves the question of the scars. And here the Ishbitzer says that even Moshe couldn't take away the scars because they were so deep. Only with the coming of *Mashiach* will the scars be healed. Only the Messiah can take away all our scars, and then we will really be free.

MOSHE'S ARGUMENT

. . . Send whomever You will send. (Sh'mos 4:13)

I WANT TO SHARE SOMETHING VERY STRONG WITH you.

Avraham Avinu had a covenant with G-d. So when a baby is circumcised, he is initiated into the covenant of Avraham. But do you know who else is there at the *bris*? Eliyahu HaNavi comes and says, "I want you to know, it's not only that now you have a covenant with G-d. It's more than that. Now you and G-d *mamesh* belong to each other."

Everybody knows that Eliyahu HaNavi never died. He is the one who lives forever. When something or someone is alive forever, it can never be separated from its source, from its roots.

Now I want you to know the most way-out thing. It is said that after G-d chose Moshe to lead the Jewish people out of Egypt, Moshe Rabbeinu argued with G-d for a week. Moshe was begging G-d to send somebody else to be the leader.

One opinion says he wanted to send his brother Aharon HaKohen. But according to another opinion, Moshe asked G-d to please send Eliyahu HaNavi.

Do you know what that means? Moshe Rabbeinu wanted the first redemption to be on the level of Eliyahu HaNavi, on the level of forever. If G-d had taken us out of Egypt and led us to Mount Sinai on that level, then the Torah would have belonged to us and we would have belonged to the Torah.

You see what it is, when it reaches this level of "belonging," I just can't stop learning and keeping the Torah. I just can't stop being one with the Torah . . . no matter what.

And this is what Moshe Rabbeinu really wanted.

YISMACH MOSHE – MOSES REJOICED

Yismach Moshe be'matnas chelko. (Shabbos morning prayer)

EVERYONE KNOWS THAT SINCE PHARAOH HAD only one daughter, his last rule decreed was that the adopted son of his daughter should become the king, which means that Moshe Rabbeinu was supposed to become the next Pharaoh. When Moshe Rabbeinu was eighteen years old, Pharaoh says to him, "I want you to become involved in our government."

And here, Moshe Rabbeinu says to Pharaoh, "I have a feeling that I'm the best slave driver in the world. I truly hate those slaves. Let me go and see them and I will come back to tell you what I think we could do with them." Can you imagine how proud Pharaoh was after hearing such words?

Now listen to this.

Moshe Rabbeinu went down on Thursday, and that Thursday was the most terrible day for all the Jews. And Moshe Rabbeinu really was the lowest slave driver. He didn't let them rest for a second. When he came home, Pharaoh was just glowing. "I hear that the way you worked those slaves today is like nobody ever did before."

"I told you I would."

"Well, do you have any suggestions?"

Listen to this unbelievable thing.

"I'll tell you something," Moshe says. "Based on the way we are working them now, their life span is very short. If you could give them one day off, they would live maybe twenty years longer."

"Great idea, when do you think I should give them off?"

And Moshe says, "I think you should give them off tomorrow night."

This is what it means when we say in the prayers of Shabbos morning, *"Yismach Moshe b'matnas chelko"* – "Moshe will rejoice with the gift of his portion." Do you see what this portion was? Moshe Rabbeinu gave us Shabbos. Moshe Rabbeinu initiated that at the end of the week, we had twenty-four hours off.

Now when slaves have off for twenty-four hours, they go home, eat, and sleep. You know what Moshe and Aharon initiated? It was that you spend those twenty-four hours learning. Moshe Rabbeinu and Aharon HaKohen secretly put the word out that they would all meet in a certain cave and learn on the day off.

The most incredible thing began to take place. Before this, whenever a Jew was hit by an Egyptian, he became downhearted. After that one Shabbos with Moshe, whenever a Jew was hit, beaten up, or insulted, one Jew would tell the other, "Remember what Moshe Rabbeinu taught us on Shabbos?" *Gevalt.*

I want you to know this awesome story.

One of the biggest Rebbes in Poland was the holy Radomsker. Radomsk is a city not far from the German border. After the First World War, a lot of *Chassidim* went to Germany, since Poland was always going bankrupt because they didn't know how to run their country.

The Radomsker was afraid they wouldn't keep Shabbos, so when a Jew left he would say, "I'll tell you what – make me a partner with you for ten percent." The most unbelievable thing was that if you became a partner with the Radomsker, you *mamesh* got rich. Would you believe that half of Berlin belonged to the Radomsker? He was a multi-millionaire.

Now listen to this.

They had a yeshiva with thirty thousand kids, and the Rebbe *mamesh* financed it personally. It was his money. You know how much it takes to feed thirty thousand kids? A lot of bread. The holy Radomsker was paying it all from his own pocket and he still remained a multi-billionaire. People would beg him to become his partner, because they knew the moment you are a partner with the holy Radomsker, you become a millionaire the next day.

His son-in-law, who was also his nephew from his brother, was most probably the greatest genius in Poland. He knew the whole Talmud by heart when he was fifteen years old. *Bavli* and Yerushalmi. He came to the concentration camp when he was eighteen. Since he knew the whole Talmud by heart, while everyone was working he was learning out loud so that everyone could learn.

I heard from somebody whose father was there, that although they were beating them up and were still physically in Auschwitz, they were sustained by the melody of his hearning – it was something else. This son-in-law was there for two weeks, and he didn't stop reciting the Talmud. It was getting on the Germans' nerves, so one morning they just took him and shot him.

Do you know what he was able to do? He redeemed those around him. He didn't take them out of slavery yet, but one thing he did do was that they knew from him that they were not really slaves.

This is what Moshe Rabbeinu gave the *Yidden* while they were slaves in Egypt.

וארא

VA'EIRA

וארא

"Friendship is so much deeper than a contract."

– Rabbi Shlomo Carlebach

This *parsha* is dedicated to:

Rami and Leora Yehoshua,
their children
and the extended
Yehoshua/TBWA "family"

Thank you for your support,
generosity and unconditional friendship.

EXODUS FROM PAGANISM

I WANT YOU TO OPEN YOUR HEARTS IN THE DEEPest depths.

The Maharal (*Netzach Yisrael* 1) says that anything that is unnatural cannot last. Imagine I would force a human being to walk on all fours. Eventually this person would rebel because nature has a tremendous force. Everyone hopefully wants to be natural.

Even those who want to be super-sophisticated and act unnaturally, eventually break down and are normal again. To be a slave is completely unnatural because G-d created us in His image, so it's absolutely not normal for someone to be a slave.

When it comes to the redemption of us *Yiddelach* from slavery, I could say that all we really wanted was to get out of Egypt and be normal human beings again.

But how does that sound to you? Is this all there was to us leaving Egypt? To stop being slaves? Was this whole big operation – Moshe Rabbeinu, the ten plagues and everything coming on so hard – just in order to stop the slavery? It's got to be more than that.

And here I want you to know something so deep.

War is unnatural and peace is normal. Do you think that all the world needs is to stop fighting with each other and be normal again? Do you really think that G-d has been preparing the world for thousands of years for the coming of the Messiah, just so that we could be natural again?

It's got to be more than that. Nature means that if I'm good, I'm good and if I'm bad, I'm bad. If I love you, I hug you, and when I hate you, I hate you. This is normal, so to speak. Do you know what it means to be in G-d's image? To be in G-d's image means I'm beyond nature. I could be beyond everything in the world.

What's the difference between us *Yiddelach* and the world of psychology? The world of psychology says to you, "You want to call someone a dirty name? Go right ahead. It's beautiful to express yourself." But it's really off if you feel the need to have a very dirty mouth.

The world of psychology says that if you want to assert yourself, who cares what the other person is feeling? Some people think they have to walk around, telling people what they really think of them and this is all in the name of "the truth." It's cute and sweet, but what it really means is that I don't really care about your feelings. I walk away thinking that I'm the holiest man in the world, always telling the truth.

That's all there is to life? It's got to be more than that.

Being normal again might be healthy, but there is something much deeper than being normal. I don't mean being abnormal. On the contrary, we human beings have something so much deeper than just being natural.

I want you to think of it in a deep way.

When I meet a girl who I love very much and I want to marry her, what am I thinking about? Do I just want to live like a normal human being? Do I want to be married since everyone else is getting married? Do I want to build a house with her because that's what all other couples do?

Everyone has children, so I want to have children. Everyone is rich, so I want to be rich. Is this all you are capable of dreaming about? When I meet someone I love very much, I want something that never happened before. I don't want to get married just because everyone else is getting married.

The *Medrash* (*Midrash Aggada* 53) says that before our holy mother Sarah couldn't have children, it never happened that a woman wasn't able to have children. In the time of the flood there were women who didn't want to have children because, crazily enough, they thought they would lose their natural beauty. They would drink some kind of poison in order not to have children.

But on a normal level, there was never a woman who didn't have children. Our mother Sarah was the first woman to never have children. She only had a child after so much praying.

Let me ask you – why did it have to be that way? Very simple. The world thinks that a man and a woman get together like putting a dollar into a Coke machine and Mazel Tov, a baby is born. Yes, you can have a lot of babies this way, but you don't have Yitzchak like this. The way a Jew looks at his or her children is something so much deeper.

I'll tell you something, I can walk on the street and buy an apple for one dollar and twenty cents. But now imagine there is an apple I paid a million dollars for. How much am I taking care of *that* apple?

Do you know why most parents are really not taking care of their children? They paid one dollar and twenty cents for them. That's all they put in, but if you put in a million dollars . . . gevalt, are you careful.

Sometimes I meet someone who says, "I'm a Jew," but you can tell it's not for real yet. They eat gefilte fish and have chicken soup on Shabbos, and they go to shul Shabbos morning. What's missing there? Everything about them is within the realm of nature, but nothing is standing out.

You know who a servant of G-d is? A servant of G-d is someone who is completely beyond nature.

When it comes to friendships, it's the same thing. I can meet up with a friend for lunch and pay their bill, but if I wake this friend up at four in the morning and say, "I need you. It's an emergency!" he might say, "Why did you call me? Don't you have other friends?"

There are so many married couples that are so distant from eachother. Everything about their relationship is one hundred percent natural. He is a man, she is a woman. They got married and they live in the same house. What is missing? There is nothing between them that is beyond nature.

You know what the world needs?

The world needs redemption. Redemption is to be beyond everything. Redemption does not mean to return to my natural state. It's to be somewhere so much deeper and so much holier.

Friends, do you know how much pain we go through to have the Holy Land? For two thousand years we are *shlepping* from one country to the other. How much have we gone through in history to be Jewish?

Do we go through so much just to be able to have some chicken soup on Shabbos, just to go to Shul on Shabbos morning and *shuckel* a little bit? It's got to be more than that.

I want you to know something awesome.

We were once learning on Shabbos *Vayechi* that Rashi (Bereishis 49:1) says that before Ya'akov died he wanted to tell his children when *Mashiach* is coming. Then "*v'nistalka mimeno shechinah*" – "G-d's presence left him." G-d didn't want him to tell.

And here you have to open your hearts.

There was a survivor learning with us and he said like this: "Do you know what kept me going in the concentration camps? We thought *Mashiach* is coming any day now. If I would have known that *Mashiach* is not coming, I would have committed suicide every day."

So here we come to the deepest question in the world. What kind of redemption were we waiting for in Egypt? Moshe thought he would come to Pharaoh and tell him, "Let my people go," and Pharaoh would say "I think you are right, Moshe. I'll let them go."

How does that sound to you? For this we are slaves for two hundred and ten years? For Pharaoh to say, "You are right, we should be more human. I'll give you freedom"? How does it sound to you? That's all there is to it?

Let me ask you – if we would have gotten free from Pharaoh like this, would we have Seder night? Would we have Pesach?

Now open your hearts.

Moshe Rabbeinu says to G-d, "[The children of Israel] will ask me, "What is Your name? What should I answer them?" (Sh'mos 3:13)

Let me ask you, friends – we are talking about the children of Avraham, Yitzchak, and Ya'akov.

They knew there was one G-d. I'm sure they were some of the greatest Kabbalists in the world. What does it mean that they don't know G-d's name?

You know what G-d answered?

"My name is, 'I will be what I will be.'"

What is G-d saying to Moshe?

But you see, Moshe Rabbeinu was asking G-d, "What kind of a redemption are you preparing us for? Do I go to Pharaoh and say, 'Let my people go,' and it might take a few weeks, but he will eventually give in? Or is it something much deeper than that? What exactly are we talking about?"

And here I want you to know something so beyond.

It is possible for one *Yiddele* to give five million dollars a month for charity, and another *Yiddele* to gives one dollar. But you know something? This one dollar came from the deepest depths of their soul while the five million dollars was to write off taxes.

I want you to know something heartbreakingly powerful.

One time in my life I had the privilege of saving someone's life.

I was in France and a girl jumped into the ocean, trying to commit suicide. I jumped into the ocean and got her out. It was an awesome experience. I could not imagine ever doing anything wrong again. It was so holy to *mamesh* save someone's life.

When the Mishnah says that saving someone's life is like saving the whole world (*Sanhedrin* 4:5), it is *mamesh* for real. It's not just a cute little saying. So the next day I asked a lifeguard how many lives he saved that year?

With the most bitter face he says to me, "I saved twenty-six children." Twenty-six children! According to nature, he should be glowing. G-d's presence should be upon him day and night. Why isn't he glowing? Because it's his job. He is supposed to save somebody. He sees someone drowning, he jumps in and gets them out, but his inside is not involved.

I want you to know the deepest depths.

To serve G-d without your inside is absolute paganism. In Hebrew, paganism is called *Avodah Zarah*. You know what that means? The Kotzker Rebbe says that *Avodah Zarah* doesn't mean paganism. It means a strange kind of service. I can serve G-d . . . but serving G-d is strange to me.

I can be married to my wife like a stranger. I can say hello to my kids like a stranger. I can come to the Holy Wall, shuckel like a herring and pray for three hours, but I do it all as a stranger.

The most important question is – how much are you a non-stranger to G-d?

You see what it is – the exodus from Egypt is not just the exodus from slavery. It's the exodus from paganism. Stop being a stranger to G-d.

When you love someone, you don't make a slave out of them.

The way it used to be was that if you are a stranger you don't belong here. And, if you are still here, I can do anything I want to with you. Pharaoh was right. The Jews don't belong in Egypt. He can kill them and make slaves out of them. He can take their children and put them into the wall.

Why not? We must realize in a very serious way that any person who feels strange with another human being is not material for the Messiah yet. You might go to Paradise, you might be the president of your Synagogue, but you haven't tasted anything of the Messiah yet.

When I see a poor man on the street who has nothing to eat, I shut the windows and I assume that he is most probably a dope addict. All year long I don't open my door and invite him into my house because to me he is a stranger. If he is hungry, let him go to a social worker.

You know what happens to me on Seder night, when I am getting out of Egypt? On Seder night, there are no strangers anymore. *"Kol dichfin yesei veyechol"* – "whoever is hungry come in and eat." (*Haggadah* of *Pesach.*)

I want you to know that the degree of being strange to G-d and of being strangers with people is the same. If I can see a poor man on the street and not bring him to my house, something inside of me is a stranger with G-d. We are not so close yet.

Now listen to this.

There are two kinds of learning. There is learning when I have a good head and someone teaches me that one and one is two.

I call up Air Canada and ask them "What time is the flight to Toronto?" The operator says, "Five o'clock."

Now listen to the other side of the story. I call up Air Canada and the operator says, "I don't feel close enough to you to tell you what time the flight is." I say "You don't have to feel close to me for this. Just tell me what time the flight is leaving."

When I study physics, I don't have to feel close to the teacher.

You know what learning Torah is? The Gemara says that unless a teacher loves the student like his own child, you have no right to teach him . . . because you simply can't.

Do you know why, sadly enough, so many kids leave the Yeshivos? Because the Yeshivos haven't learned yet that unless the teacher loves the children like crazy, you can't teach them Torah. You can't. It doesn't go in. It just doesn't go in.

In the Sixties, when the youth woke up a little bit, what did they want? They didn't want information. They would have bought a book for information. They wanted a teacher. They wanted someone who would be close to them. And this is what G-d says to Moshe in the beginning of our portion. "Let me tell you something Moshe – redemption is not just about getting out of slavery."

Now listen to the deepest depths.

When Moshe Rabbeinu came and told the *Yidden* that G-d is redeeming them, they believed Moshe because it was still in the framework of nature. Every slave has to be freed eventually. But after G-d told Moshe that redemption is much deeper than just getting out of Egypt, *"v'lo sham'u el Moshe"* – "they had no vessels to hear it" (Va'eira 6:9.) They could not fathom this kind of "beyond nature" redemption.

According to our holy tradition, when people get married, the beginning of the wedding is that the groom covers the face of the bride. You know what that means? Do you think a marriage is a very normal thing? I find this girl, I like her and she likes me. Her father likes me. I can't stand her father but he has money so I tolerate him and I marry her. For that G-d has to call out who my soul mate is forty days before I'm born?

When I cover my bride's face, I am letting her know that I want something so much deeper. I want something which never happened before and which neither of us can see yet. It's not in the world yet. This is what G-d says to Moshe, "Tell them my name is "*Eh-yeh Asher Eh-yeh*" – "I will be what I will be." (Sh'mos 3:14)

You know what our dreams are?

I'm not dreaming based on measuring what I have today. If I have a hundred dollars, do I dream to have a thousand? For that you don't need dreams. You can figure it out on a piece of paper.

You know what dreams are? Dreams are the deepest depths of my soul. When the Messiah is coming it says, "*Beshuv HaShem es shivas Tziyon, hayinu k'cholmim*" – "We will know what we were dreaming about." (*Tehillim* 126:1)

G-d says it hasn't happened yet, but *Eh-yeh* – "it will be." How was a *Yiddele* to know that it really will be? Because it cannot be that G-d is putting me into slavery for two hundred and ten years just so that I can go to Israel to pluck oranges like a free man.

What does Israel mean to most of us today? Instead of going to Acapulco, I go to Tel Aviv. I go to the Holy Wall to say "Hi" to G-d. And since I'm already there, I might as well buy my wife a fur coat. It's got to be more than that. It has got to be more than that.

We have to give the world a different message. The message is not that you didn't have money for bagels yesterday, but from now on you will have because there is peace in the world. Yesterday you were shooting each other. Tomorrow you will say "Hi." Has mankind been going through fire for thousands of years just be able to say "Hi" in the morning?

Who do you think G-d is?

This is what G-d is saying to Moshe. It is not that He can't get the Jews out in one minute. G-d can perform a miracle and take them out in a split-second. But we first have to find out what we are made of. And this is what the ten plagues were all about. To get out of Egypt was a secondary thing.

The ten plagues weren't so much for the Egyptians. They were mainly for us *Yidden.* Because each time there was a plague, we got a little bit more out of Egypt. It was not just that we were slaves to Pharaoh and had to work for him.

We were slaves in Egypt mentally and spiritually. Each time a plague took place, we Jews got deeper and deeper. Our vision of G-d, our vision of redemption got so much deeper. And this kept on happening until Seder night, when we *mamesh* reached the absolute deepest level.

So you see what it is – G-d did not just want to redeem us from slavery. What G-d really wanted was to make us different human beings.

PRECIOUSNESS

RASHI SAYS THAT THAT THE MOST PRECIOUS learning is *"Girsa Deyankusa"* – "the learning of a child" (*Shabbos* 21b.) Does it mean to learn like a child? It really means that what you are learning is not clear to you yet, but at the same time, something special is going on.

I'm learning Gemara but I don't really know it yet. I just know a little bit, but that little bit is so precious to me. When I know everything and everything is clear to me, it's beautiful . . . but it stops being precious. The highest level in the world is when I really understand what I am learning, but it remains precious to me like the way it was before I knew it.

Now imagine on the deepest, highest, most glorious level.

I'm sitting on the subway on 72nd Street in New York City, and I see this absolutely beautiful girl, and I catch her right before she goes through the door. I ask her what her name is. She tells me her name and her number. This name and this number are so precious to me. I learn it one hundred and one times.

This happened to me, and thank G-d, we end up getting married and have ten children. At this point in life, when you ask me what my wife's telephone number is, I will say it straight out, without even thinking about it. But in all honesty, does it have the same preciousness like the time I first met her on the subway when she told me her number? The saddest thing in the world is that by now, knowing her number doesn't do anything to me.

So you see what it is – the highest level in the world is to be able to reach that level after you are married for sixty years and you have great-grandchildren and your wife's name or number is as precious to you as that moment when the door is being closed on that subway on 72nd Street.

And here I want you to open your hearts.

So many people go through so many struggles in their lives until they reach the level where they are supposed to be. A struggle is a very holy and precious thing. In a certain sense, there is no other way to make it to the other side. You don't just wake up in the morning and reach that which you are longing for.

Everyone knows that you shouldn't get angry every two minutes. It's clear to you like daylight and yet you might have to work on it your whole life until you reach the level that you don't blow up over every little thing. But everyone wants to know, "Why do I need to go through the whole thing? G-d can simply remove the struggle from me so I can just be holy and sit and learn all day."

And here I want you to know that this is what G-d is telling Moshe in our *parsha* "I have a plan but I want the *Yidden* to taste the preciousness of the struggle." Until you taste the preciousness of when things aren't so clear, you might be leaving Egypt but you will walk right back there.

You know what it is, having clarity without struggling and without pain is so empty. But if it's clear to you that *gevalt,* "I went through so much till I got here," then you experience life so much more deeply.

In 1840 approximately, there was a Jew in Lemberg who denounced all the great Rebbes, all the holy *Tzaddikim,* saying that they are a danger to young people. He would tell the authorities that they are dreamers, that they tell young people to dream about the Messiah and about G-d's kingdom and that they are a danger to mankind.

At that time, Reb Mendele Riminover was in the *Beis Medrash* of Lemberg and all the holy people were with him. The police came and arrested them. The Ropshitzer was the sharpest of them all. He saw the police coming and jumped out of the window because he thought that at least one of them had to be outside.

The Ropshitzer made himself strong, walked over to the police the next day and said that he wants to talk to the head of police.

The head of the police asked him, "What do you want?"

He said, "I heard you arrested all those rabbis, the dreamers."

"Yeah, we did it all right. They are terrible people."

So the Ropshitzer says, "Oh, really? I'm one of them." The policeman says, "What? You are one of them? If you are one of them, I will release them all right away."

Anyway, this person from Lemberg was constantly making trouble. The *chassidim* realized there must be a Rebbe somewhere who could take care of this troublesome Yid. So there was one Rebbe, the *Heilige* Reb Baruch Zvarsha. Reb Baruch Zvarsha was so holy. He called every Jew "*tzaddik*."

He was once with his wagon driver, a simple-minded man, and he said to him, "*Tzaddik*, go left, *tzaddik* go right." So the wagon driver says "Rebbe, you say that I'm a *tzaddik* and the whole world says that you are a *tzaddik*. I have a son and you have a daughter. Let's marry them off." So Reb Baruch Zvarhsa says, "Listen, there are all kinds of *tzaddikim*. Your son has to marry his kind of a *tzaddik* and my daughter has to marry her kind of a *tzaddik*."

But anyway, the real *tzaddikim* thought that if Reb Baruch Zvarsha can curse this person who is making so much trouble with the police, all their *tzoros* (troubles) would come to an end.

So the holy Ropshitzer comes to Reb Baruch Zvarsha – it's a long story and I'm just giving you the short version – and the Ropshitzer says to him, "*Heilige* Zvarsher, you have to curse this person."

The Zvarsher says, "Ropshitzer Rav, come with me. Come down with me to the cellar." They go down to the cellar and there was a huge barrel of water.

So he says to the Ropshitzer, "Do you know what's in here? In this barrel are the tears I have cried before G-d that I should never say anything bad about another person. Please don't take these tears away from me."

You see what it is – can you imagine what the Zvarsher had to go through until he was able to look at *Yidden* and call each and every one of them a *tzaddik*? He wouldn't let anyone take away the pain and tears he had to cry in order to reach this level of tasting each person's preciousness.

Can you imagine how much Avraham Avinu went through until he reached the level of being Avraham Avinu? Some of us think that he was born a way-out hippie, sharing everything with everyone. And we might think that Sarah was walking around with beads, always happy to let all the people come to their house.

The holy Sanzer says that Avraham Avinu was born with the stingiest soul in the world, but he *mamesh* worked his way up to be able to give everything away.

You see what it is – anything which falls into my lap, I'm not able to give over to my children. Whatever I work on like a dog is what I give over to my children. Avraham, Yitzchak, and Ya'akov worked so hard till they got there, spiritually, mentally and divinely.

They turned their *kishkes* over a million times a second, paving the way for us.

The real "*yerusha*," the real "inheritance" you leave for your children, is not the few rubles you leave. What you leave for your children is what you went through. The journey toward the purification of your heart is what is left for your children.

All those *Yidden* who are, so-to-speak, *"frum"* but don't work on it . . . their children don't care. Their children may end up *frum* because of a miracle or maybe someone else will turn them on.

So here G-d says to Moshe Rabbeinu, *"Va'eira el Avraham el Yitzchak v'el Ya'akov b'Keil Sha-dai."* What was difficult for Avraham, Yitzchak, and Ya'akov? It was that when they received G-d's word it wasn't shining from all four corners. *"U-sh'mi HaShem lo noda'ti la-hem"* (Sh'mos 6:3) – "I didn't tell them My Name."

It wasn't that clear that this is G-d's word, but one thing was clear to them – that unless they turn over their *kishkes* a million times to do what G-d says, they won't really understand what He wants from them. The preciousness was that G-d never made His word completely clear to them, which is what brought them to work so hard on themselves.

Sometimes the *Ribbono shel Olam* tells you something and it's not clear yet, but *gevalt* is it precious! Sometimes G-d tells you something and it's clear. It might be very beautiful but it has no preciousness. Was there ever a moment when things were clearer to us than on Mount Sinai? G-d spoke to us face-to-face, but what does G-d tell us on Mount Sinai? *"Remember, I took you out of Egypt."*

You know what G-d was telling us? "Don't forget how precious you were when you knew there was one G-d, while you were still slaves in Egypt." *Gevalt,* was it precious.

This is the first way a *Yid* learns how precious something is.

The Ishbitzer says that whenever the *Ribbono shel Olam* sends us a little word, we *Yidden* become *"choilas ahava."* We get sick with longing over it. We are living in a world where most people don't know anything about *Yiddishkeit*. Whatever they hear about *Yiddishkeit* is still in exile by them. But for them, it's so precious.

Then you meet a *Yiddele* for whom it is already clear, but it has lost its preciousness. It's not so precious anymore and he doesn't even learn from it. The reason he doesn't even learn from it is because he needs someone to make the word precious even after he knows it. I want it to be precious after I know it.

You know why some of us are so angry (a little bit) at the people in Israel? They took away the whole preciousness. There is a State of Israel and that's it. The State of Israel began with Herzl or the moment Weizmann or Ben-Gurion came to Israel. It's cute, but where are the two thousand years of crying for it? What happened to that?

I'll tell you something crazy.

Two weeks before the Yom Kippur war, I was taking a cab from the Hilton to somewhere. The taxi driver had his girlfriend in the car. I was talking about something and I used the word *"Yidden."*

She turns to me and says, "I'm not Jewish. I'm an Israeli."

"You are not Jewish? What do you mean you are not Jewish? You are ashamed to be related to the Six Million Jews? You are ashamed to be related to people who went into the fire for G-d during the Inquisition?"

So she says to me, *"Ein li shum esek itam"* – "I have nothing to do with them." Sometimes I have patience and sometimes I don't. It was Friday afternoon and I just didn't have the time. She doesn't need Jews. She just needs Israelis.

A year later, *min HaShamayim,* he was still a taxi driver at the Hilton. I meet him again and *nebach,* the saddest thing is he only has one foot. He says to me, "You know something, my girlfriend and I were looking for you. I now know that I'm a Jew. *Gevalt,* do I know I'm a Jew! When I was out there in the Yom Kippur war, I knew that I am a Jew. Not an Israeli." You know what he tasted? The preciousness of being a *Yiddele.*

Here I want you to know the deepest depths.

What's the difference between Torah and *tefillah*, between learning and praying? Torah is when I understand what I am learning. *Tefillah* is also saying words of the Torah but I only understand a little bit. I can read what it says, but *gevalt* is it precious to me.

I want you to know, when we put on a *tallis* when we daven and we say, "*Ma yakar chasdecha Elokim*" – "How precious is your kindness, O' G-d" (*Tehillim* 36:8), because davening is so precious.

You know why the Holy Temple is destroyed? The Holy Temple is the place of davening. What happened to us? Things stopped being precious to us. It wasn't so precious anymore.

And here I want you to know something, sweetest friends.

When I know how precious every Jew is, I don't hate them. Only when I don't know how precious they are, do I judge them. You know something, when it comes to our love for our children – if the whole world, the *Shechinah* and G-d Himself, would tell me that my children are evil, I still wouldn't believe them because preciousness is the strongest thing in the world. My children are always the most precious in the world for me.

And here I want you to know something awesome.

When I learn, I don't have to do it together with other people. When *Yidden* daven, it's *mamesh* together with ten other *Yidden*. You know what that means? Is it possible to be together based on the fact that we share the same knowledge? You're a lawyer, I'm a lawyer. You're a doctor, I'm a doctor, You're a stockbroker, I'm a stockbroker. No! When we have the same things that are precious to us – *gevalt* does that bring us close!

Now here I want you to know the deepest depths.

On the deepest level, preciousness comes from Avraham, Yitzchak, and Ya'akov. This strength, that the Torah strikes something in us, makes us feel how precious it is . . . this is what we inherited from our three fathers and four mothers. You know friends, for us *Yiddelach,* Jewish children are so precious to us because of our mother Sarah. Was there anybody in the world to whom a baby was more precious than to our mother Sarah?

I want you to know something.

When the angels came to Avraham, they said, *"Ayeih Sarah ishtecha"* – "Where is your wife Sarah?" So he answered, *"Hinei ba'ohel"* – "she is in the tent." (Bereishis 18:9) The Vorker says like this – the angels were asking Avraham, "Who is your wife? She is turning over heaven and Earth. Everyone is talking about Sarah. Where is she? What's her level? Can you tell us something about her?"

"Hinei ba'ohel" – "She is in the tent." Avraham is saying, "She is so hidden that even I don't know. She is beyond me." So I just want to add that preciousness is when I know something is holy and special, but I have no concept as to how much it really is so.

So I want to say like this.

Sarah was the first one who knew how precious a Jewish baby is. You can only give over *Yiddishkeit* when you give over how precious it is.

So the angels asked Avraham, "What does Sarah know?" *"Hinei ba'ohel."*

What do you do when something is very precious? You hide it. So Avraham Avinu answers, "She is the master of hiding." The first sign you love somebody is not how much you know them. It's how precious they are to you.

INFINITE LIMITATIONS

I revealed myself to Avraham, Yitzchak, and Ya'akov as El-Shaddai. . . . (Sh'mos 6:3)

IMAGINE THAT I TELL YOU THAT I CAN NEVER GET married because I cannot limit myself to one woman. Or I say that I'm a universalist and I cannot limit myself to one religion. As for Shabbos? How can I limit myself to just one day? For me, Shabbos is Sunday, Monday and Tuesday. I also can't limit myself to just buying kosher meat.

I'm so universal and so into meat that whenever I pass by a meat store, I just have to go in and buy some. And I also can't limit myself to live in one house. I have to live in the subway and all night long I'm going from one place to another. But to live in just one house, have one key, sleep in one bed? I'm a universalist and I can't limit myself.

How does that sound to you?

Here I want you to open your hearts.

The more serious anything gets, the more you have to narrow it down. I once asked a group of people to tell me how much paper they would need to write down their secrets. One girl said, "Thousands of notebooks."

Finally it was my turn. I told them that I could write my secrets on the top of one nail and my nail would still be half empty. You see, the more you get into what is real, the more you narrow it down.

When we say, "*HaShem Echad*" – "G-d is One," it doesn't just mean that there is one G-d. It means that when it comes to the real thing, it is only one, just one. And what is more real than G-d? And here the Ishbitzer says the deepest Torah.

Everybody knows that the deepest covenant between G-d and Israel was not through Moshe at Mount Sinai. It was through our forefathers, Avraham, Yitzchak, and Ya'akov. Like we say in *S'lichos, "Z'chor lanu bris avos"* – "Remember the covenant of our fathers." The biggest *tzimtzum,* the biggest limitation, is making a covenant. A covenant means I narrow down my focus, making a relationship with just one other being.

What does it mean to have a covenant with G-d? Do I have to stop being universal? Not at all. It means that I'm *mamesh* getting into the deepest depths of being close to G-d.

Without sounding coarse . . . if I cannot get married because I can't limit myself to one woman, that means I cannot make a covenant. I can't commit myself. I can't narrow myself down to one. If I think I have to have everything on an equal level, if I have to change all the time or if I have to go from one thing to another – then really, I have nothing.

But if I can narrow down to the deepest, most important point, then I really have everything.

I once met a kid who told me, "I'm universal. I can't limit myself to *Yerushalayim.* For me, Paris and Bombay are also holy."

What is his problem? He thinks that this way he has more. But in the deepest depths, he has nothing.

Now listen to what the Ishbitzer says (*Beis Ya'akov* HaKollel, "Va'eira el Avraham.") We know G-d by different names and each name has a different meaning. G-d's name of *Shin, Daled, Yud* is basically the name of *tzimtzum,* of restriction.

You see, HaShem created this big world filled with so many things. He then put His name of *tzimtzum* into it. And this way, He made it possible for us to narrow ourselves to one point, to concentrate on one page. If He hadn't put this name *Shin Daled Yud* into the world, we wouldn't be able to focus on any one thing. We wouldn't even be able to talk to one person at a time.

Have you ever seen people who have one eye on you and the other eye on something else while they are talking to you? They aren't really with you. They are already somewhere else. They think that concentrating on you is too limiting and they want to have more.

But they have nothing this way. Even a dog responds to you when you talk to it. People like this are not connected to the name *Shin Daled Yud.*

When G-d added the concept of *tzimtzum* to His name, He was actually setting limits in the world. Day is day, night is night. Summer is summer, winter is winter. A tree is a tree. Each thing is just what it is, and nothing else.

Imagine if an apple would say, "I cannot limit myself to just being an apple. I want to be universal. I want to taste like an orange, look like a grape, smell like an onion and be sweet like Coca Cola." Crazy! Is it an apple or not? If it's not an apple, then it's nothing.

I've never seen an apple coming to a psychiatrist complaining that it is having an identity crisis or that it can't identify as an apple. Only we human beings have this kind of problem.

You see what it is – G-d's name on the outside of a *mezuzah* is "*Shin Daled Yud,*" and His holy name of "*Yud Kei Vav Kei*" is on the inside. Do you know how deep this is? Do you think G-d is narrowing us down? It's just the outside. From the inside we have the whole world.

When I narrow myself down to that which is most precious in life, then I have the whole world. I have everything. People who think they have everything really have nothing because they never found that one thing they want to tie themselves to. They never found the covenant.

Most of the time, when I have something, it makes a wall between G-d and me because I think it's mine. Do you know how easy it is to make a wall between people? I have something and you don't have it. It makes a tiny wall. Can you imagine the depths of closeness between people when something belongs to both of us?

The closeness between husband and wife is that whatever they have belongs to both of them. The moment I say, "It belongs to me," I'm already making a wall. So I put a *mezuzah* with *Shin Daled Yud* on the door to my house, so everyone will know that nothing belongs to me. Whatever seems to be mine really belongs to G-d.

And when I go out on the street, it's usually to get more than I already have. And lots of times I get lost. So when I leave my house I kiss the outside of the *mezuzah*, the *Shin Daled Yud*. Before I go out to the street, I have to remind myself not to forget my roots. And when I am inside my house, I have to always remember that the whole world belongs to G-d.

*

I remember that one time, at the beginning of my humble career, I met a group of one hundred Jewish kids from Germany who were travelling all over Europe on buses.

These poor kids didn't know what to do with themselves. On the one hand they'd been told that all the *goyim* are terrible and that they had killed all the Jews. Then their parents said that the Jews are the chosen people, but they didn't observe anything.

These kids couldn't figure any of it out and they knew nothing about *Yiddishkeit*. It was *mamesh* heartbreaking.

Anyway, I saw them on their bus, and I started talking to them. And they were really open to what I had to say. It was Shabbos when I met them, so I told them a little about the day and invited them to come back with me for *shaleshudes*, the third meal. They really wanted to come. They were with me all the way.

Now these kids had an Israeli guide with them. He saw what was going on and he couldn't bear it. He pulled me away from the bus and said, "Stop telling these kids nonsense. All this stuff about Shabbos . . . it's too narrow. It makes us small. For me, Shabbos isn't one day. It's every day." With that he got on the bus, slammed the door and they drove off.

Imagine that I'm drowning and someone throws me a rope. And I say, "Listen, I'm universal. I'm not holding onto only one rope. Either you throw me all the ropes or leave me alone and I'll just drown." But there is only one rope. *"Eitz chayim he lamachazikim bah"* – "The Torah is a tree of Life to those who are holding onto it." (*Mishlei* 3:18)

Now listen to this. It's the deepest depths.

The roots of a tree sometimes aren't so big, and in any case, you can't see them. They're deep under the ground. But above the roots, above the ground, the tree can have thousands of apples.

This is how it also is with us *Yidden.* We have one system of roots – one Avraham, one Yitzchak and one Ya'akov. And when we make a covenant we're connected to those roots, to the roots of our roots. Then we can be connected to everything in the world.

So you see what it is – on one hand, when I think about G-d's names, I want them to really take over, to *mamesh* shine everywhere. Why doesn't that happen? As Moshe Rabbeinu said to G-d, "Here You are giving me Your names. Why don't they expand all over the world?"

And G-d answered, "Don't you understand? One of the names I'm giving you is *Shin Daled Yud.* First I'm fixing the roots and while I'm doing this, it looks like nothing is happening. But ". . . *va'ezkor es brisi.*" (Sh'mos 6:5.) First I'm fixing the covenant, and then you will see. It will expand."

There are two kinds of people in the world. Sometimes when you meet a person, everything is clear between the two of you. This is very holy. And then there are times when you meet people and nothing seems to be happening. Do you know what these people are doing? They are fixing your roots. You walk away and you still don't know it, but your roots are fixed.

And do you know what *Yerushalayim* is? When the Holy Temple is standing, it shines G-d's light. It expands everywhere. But now, when the Temple is destroyed, do you know what is happening? The Holy Wall is fixing our roots. A lot of people go to the Kotel, and when they come away, they still eat *treif* and they still drive on Shabbos. But they are more connected to their roots.

Whenever you don't know what to do, you have to limit your attention to see what the most important thing in your life is. If what you're thinking of doing connects you to that important thing – to your roots – that's okay. If not, then it has nothing to do with you.

You see what it is – when you are connected to your roots, you know where you are going. Your head is so clear. How can you know if the *Yeshiva* you are learning in or the Rebbe you are learning with is right for you? If you walk away and you add more Torahs and everything connects, then you know that it's all part of your roots.

This is the Shabbos of roots, the Shabbos of that deep connecting.

This is the Shabbos of *tzimtzum,* of focusing on the most important point. It is the Shabbos of *Shin Daled Yud.*

*

What does it mean to have a covenant with G-d? It means that G-d is looking just at me. But how can I limit G-d just to me? How can I limit G-d at all?

It's the strangest thing in the world. When you love somebody very much, you don't think of anything other than the person you love. From the outside it looks like you are limiting yourself and seeing just one person. But *gevalt,* when you love somebody, the whole world seems so much more beautiful.

So you see what it is – from the outside it seems like I'm making G-d smaller when I think He is looking just at me. But really, this is when I most clearly see G-d in the whole world. And then, *gevalt,* am I making G-d's name big.

How does the *Ribbono shel Olam* tell Moshe Rabbeinu who is the master of *Yud Key Vav Key,* G-d's universal Name? *Va'eira el Avraham.* G-d appeared to Avraham, to just one person. To Yitzchak, just to Yitzchak. And to Ya'akov, just to this one person, Ya'akov. *Gevalt,* this is so deep.

Chassidim used to say that the Holy Baal Shem Tov was *mamesh* shivering when he said hello to a new person. So they asked the Baal Shem, "Why do you shiver when you meet somebody?" And the Ba'al Shem Tov answered, "The Torah tells us, *"v'ahavta l'reyacha kamocha"* – "Love your neighbor like you love yourself." People think *"reyacha"* means "your neighbor," but really it means the person you are talking to. So I *mamesh* have to completely give my heart to each person I talk to. It's a heavy thing. *Gevalt,* is it hard."

You see, we always walk around meeting people, saying, "Hi. How are you?" But we are missing out on the whole thing. It's not enough to just say "Hello" to people. You have to give them your heart. How do you do that? By focusing your whole attention just on them.

*

Everyone knows that Pharaoh also believed in G-d.

So why did the Egyptians and all the pagans have so many deities? Because they didn't think that G-d could narrow down His focus to take care of every little thing. So they had many gods to cover all areas.

The Rambam says that the Egyptians believed that G-d is just everywhere. He is everything. Pharaoh called Him *"Eloha de'eloha"* – "He is the G-d of all the gods." He is the Big Master, taking care of the big picture. And He has other gods working for him, taking care of all the details.

But we know that the *Ribbono shel Olam* is *mamesh* taking care of everything . . . the whole and also all the parts. Take the big Rebbes. The really great people were not trying to take care of the whole world at once. What was so special about them? Whenever they spoke to one person, they forgot the rest of the world.

In Lubavitch, what was the whole thing of *yechidus*? It wasn't just that one *Chassid* met alone with the Rebbe. The special thing about *yechidus* was that, in the moment of meeting his follower, the Rebbe *mamesh* extracted himself from the rest of the world and turned all his attention to this one *Yid.*

If G-d can narrow down His focus towards each of us, why can't we narrow down our focus towards G-d? We think that the moment we limit ourselves, we make ourselves small and can't relate to the whole world. So here the Ishbitzer says like this – Yosef was the master of *tzaddik yesod olam,* the righteous one who is the foundation of the world.

Gevalt, was Yosef able to control himself! Not only could he commit himself to one woman but he didn't even want to look at someone who was not his wife.

But do you know what Yosef was doing? He was feeding the whole world. There was nobody in the world who was more universal than Yosef. He was *mamesh* the master of the *bris,* the covenant . . . the greatest *tzimtzum.* And at the same time, he was the master of *hashpa'a,* giving sustenance to the whole world.

Torah she-b'ch'sav, the written Torah, is universal. The Gemara says, "*Torah munachas b'kerem zavis*" – "the Torah was placed in a corner," anyone who wants to may come and learn." (*Kiddushin* 66:1)

Torah she-be'al peh, the oral Torah, is "*va'ani zos brisi osam amar HaShem*" – "And for Me, this is My covenant with them, said G-d." (*Yishayahu* 59:21)

The Ishbitzer says that the *bris,* the covenant, is the biggest form of *tzimtzum* in this world. *Torah she-be'al peh* means that I'm sitting over this one *Tosafos* or over this one Rambam, and I can't move.

Here is this big world and I narrow my focus down to one page.

But in this one page I taste everything.

TWO TYPES OF REVELATION

THERE ARE TWO TYPES OF REVELATION FROM above.

There are the ten sayings with which G-d created the world, *"ba'asara ma'amaros nivra ha'olam,"* – "The world was created with ten sayings" (*Mishnah Avos* 5:1.) When G-d says, "Let there be fish," G-d's very words saying there should be fish, created the fish. When G-d says, "Let there be light," G-d's words saying "let there be light" are light itself.

But then there is another type of revelation, when things take much longer to happen and here you have to open your hearts, my friends.

At the end of the portion of Sh'mos, G-d says to Moshe, "Go to Pharaoh, give him over My words. I want him to let the Jews go."

Moshe Rabbeinu comes back to G-d and he says, "Nothing happened." Here I have to fill you in.

Moshe Rabbeinu was adopted by the daughter of Pharaoh. The last will of Pharaoh was that Moshe Rabbeinu should be the next Pharaoh. Moshe was able to trick Pharaoh into giving the *Yiddelach* one day off from slavery and he gave them Shabbos.

After Moshe Rabbeinu killed an Egyptian, who was one of the most evil people in Egypt, he had to leave Egypt. Here he is coming back, and he comes up to Pharaoh and demands, "In the name of G-d, let my people go."

You know what Pharaoh did? The first thing he said to Moshe is, "I'll show you what I will do. Because of you I let them have Shabbos for so many years. No more Shabbos for the slaves. No more Shabbos for the slaves."

Until Moshe Rabbeinu came, the Egyptians were feeding us just a little bit. From now on, there was no more food for us *Yiddelach.* You are hungry? Find it yourself!

Until Moshe Rabbeinu came, they were given straw and all kinds of materials to build those bricks for the pyramids. From now on, nothing! "You get your own material." Every Jew was supposed to make a certain amount of bricks and if you didn't bring that amount of bricks, you were whipped to death.

And lastly, until that time they were only working for the Egyptian government. After Moshe Rabbeinu comes to Pharaoh and says, "Let my people go," Pharaoh issues is a new decree. During the day you work for the Egyptian government, but at night any Egyptian can grab you and make you work all night long. How long can a human being exist like that?

Here Moshe Rabbeinu finds out that Pharaoh took away their Shabbos, their food and their material to build the bricks. So he comes before G-d and he says, "*Lama hare'osa la'am ha-zeh?*" "*Gevalt!* How can You let this happen?" (Sh'mos 5:22)

Can you imagine how much Moshe Rabbeinu was crying? What hurt him the most is that he thought he was the cause of all this. Moshe Rabbeinu thought that Pharaoh didn't listen to him because he, Moshe Rabbeinu, isn't holy enough to bring over G-d's word. But deeper than all this, Moshe Rabbeinu was asking G-d, "If Your word is for real, not only did it not help, it made things worse." (Sh'mos 5:23)

Sometimes we pray and we do what G-d tells us to do, but nothing seems to change. Moshe Rabbeinu thought that once he would approach

Pharaoh in the name of G-d, a miracle would happen and the *Yidden* would be freed. But the truth is that it's so much deeper than that.

And here is the second type of revelation.

The Gemara says "*tefilos avos tiknum*" – "the prayers were initiated by our forefathers." (*Brachos* 26b.) Avraham initiated the morning prayer, Yitzchak the afternoon prayer, and Ya'akov the evening prayer. But it means more than that. It means that in a certain deep way, praying depends on the parents.

If my child is crying and I say, "Keep your mouth shut," this child knows that nobody answers when I cry, so I'm not going to pray to G-d either.

But if children know that when they cry, their parents jump out of their skin and will do anything for them, then they also know that there is someone up there who listens to every prayer.

When my child is crying and I say, "Stop crying, you are grown up now," the child starts thinking that crying doesn't help. When my child is crying and I'm crying with him or her, my child knows that G-d is counting all the tears. And even if it takes time, it's okay. There is someone crying with me.

Here the Ishbitzer says the deepest depths.

What happens to a seed when you put it in the earth? Imagine I will interview that seed before it's put into the earth. "Seed, what are your plans?"

"My plans are to spend a little while under the ground and come out as an apple tree." Unbelievable! I wish you luck. Two days later I'm coming down to the seed. No apple tree yet. I say, "Seed, how are you doing?"

"Well, to tell you the truth, I really thought I would become an apple tree, but it was a mistake. I'm just disintegrating and nothing will ever become of me."

Two months later I speak to the seed again. I say, "Hey, seed, how are you doing?"

The seed says, "You know something? There is nothing left of me. I was small at the beginning, but now there is nothing left of me."

And here I want you to open your hearts.

Do you know what disintegrating means? It means that anything which is not the essence of the seed doesn't exist anymore, because an apple tree does not come out of the seed. It comes when the seed reaches the deepest depths of its existence. It's almost not there anymore, but when its essence connects to the earth, it begins to grow.

You know, friends – when do we grow? Here I heard a lecture on Judaism and think I'm growing. I'm a better Jew tomorrow. It doesn't actually go this way; I read this book on happy marriage, and now my wife and I are growing together. It's cute, but it's only good for another article in *Readers Digest*. In reality it doesn't help. In order to grow, you have to hit the essence of the essence of the essence of the essence.

Let me tell you – the same thing is happening when it comes to learning. I'm learning this one page of the Gemara. I understand it and I'm ready to write a book on it. You might be able to find a printer, but the book has no taste.

Real learning is when I spend days and nights over what I'm learning and I don't understand a word. I'm just about giving up, but at the last second G-d enlightens me.

This is one of the deepest stories.

The Sochatchover had a big Yeshiva with hundreds of students. One day he sends a letter to the father of one of his students, "I'm sorry to ask you, but please take your son home because he cannot stay in my Yeshiva."

The father is so heartbroken and he comes to pick up his son. He says to the Sochatchover, "I'm so sorry my son is not learning."

So the Sochatchover says, "G-d forbid. He happens to be the best boy in my whole school."

"So why don't you want him to stay and learn?"

The Sochatchover says "Well, to tell you the truth, I have never seen tears in his eyes when he is learning."

You see friends, there is learning where I understand everything because I'm a genius, but this is not G-d's word. This is like any university. Since you are a genius and have a good head, so therefore you are learning. G-d wants something so much deeper of us, but you cannot get there if you don't dedicate your heart and soul to every word.

Someone came to Reb Nachman and said to him, "You are such a great Kabbalist. Can you please give over the secret of *tzitzis?*"

Reb Nachman says, "If you will cry over the *tzitzis* as many tears as there are threads in your *tallis,* then you will understand it." Not so simple.

Now let's go back to the beginning.

Moshe Rabbeinu says to G-d, "You told me to tell Pharaoh to let them go. Why didn't it help?" The Ishbitzer says that redemption is like a little seed. Someday, there will be no weapons in the world and people will love each other. But it won't happen like the ten sayings of the creation, where G-d says "Let there be light," and there is light.

When G-d sends the Messiah, it's like a seed. It's disintegrating. You have to go through so much. So G-d says to Moshe, "Do you know why they have to go through so much pain? It's because the exodus of Egypt is reaching the core of their being."

I want to share this story with you – one of my favorite stories.

I saw an old movie which showed the last two hours of the Titanic. The ship sunk at midnight, January 1st. The focus of the movie was on a father and mother. A typical wealthy family. It cost a fortune to be on the ship. They were married, coexisting. The father is sitting with another woman by the bar, while the mother was sitting with another man. Every half hour they each found another man and woman to sit with. They had two kids, a boy of five and a girl of seven.

The kids are getting tired. Someone has to put them to sleep. They come to their father, "Can you please put us to sleep?" So the father tells them, "You see I'm busy, go to your mother."

They come to the mother and get the same response. In the meantime, these lonely kids fall asleep on the deck. Exactly at twelve the sirens go off and they announce. "The ship is sinking and there are only enough life jackets for the children. Collect your children and bring them on deck."

How do this father and mother feel at that point? They don't even know where their children are. "*Gevalt,* did we neglect them." They start yelling for them from the deepest depths of their heart. They are running up and down the ship. Finally, they find the two kids lying on the deck, sleeping.

The captain comes up to them and he says, "You have three minutes to say goodbye."

They would give two million lifetimes just to put their kids to sleep one more time. They would give two hundred thousand lifetimes just to sit together at the same table one more time. You know where they reached in those three minutes? Suddenly it was clear to this man and woman how much they love each other and how much they love their children. The thing is, it was too late. It was too late.

The greatest thing is that when G-d blesses you, you "disintegrate" while you can still fix it. And you know something? You have to believe that on a certain level, you can always fix it. It's never too late.

I want you to know something.

Sometimes a husband and wife have a fight. People who never fight are not normal. If they end up having a little fight, there are two ways of handling it. They can go to a marriage counselor and say, "Let's have peace again." *Mazel tov.* It's all cute and sweet, but did we have to hurt each other's feelings for that? Did we have to go through so much pain for that? Unless it is two million times deeper, unless I love you like I never loved you before, then causing each other pain just isn't worth it.

This is the difference between the two revelations. One revelation in the world is when G-d created the world. He proclaimed something and it happened right away. But then there is another revelation where G-d's word is like a seed. G-d says there will be redemption, but redemption has to first penetrate the deepest depths of my being.

ARE YOU CLOSE ENOUGH TO CRY?

. . . I heard the groaning of the children of Israel. (Sh'mos 6:5)

I WANT TO SHARE SOMETHING SO DEEP WITH YOU.

Moshe Rabbeinu says to G-d that when he will come to the *Yidden* to declare the beginning of the process of freedom, they won't believe him.

So G-d says, "Okay, let the level of the redemption be on the level that I can do it and show them miracles."

You know what that means?

Miracles show that G-d can do anything. Redemption is not about what G-d can or can't do. So here Moshe Rabbeinu says to G-d, "Why did you send me? I think I ruined the whole thing by telling You they won't believe me because You then reduced the redemption to the level of miracles."

G-d has all kinds of revelations. There is a revelation that it has to be clear to everyone that G-d can do anything in the world. There is nothing in the world that G-d cannot do, but my connection to G-d is so much deeper than that.

My connection to G-d is not because G-d can do anything. I'm so glad that I know G-d can do anything, but the redemption is so much deeper. The revelation of the redemption is that I can cry to G-d and G-d hears me. *Gevalt,* what a great privilege it is to have it in this world.

And here I want you to know something awesome.

I am so close to G-d that he can give me orders, and I want to listen to them. But do you think the Torah is only about taking orders? It's really about how close I can be to Hashem.

The first stage of the redemption was the praying: *"Vayitzaku b'nei Yisrael el HaShem"* – "and the children of Israel cried out to G-d" (Sh'mos 14:10). My first connection to G-d is not because G-d is the Master of the World. My first connection to G-d is because G-d listens to me.

So you see how deep this is.

The first message was not "I'm redeeming you." If you read the portion properly you will realize that the first message of Moshe to the *Yidden* was that G-d heard you cry. Imagine if it will be clear to me that each time I pray, G-d hears me. You would taste redemption . . . you would *mamesh* taste redemption.

When we daven, first we say, *"Ga'al Yisrael"* – "Redeemer of Israel," and only then do we start the *Shemoneh Esrei,* the silent prayer.

You know what the deepest redemption is? It's that I know that I can pray and G-d hears me. This is the deepest redemption in the world.

Then G-d says, *"V'gam ani shamati es na'akas b'nei Yisrael"* – "I also heard the crying of the children of Israel." (Sh'mos 6:5) G-d says "I also heard the crying of the Jews." Everyone is asking, what's this *"v'gam"* – "also"?

There are all kinds of Torahs. I want to share this one with you.

In the deepest depths, when I'm suffering, I don't only want to be helped, I long to be heard. I want someone to hear me. So G-d says, *"V'gam ani shamati."* The *Ribbono shel Olam* says, "I, Master of the Universe, I heard their crying."

When little children cry, it's so deep. Lowlife parents think their kids want something. But they want nothing . . . they just want to cry and be heard. At night, when they cry, parents come in and ask, "What do you want?" This is an exile relationship between parents and their children.

You know what exile is? In exile we also still believe that G-d can do anything, but we don't have this closeness that I just want to cry to G-d.

Eretz Yisrael is *"Eretz asher . . . einei HaShem Elokecha bah"* – "the land where G-d doesn't take his eyes off it." G-d is looking at us all the time. (Devarim 11:12)

So is *Eretz Yisrael* the land of miracles? It is, but it's so much deeper . . . so much deeper.

Do you think the spies were crazy? They had clear prophecy. They were Moshe Rabbeinu people. You know what they saw? They saw the destruction of the Temple and they saw the blood from *Yerushalayim* flowing to the four corners of the world.

Do you know what else they saw? They saw that on the level of Torah and mitzvos we don't deserve it yet, *"ki chazak hu mimenu"* – "for they are stronger than us." (Bamidbar 13:31) They felt that if the *Yidden* want to come to *Eretz Yisrael* based on their own credit, they can't come in yet.

So what was the spies' mistake? You don't go to Israel because you deserve it. That's not what coming to the Holy Land is all about. The spies thought *Eretz Yisrael* is the land of miracles, but that's not what *Eretz Yisrael* is all about. Redemption is something else.

Now let's go back to the beginning.

At the end of last *parsha,* Moshe Rabbeinu can't understand what's going on. After going to Pharaoh and giving him G-d's word, the situation was only getting worse and much darker. "|*Lama harei'osa la'am ha-zeh*?" G-d, why are you making it so hard on the *Yidden*? *"Lama zeh shelachtani?"* – "Why did you even send me to Pharaoh in the first place?" (Sh'mos 5:22) Did You send me to make it worse?

So G-d says to Moshe, *"Ata sire'h,"* – "Now you will see what I am all about." (Sh'mos 6:1)

Our portion begins with G-d saying to Moshe, "I want you to know that I revealed myself to Avraham, Yitzchak, and Ya'akov by the name '*Shin, Daled,* and *Yud.*' But to you Moshe, I reveal myself with the name '*Yud, Hei, Vav* and *Hei.*'"

Everyone knows, the name "*Shin Daled Yud*" stands for "*She'amar l'olamo dai*" – "the One who said to His world, 'Enough.'" (*Chagigah* 12a.) It's the name of G-d that keeps the world together. It's like the scotch tape of the world.

It's one thing to believe that G-d can do everything. Avraham, Yitzchak, and Ya'akov believed that G-d can do everything.

Redemption is not that I believe that G-d can do everything. It's so much deeper than that. It's not that G-d shows you, "I'm stronger than Pharaoh." That's not the point. The revelation of the name *Yud Kei Vav Kei* is not what G-d can do or can't do. It's much deeper than that.

You see what it is – redemption is not what G-d can do. This is not what redemption is all about. Redemption is so much deeper. You know where redemption comes from? It comes from being close enough to cry.

THE FOUR STEPS

Based on the Beis Ya'akov of Ishbitz (Beis Ya'akov Va'eira 21, Beis Ya'akov Hakollel Va'eira, Lachen Emor)

ON SHABBOS *VA'EIRA* WE READ ABOUT THE FOUR steps of getting out of Egypt. The first thing is *"Vehotzeisi"* – "I will take you out." Next comes *"Vehitzalti"* – "I will save you." Then *"Vega'alti"* – "I will redeem you." And finally, it says, *"Velakachti eschem li le'am"* – "I will take you to be My people." (Sh'mos 6:6–7)

What's the first step toward redemption?

G-d says, *"Vehotzeisi eschem m'tachas sivlos Mitzrayim"* – "I will take you out from under the *sivlos* of Egypt." (Sh'mos 6:6) *"Sivlos"* is usually translated as "burdens" or "sufferings," but it comes from the word *"lisbol,"* to be able to put up with or to tolerate. So G-d is really saying, "As the first thing, I will take you out from being able to tolerate being slaves in Egypt."

You see what it is – the first step toward getting out of exile is that you have to stop liking it. If I like being in exile, then nobody can take me out.

I was once talking to someone about Jerusalem, and she said to me, "Listen, I'll tell you the truth. I like the Bronx." So what can you do with her? The Messiah could come and give her a free ticket to Israel, but she likes the Bronx. She will never move and there is nothing you can do about it.

Do you know what the saddest thing about the Exodus is? Only one fifth left . . . only one fifth of the Jews left Egypt, because the others liked it there. And why did they like it? Basically, it's the strangest thing in the world. Everybody talks about freedom, but it's a very heavy thing to be free.

So the first stage of redemption is that G-d will take you out from being able to put up with exile. You won't like it anymore.

Do you know what a slave is?

A slave is someone who is burdened by small things. When you ask a slave, "What are you concerned about?" he will say, "I'm hungry. I've got to eat some lunch." Later, in the afternoon, you can say to him, "Listen, you look so sad. What are you worried about?" And he'll tell you, "I need a little bread for dinner." Finally, you ask him again at night, "What do you need now?" And he'll say, "I need some straw for a bed."

It's heartbreaking, but you can't get to freedom this way. If your concern is lunch, dinner, and straw to sleep on, then when you're free you'll still be thinking about the same kind of things. So G-d says, "The first thing I have to do is to take you out from under small things. I have to free you from smallness."

I want you to think about this in a very deep way.

It took a long time to get the Jews out of Egypt. And we always think that it took so long because Pharaoh gave us so much trouble. But this is only one side of the story. The truth is that it had to take a long time because we were *mamesh* not on the level.

Imagine that the Messiah would come right now and say, "Listen, today I'm bringing you a brand-new world, a beautiful new world." How many people would be interested? One fifth? Do you think our holy rabbis were wrong when they said one fifth? To say that one of five would be interested is already a very high percentage. Maybe today it is one out of a thousand, but let us hope it is at least one out of five.

So the Holy Ishbitzer says, "G-d told Moshe, 'Do you know what you have to do first? You have to take them out of their smallness.'"

*

Now when I am really concerned with very big things, very high things, you'd think I would walk around with my shoulders hanging down because I am carrying such a heavy load.

But it's really the other way around. When I am connected to high things and meaningful matters, it suddenly doesn't feel like such a burden. It doesn't knock you down. It lifts you up. It's only when I'm only thinking about very small things that it all feels so heavy.

Imagine I am concerned with the little hamburger I want to have for lunch. All I can think about is where I will get this hamburger, how much it will cost and whether it will fill me up.

Or, on the other hand, imagine I am concerned about the redemption of the world. You might think that if I'm walking around thinking about our final redemption, I wouldn't be able to walk because it's so heavy.

But it's not true. In fact, the opposite is true. Only small things weigh on you so heavily. High things don't weigh so much. "*Sevel*" means "to put up with," and it also means to carry, to *mamesh* carry burdens. So G-d told Moshe, "I have to take the *Yidden* out from the burdens of Egypt." And the Ishbitzer comments, "Do you know what burdens are? Small things. Small things feel so heavy."

You see what it is – someone asked me about a person who doesn't keep Shabbos. It's a heavy question. So I answered that for me, personally, a person who doesn't keep Shabbos is someone who is so involved with small things that he doesn't even remember there is such a thing as keeping Shabbos.

The small things take up so much of his heart and his mind that he is completely cut off from the world of Shabbos.

A slave is someone who is so consumed with small things that he *mamesh* doesn't even remember that there is such a thing as freedom. Okay, maybe he can talk about freedom like they do in the newspapers, but he is so involved with smallness that freedom, his own freedom, isn't real to him.

So we all have to get out of the smallness and be involved with higher things. There are thousands of stories about this, especially from the Holocaust. The Holy Radomsker had a son-in-law who was one of the greatest geniuses of his generation. Already in his teens he not only knew every word of the Gemara, but he also knew Gemara Rashi and *Tosafos* by heart.

He was taken to Auschwitz, and what did he do there? He was learning and teaching the whole time, day and night. Maybe, sadly, he was physically in the concentration camp but, at the same time, he really wasn't there. His feet were there, his skin was there, but his soul, heart, and mind were *mamesh* somewhere else. So he was never really a prisoner . . . he was never really a slave.

Sometimes you meet people and their minds are so great and so special. They are so high and they have such deep ideas. And then again sometimes you meet people who are so small. Even the way they think of the redemption of the world is so small, so small.

We *mamesh* have to get out of all the smallness and attach ourselves to something bigger, something higher.

So the first thing G-d says to Moshe is, "Take them out of all the smallness." You have to empty your mind of all the small things. And the moment you are not filled with the smallness, you can really know, "*Gevalt*, I'm in slavery. But I'm really not a slave. I'm bigger than that. So I have to get out of here!"

Only small people can be slaves. Great people are never slaves. Wherever they are and whatever is going on with them, they are always free.

So, this is the first step.

Next G-d says, *"Vehitzalti eschem me'avodasam"* – "I shall rescue you from their labor." (Sh'mos 6:6)

You see what it is – first G-d takes me out of my smallness and suddenly I am becoming high again. And the moment I am high and divine, I suddenly realize that I am in the wrong place. I'm not a slave . . . I can't be a slave. So G-d says, *"vehitzalti eschem"* – "I will also save you from slavery. I am with you all the way."

But let's go one level deeper. This is not the end yet.

Sometimes you meet young people who are the highest in the world. Then you go visit them in their parents' house. And without saying anything too bad, in their parents' house they are not the same, because their parents make them small.

If there is somebody or something that can make them small, that means they are not completely free yet. Maybe their ideas are free but the rest of them is not, because there is still something very deep inside of them over which somebody else can have dominion.

So G-d says, *"Vega'alti eschem"* – "I will redeem you." If there is one deep place inside you where someone can rule over you, I will take that place out of you and set you free.

And finally, G-d says, *"Velakachti eschem li le'am"* – "I will take you to be My people." (Sh'mos 6:7) Do you know what it is to be G-d's people? To be G-d's people means that suddenly it's clear to all of us that nobody in the world has dominion over us but G-d.

I want you to think about this in the deepest way.

Egypt was a preparation for all the exiles to follow, because *Mashiach* didn't come when we walked out of *Mitzrayim.*

We have a long way to go before the Messiah comes because the world isn't ready yet. So the redemption from Egypt was a preparation for all the generations to come.

What is the strongest preparation? It is to know that no one has dominion over us. Absolutely no one. We are *mamesh* completely and only under G-d's rule, not only from now on . . . we really were never under any other domination.

This is what it means to be G-d's people.

BEING READY FOR FREEDOM

HOW LONG DOES IT TAKE FOR SOMETHING TO get into your soul?

There is a passage which says, *"Ki mi-Tziyon teitzei Torah"* – "For out of Zion will come forth the Torah," the teaching; *"u-d'var HaShem mi-Yerushalayim"* – "and the word of G-d from Jerusalem." (*Yishayahu* 2:3)

So the Ishbitzer asks, "Isn't the Torah also G-d's word? Why does the prophet put it in two categories? The Torah will come out of Zion, and the word of G-d from *Yerushalayim.*"

The Ishbitzer says that when I receive the word of G-d on the level of information, it's Torah. It might be the holiest teaching in the world, but until it gets into my bones, until my toenails know about it, until it stops being knowledge, it takes a very long time. Until it's so much inside of me – in my heart, my soul, my mind, in my everything – until then, it is not called G-d's word.

You know something . . . it's strange.

There are a lot of things I would do in life, but I don't do them because it is not fully clear to me that this is really G-d's word. If it was *mamesh* clear to me that this is G-d's word, I would do them. It's not enough to say, "Okay G-d, make it clear to me that this is Your word, and I will do it." It just doesn't go this way.

You have to plow yourself right through it. First G-d gives you a little knowledge and then you have to work on it so hard. *Gevalt,* what you have to go through until you get to it!

For instance, when it comes to anger, I can have this deep information that I shouldn't get angry. So each time I want to get angry, my information tells me, "Don't get angry." And yet I struggle with anger my whole life.

Do you know how this could be? My problem is very simple. My problem is not anger. My problem is that I have yet to reach the level of *"D'var HaShem"* in regards to anger, because if it is the word of G-d, it gets inside of me so much that I'm not able to get angry anymore.

I want to share something very deep with you.

A person can know the truth a million times and still be off. The truth does not prevent me from doing something wrong. There is only one way – *"u-d'var HaShem mi-Yerushalayim"* – "the word of G-d from *Yerushalayim.*" If it becomes so clear to me that it is *mamesh* G-d's word, it shines into me in such a way that it changes me forever.

I can keep Shabbos all my life and yet the word Shabbos never became G-d's word to me. Shabbos becomes G-d's word to me when it is going into the deepest chamber of my soul.

So the first step of the redemption is *"V'hotzeisi"* and the Ishbitzer says this means that G-d will literally take us out from our smallness (*Beis Ya'akov Va'eira* 21). As long as you are small, you don't even realize you are a slave. And as long as you don't realize you are a slave, G-d can give you any type of freedom in the world and it still wouldn't get you out of Egypt.

The freedom we are talking about here means that G-d is freeing you from the possibility of ever becoming a slave again. As long as there is something which can make you into a slave, you are still a slave even if you feel free.

For instance, if I think someone has dominion over me, and I am moving to Bermuda because I am free there and I can do whatever I want, you're not really free. If it takes you moving to Bermuda in order to be free, that means there is a possibility for you to still be a slave.

The highest level is to be G-d's people. Being G-d's people means that nobody can ever make me small. Nobody can ever put me into slavery.

So you see what it is – you can have freedom on a knowledge level, on a *ki mi-Tziyon teitzei Torah* level, but this does not make you really free yet.

NOT WANTING TO MOVE

They did not listen to Moshe from shortness of breath . . . (Sh'mos 6:9)

SOMETIMES YOU ARE IN A PLACE AT A MOMENT that you don't want to ever end. You can know how much you love a person by how much you don't want your time with him or her to be over.

Imagine you're standing with someone on 42nd Street and 8th Avenue, which is really not the most wonderful place in the world. When you're there with someone you love very much, you can stand there for two thousand years.

Now open your hearts.

When you inhale, you exhale. Do you know what it means to be out of breath? That's when you are afraid to exhale because you don't know if the moment will ever happen again.

"V'lo sham'u el Moshe mikotzer ruach. . . ." (Sh'mos 6:9) *"Mikotzer ruach"* is often translated as "from shortness of spirit." But really it means "from shortness of breath." The people didn't listen to Moshe from shortness of breath.

You see what it is – Moshe came to *Am Yisrael* and told them, "G-d says He will take you out of Egypt and you won't be slaves anymore."

Can you imagine how much it meant to the *Yidden* to hear that? It was so precious to them that they didn't want to exhale because they were afraid the moment would disappear. They wanted to hold that moment, to hold the idea they would be free forever. And they didn't want to hear anymore.

HEBREWS

Speak in the name of G-d of the Hebrews. (Sh'mos 7:16)

WHEN G-D SAYS TO MOSHE TO TALK TO Pharaoh, he tells him to speak in the name of G-d of the Hebrews (Sh'mos 7:16). In English this word "Hebrews" sounds cute.

But why are we called Hebrews? *Ivrim* does not only mean Hebrews. *Ivrim* also means "those on the other side." The whole world is on one side and we *Yidden* are on the other.

And here I want you to know something very important.

The strongest imprint on a person is the environment. A servant of G-d is somebody who is not influenced by the world. I don't want to do good because you're doing good and I don't want to do bad because you're doing bad. I only want to do what I think.

You know something friends. It's not the worst thing in the world to do wrong but it's horrible if you do wrong just because somebody else wants you to.

So the ordinary translation of *Ivrim* is to be on the other side, but the Ishbitzer says something even deeper: Moses says to Pharaoh, "Do you know who those people are? The ones you say are slaves? They are on both sides."

What does it mean to be on both sides? I want you to know that it is possible to be a slave to freedom also. You can be a slave to freedom and then you are also not free.

We *Yiddelach* are masters of being able to be on the other side of anything which is not for real.

CONNECTING BACK TO OUR ROOTS

These are the heads of their father's houses. . . . (Sh'mos 6:14)

RIGHT AFTER MOSHE IS SENT ONCE AGAIN TO Pharaoh, to tell him to set us free, we start learning of something else.

"Eileh rashei beis avosam." (Sh'mos 6:14) "This is the story of Reuven, Shimon, Levi, Moshe and Aharon."

Now listen to this.

What did we inherit from Avraham, Yitzchak, and Ya'akov? Why do we say they were the first people who had faith in G-d? There were a lot of others who maybe believed in G-d before Avraham. Do you know what the difference was? It was that those other people's belief in G-d wasn't precious to them.

What was the basic difference between Avraham and Noach? Noach also believed in G-d. But Rashi says Noach was *"ma'amin v'eino ma'amin"* – "He believed and he didn't believe." (Rashi, Bereishis 7:7) What does this mean? His faith in HaShem wasn't precious to him.

Avraham Avinu was the highest of all the believers, but not just because he believed in G-d. The biggest question is not whether or not you believe in G-d. The biggest question is whether you could live without G-d? Can you visualize what it would be like to live without G-d? We only *mamesh* believe in G-d if we know how precious it is that we know that G-d exists.

You see what it is.

When we want to get *Yidden* out of Egypt and it just doesn't go, there is only one thing for us to do. We have to connect every *Yid* to Avraham, Yitzchak, and Ya'akov. It's not yet the time to explain things better to them. First we have to make things more and more precious to them.

So the Ishbitzer says (*Mei Hashiloach* 1, *Va'eira, Vayedaber* 2) that right away, as soon as Moshe comes to tell the people that G-d will take them out, the Torah begins to connect us to our roots – "*Eileh rashei beis avosam. . . .*"

בא

BO

בא

In remembering our unforgettable wedding during the week of *parshat* Bo, this Torah portion is dedicated to my loving wife:

RUTH HANNAH bat EPHRAIM CHAI

May she continue to host the most amazing Shabbat meals, give over the most *gevaldic* Reb Shlomo Torahs and get *nachas* from the *gantza mishpacha* and her *chevre, ad* 120.

זכר לקריאת פרשת בא בשבת שבע ברכות שלנו,
פרשה זו מוקדשת לאשתי האהובה והיקרה:

רות חנה בת אפרים חי

שתזכה להמשיך בהכנסת אורחים הבלתי רגילה שלה,
הפצת התורות הכי גבוהות ועמוקות של רבנו הקדוש,
וקבלת נחת מכל משפחותיה וחבריה עד 120.

HOW DO YOU APPROACH THE ABYSS OF EVIL?

Come (with me) to Pharaoh . . . (Sh'mos 10:1)

ON THE FIRST SHABBOS IN THE MONTH OF *SHVAT,* we almost always read about how G-d says to Moshe, *"Bo el Paroh"* – "let's go to Pharaoh [together]." (Sh'mos 10:1) The Zohar Hakadosh says (Zohar *Bo* 34b) that since Moshe Rabbeinu was afraid to go to Pharaoh, G-d said to Moshe, *"Bo"* – "Come with me. I'm going with you."

And here you really have to open your hearts.

Why is there a division between the first seven plagues which are in the portion of *Va'eira,* and the last three plagues which are in *Bo*? The Ishbitzer says that the first seven plagues were to fix the consciousness of the *Yidden* . . . to get their consciousness out from Egypt. The last three plagues are deeper than consciousness because they are dealing with the infinite, with the sub-consciousness. It is only our consciousness that is finite, but our sub-consciousness, our inside, has no limits.

And here I want you to know the deepest depths.

It's not that Moshe Rabbeinu was afraid that Pharaoh would teach him how to be bad. That is not the point. Moshe simply didn't want to ever see such utter darkness. So when G-d says, "I am going with you," G-d is letting Moshe know, "You are about to approach the bottomless evil which exists in the world."

But friends, this was only because G-d was about to reveal the endless goodness which exists in the world. You cannot be confronted with absolute bottomless evil and just say a little cute Torah'le to get you out.

Unless you are aware that something exists in the world to counterattack this bottomless evil, it is absolute destruction. *Mamesh* destruction.

What is a sign of bottomless evil? Bottomless evil is the way our worst enemies treat children. You can be sick for years when hearing stories of how the Germans treated babies. *Mamesh* the abyss of evil.

Consciously they still wanted to pretend they were human beings, but if you would x-ray their unconsciousness, you would see that they were not human.

Friends, let me ask you . . . how old were the Jewish children in Egypt when they had to work? Most probably from the age of three, and they had to work day and night until they *nebach* died from the whipping and hard labor.

But here comes Pharaoh with an official new statement – he says he loves children. Khrushchev and Stalin were always taking pictures with children. *Yemach sh'mo,* I don't want to mention his name . . . in Germany . . . whenever he was in public, he was taking pictures with children.

This is when Moshe Rabbeinu gets a taste of the bottomless evil in the world . . . when Pharaoh says with utmost cruelty, "You can go, but leave me the children. Your babies stay here."

Do you know what that means? Pharaoh was trying to make it even more cruel than all that was before, because as bad it was in Egypt, there was still a little bit of family life. The most evil thing in the world is to separate parents from children.

Now remember, the month of *Shvat* belongs to the tribe of Asher. By Asher it says, "*Baruch mibanim Asher.*" Asher is the one who is closest to his children. From all twelve tribes, there was nobody who knew so much about endless goodness like Asher.

When the holy tribes came back from Egypt, they had to tell Ya'akov Avinu that Yosef HaTzadik was alive. They were afraid he was going to have a heart attack when hearing that after twenty-two years of missing his child, his child is still alive. So they decided to choose Asher's little girl Serach believing that she would know how to tell this to Ya'akov Avinu. She was sitting by Yaakov, singing a little song.

And Ya'akov asked her "What are you singing?"

Serach said, "I'm just singing to myself, making up some songs."

In the middle of one of her songs she began chanting, "Oh, Yosef is alive. Oh, Yosef is alive."

Since Serach was the one who brought Ya'akov Avinu the news that Yosef is still alive, she gave Ya'akov Avinu back his soul (*Sefer Hayashar, Vayigash* 14: *Midrash Hagadol, Vayigash* 45:26.) And according to our tradition, she lives forever (*Kalla Rabbasi* 3:23). Serach was the daughter of Asher, and Asher was known to be the closest to his children. Nobody was an expert on closeness between parents and children like Asher.

You see what it is. We don't just need to get out of Egypt or out of Western culture. We need to get out of the absolute corruption of Western culture. It's the deepest corruption there is. The way they teach children about life, about G-d and about themselves is absolute corruption.

What needs to happen for the world to realize that our whole school system is terrible? We are in Egypt. We are completely drowning in tree of knowledge culture. It's all tree of knowledge.

You might be the best person in the world but according to our system, if you are not a good student, you are a failure. Yet a disgusting kid who knows that one and one is two might be hitting everyone and he might have disgusting language, but he is considered a success.

Corruption! This is a taste of the abyss of evil. When you are ready to go and taste this darkness, G-d says, "I'm coming with you."

*

By the eighth plague, something new began. G-d usually told Moshe what type of plague was about to come down, but here G-d didn't really tell him what to expect.

Still, Moshe Rabbeinu knew it was locusts. How so? Locusts have no king. All animals have a king, all animals have a leader. Bees have a leader, wolves have a leader. But locusts have no leaders and yet they love each other and live in harmony.

After the seventh plague, suddenly G-d says to Moshe, "Go to Pharaoh."

So the Ishbitzer says that Moshe Rabbeinu knew it was locusts because they are one . . . they completely have G-d's oneness. And Pharaoh is completely anti-G-d's oneness. Not only is he anti-good, he is against G-d, against the oneness of G-d.

What happened after that? *Makas choshech,* the plague of darkness. Moshe Rabbeinu didn't go to Pharaoh to tell him there will be darkness because *gevalt,* is Pharoah dark! The plague of darkness was not something new. ". . . *U-l'chol b'nei Yisroel haya ohr b'moshvosam*" – "And for all the children of Israel there was light in their dwellings." (Sh'mos 10:23) By us *Yidden* there was light, and we were finally able to see how dark Pharaoh is.

I want you to know something so deep.

When G-d revealed to Moshe the depth of the darkness of Pharaoh, G-d also revealed to Moshe the depths of the oneness and the beauty of us *Yidden.*

*

Before the seventh plague, Pharaoh was ready to let us go as long as we leave our children in Egypt. The adults can go, but the children have to stay. Just think of the cruelty.

We adults could have made it out after seven plagues, but our holy sages make it very clear that the last three plagues were brought down just in order to get our children out of Egypt.

I want you to know something so deep and so far-reaching.

Why is the last plague the killing of the first born? On a very simple level, it's because Pharaoh was a first born and he was frightened for himself, but it's got to be more than that. The question is – when you bring your first-born to the world, where does it touch you? Where do your children reach in you? Does the awesome privilege of being a parent reach the absolute highest place of your being?

I want you to open your hearts.

With each plague G-d's light was shining deeper. Each plague was simply a revelation. The first seven plagues were reaching our consciousness . . . cleaning our consciousness from slavery. The last three cleansed our beyond consciousness, our super-consciousness. The deepest question by G-d is – do your children reach your deepest sub-consciousness? How much are you a father or a mother in your sub-consciousness?

One of the saddest experiences I had was in the late '60s in San Francisco. One of my friends thought he was getting very spiritually high through some drugs. One morning, he came over to me and said, "While I will be spiritually high later today, I want you to ask me certain questions." He wrote down twelve questions that he wanted me to ask him while he was under the experience. He was a very high person but obviously not the highest.

I asked him, "Can you name one of your seven children?" For the life of him, he couldn't remember the name of even one of his children. Do you know what that means? His consciousness was so off that it never reached his unconsciousness. Inside he was empty.

Now listen to me, my beautiful friends. This is unbelievably beautiful.

We have five books of Moses. In the fifth book, Moshe Rabbeinu began retelling us the whole Torah, and when does this happen? It happens on *Rosh Chodesh Shvat*. *Shvat* is the month of children. This Shabbos is the final exodus out of Egypt, and *Rosh Chodesh Shvat* is when Moshe Rabbeinu is beginning to explain the Torah.

Now listen to the deepest depths.

On what level was Moshe beginning to explain the Torah to us? "*Arbeh*" (locusts) is the eighth plague. "*Arbeh*" simply means "more." Do you know what it means to explain the Torah? Not that we didn't know it before, but it's on the level of "*arbeh*" – on the level of "more."

If I get a business letter, I'll read the letter once. When I get a letter from somebody I love, I'll read the letter twice. If I get a letter from someone I love the most, I can't stop reading it.

Each time I read the letter, it becomes deeper. It's not "more" on a conscious level, because all it says are the same words, but inside it's becoming deeper and deeper.

WHAT DO YOU DO WHEN IT'S DARK?

For all the children of Israel there was light in their dwellings (Sh'mos 10:23)

DURING THE THREE DAYS OF DARKNESS IN Egypt, nobody saw one another. By us *Yiddelach,* there was the same darkness, but the Torah says that for Israel it was light. (Sh'mos 10:23)

So the ordinary meaning is that for Egypt it was dark and for the *Yiddelach* there was light. But the real deeper meaning is that when it was dark in Egypt, they weren't able to see anybody else. What do us *Yiddelach* do when it is dark? We look for somebody else.

I'll tell you something so deep.

When there is light, you don't feel so lonesome. But when it's dark, you *mamesh* need someone. What do we *Yiddelach* do when it's dark? We walk around looking for people who are also lonesome.

Before *Mashiach* is coming it's getting a little bit dark, but suddenly we're aware that there might be someone else who is in even more darkness than me.

I have got to find that person.

NO MORE SLAVES

Let each man request from his fellow . . . (Sh'mos 11:2)

WHAT IS THE DEEPEST SENSE OF A RELATIONSHIP? It's not only when I can talk to you, but it's also when I can shine my soul into you. The greatest privilege in the world is when my whole heart is shining into you and your whole heart is shining into me.

In the Haggadah of Pesach we say, *"Ani ve'lo malach, Ani ve'lo saraph, Ani ve'lo shaliach."* G-d says, "It is I who am coming to redeem you. Not through any messengers. Just me."

The Alter Rebbe's Seder was obviously beyond words. When he would get to the words *"Ella HaKadosh boruch Hu"* – that it was *mamesh* G-d Himself who took us out – he would always faint. It took a long time to revive him. Do you know why? Because G-d was literally shining into him.

On Seder night, G-d is shining into me something you cannot reach in two thousand lifetimes. And the moment G-d is shining into me, all slavery ceases to exist. I'm usually afraid of this person or I'm nervous around that person or I think this one is my master. But on Pesach it's clear to me that nobody is my master. Nobody is my master.

And here I want to share something so special with you.

What do you think the Egyptians felt that night when we left Egypt? They had the highest G-d revelation in the world as well. On that night it was clear to them that Pharaoh is not really their master.

I want you to know something which is not to be believed.

G-d says to Moshe, "*. . . V'yish-alu ish may'eis ray-ayhu v'isha may'eis re'usah k'lei chesef uchlei zahav . . .*" – "Tell the *Yidden* to borrow gold and silver from their neighbors." (Sh'mos 11:2.) *Ray-ayhu* does not only mean your neighbor. It means your equal.

One would think that when you have the highest G-d revelation, you should walk up to every Egyptian who has been hitting and whipping you for so many years and get some revenge. But we *Yidden* are told, "Go and borrow from your equals." From my equal? They are the lowest creeps in the world! But you see, that night, when we left Egypt, was a taste of what it will be like after *Mashiach* comes. No one is a slave to anybody else.

Not only did the Jews walk out, all of the slaves of Egypt walked out with us.

INITIATION OF *YIDDISHKEIT*

This month shall be for you the first of the months of the year . . . (Sh'mos 12:2)

AS WE WERE COMING OUT OF EGYPT, G-D TOLD US, *"Hachodesh hazeh lachem"* – "This month is your month. It's a new month." (Sh'mos 12:2)

G-d was letting us know and asking us, "Do you know what it is to be free? It's that I give you the power to renew yourselves and feel like new people. *Mamesh* like new."

You know what a new person is?

Imagine I have a little fight with someone I love, but we forgive each other. As long as I remember that we once had a fight and forgave each other, it's cute and sweet, but we are still slaves to the old story.

You know what that means? It means that there is a little scar in my heart. A new person has no scars. The scars are completely wiped out. Forgotten.

It doesn't mean that I know who you are only from today. I know you from forever but I don't ever remember that we fought. I don't remember that we were angry at each other. How can I be angry with you when I love you so much?

You see, the difference between Yom Kippur and Pesach is like this:

On Yom Kippur I'm standing before G-d and I say, "I did this wrong and that wrong. Please forgive me." But when I come out from Egypt

I don't begin talking about my mistakes, because even asking for forgiveness would be a form of slavery. I am *mamesh* a new person.

Imagine if each time I keep Shabbos, I would remember that last year I didn't keep Shabbos, and I spend my Shabbos regretting the Shabbos I didn't keep. What kind of a Shabbos is that?

It's very beautiful for the golden age club, for people over ninety-five who have nothing else to talk about besides for their past. They have to tell each other when they fought and when they made up. Is this all you're capable of? Aren't you capable of something deeper than that?

Sadly enough, do you realize with how many scars we look at each other? "Listen, you are my good friend and I love you, but how could I forget what I know you did?"

This is not what a Jew is supposed to be like. This is not a free Jew. If you want to become a servant of G-d, you have to get out of the whole thing.

I want you to know something even deeper.

The way we look at ourselves is with so many scars. I walk around and I do *teshuva,* then I don't do *teshuva.* If I could wipe out the words "*Teshuva* Movement" today, it would bring *Mashiach* the next minute. You know what I do when I say that this person did *teshuva*?

It means I take all the mud and all they did wrong and I place it on them with a big label. And people do this to themselves too. "When I was eight I did this, four years later I did this. When I was nineteen I sank even lower and then when I was twenty-nine, I was just the lowest. Then I did *teshuva* here and some more *teshuva* there, and now I'm a full paying member of the *teshuva* movement.

Does it get any more shallow than this?

The world thinks there are two kinds of Jews in the world. One Jew never did anything wrong because he ate kosher latkes all his life and the other Jew did wrong his whole life because he had ham and cheese.

I'll tell you the truth . . . I'm not so sure who has to do more *teshuva*. Maybe while he ate kosher latkes he was yelling at his wife, and this ham and cheese *Yiddele* was so sweet while he was *nebach* eating *treif*.

What do I know? They both have to do *teshuva*. I don't know who has to do more *teshuva*. Maybe this *Yiddele* didn't keep Shabbos but at least he was kissing his baby on Friday night. This *Yiddele* kept Shabbos but he was knocking his child off. What do I know? So who is desecrating Shabbos more?

But besides for all this, if you want somebody to be a Jew, the first initiation to *Yiddishkeit* is not Yom Kippur. The first initiation to *Yiddishkeit* is "*Hachodesh hazeh lachem*." This is the first beginning.

Every morning I wake up and I want to become a Jew again. I don't know anything. All I know is that I'm *mamesh* a new person. To have this newness between people, to have this absolute holiest gift that G-d gave to the world, is awesome.

On Seder night, basically what we are doing is *kadesh ur'chatz* – "Being holy and washing your hands."

I'm *mamesh* a new person.

*

Friends let me ask you . . . when did slavery begin?

We became slaves after the sin of the Tree of Knowledge.

"*B'itzavon tochalena . . .*" – "with suffering you shall be eating for the rest of the days of your life." (Bereishis 3:17) We eat bread with sadness. Reb Nachman says that Egypt was simply the outcome of the Tree of Knowledge. Therefore today we are slaves to bread. (*Likutei Halachos*, Hilchos Netilas Yadayim 6:22)

Matzah is *mamesh* the first time we are eating bread *be'simcha*.

You know what the greatest fixing is?

The fixing of death is not by living forever.

The greatest fixing is knowing how precious time is.

"Hachodesh Hazeh Lachem"

Moshe Rabbeinu says to the *Yidden,* "You want to fix the sin of the Tree of Knowledge? The fixing is, "*Hachodesh hazeh lachem.*" Time is in your hands. Time is so precious.

*

We all need the new and the old.

On the one hand I need that which is old so much. *Gevalt,* do I need what is old.

Imagine I could bring you a prayer book which your great-great-grandfather prayed from three hundred years ago. It would get right into your bones. Can you imagine saying, "Forget it, Birnbaum translated the prayer book and it's much more beautiful print."

Which one would you take? Honestly? You're giving me the prayer book of my grandfather who prayed from this book in 1640 and you can see that the pages are still wet with his tears. Of course, this is the *Siddur* I want.

Imagine I walk up to a young woman and I say, "I can either give you a candelabra which was just made in Jerusalem by Betzalel or I can give you a little Menorah from your great-great-grandmother who used it to kindle lights in the 18th century."

If she would take the Betzalel menorah she wouldn't shiver when she kindles it. But if she'll kindle the one her great-great-grandmother kindled, *gevalt* will she shiver.

So there's an absolute need for the old. But on the other hand, I also need the new.

Now open your hearts in the deepest way.

Do you know what it is to be in exile? It's when my new stuff has nothing to do with my old stuff. Going out of exile is when I experience the highest I can reach in my lifetime. But this is not all. There has to be one more thing. The question is . . . can you experience this new light when it's not there yet?

"Hachodesh hazeh lachem." (Sh'mos 12:2) Here G-d says, "I'm showing you just one ray of the new moon. I'm not shining it fully yet . . . just one ray."

Here I want you to open your hearts in the deepest way.

New does not mean I have a new suit or that I have a new teaching.

New means I have the vision of tomorrow before it even happened.

When do I choose to marry someone? When I begin to sense that with this person my life is full of newness. I didn't get married yet and we didn't start a new life yet, but I already have this vision.

This is what *Rosh Chodesh* is all about. There is only one ray of light. The moon is just beginning to renew itself but I am already feeling the whole thing.

*

Here we are reading about the first mitzvah which is sanctifying the new moon. The Talmud says that when G-d told Moshe Rabbeinu about this first mitzvah, Moshe Rabbeinu asked G-d, "Please G-d, tell me what you mean. Promise me to see the new moon."

So the Talmud says that G-d said to Moshe, *"Kazeh re'eh v'kadesh,"* – "When you see it [the moon] like this, then bless it." (*Rosh Hashana* 20:1) "You see, Moshe, this is the moon, this one ray, and this is it. *Re'eh,* look at it. *Ve'kadesh,* and make it holy."

You know my beautiful friends, what is the most glorious way of serving G-d? It's very easy to sit down and tell another human being everything which is wrong with them. And if you really concentrate, I'm sure you could write a book on how wrong every human being is. It doesn't take much.

But "*Kazeh re'eh ve'kadesh.*"

When you meet this person and you see one good thing about them, one ray of light, let it blow your mind. "*Re'eh ve'kadesh*" – if you see one good thing about another human being, don't wait. Make this person holy in your eyes.

It is possible to know another human being for two thousand years and not know anything about them. You know why? Because it could be that at that very second when you weren't looking, maybe they did something so holy that they shook up heaven and earth. Maybe for one minute in their life, the whole world was on fire because of them.

*

You know something friends, the world is always ready for atomic explosions of light, but what about one little ray of the moon?

During the time of the Holy Temple, we sanctified the new moon by two people who saw one little ray of the moon.

You know why there is no peace in the world? Because the world is always looking for experts. What about when someone simple comes to you and says, "I saw a new light." Isn't that enough?

The laws of witnesses are a very serious matter in Jewish law, but not when it comes to *Kiddush Levanah*, sanctifying the new moon.

The loneliest *shlepper* could be sitting outside his house one night when suddenly he sees one ray of light. He jumps on his horse, goes to *Yerushalayim* and says, "I saw the new moon." Another little *Yiddele* who lives a few hours away couldn't fall asleep that night. He is sitting on a mountain top and suddenly he sees a new light.

He jumps on a horse and goes to *Yerushalayim*. And because of the moon he saw, it's a new month. Because of them it's Shabbos, it's Yom Tov. Because of them time continues to go on.

You see what it is, the world doesn't need experts and geniuses. The world doesn't even need good people. There are enough good people in the world. What the world needs are whole people.

You know what the difference is between a good driver and a terrible driver? A good driver is someone who makes you forget you are out on the road, because you are sitting in the car and it is so smooth. A terrible driver is someone who begins to drive, then he stops, then continues, then goes faster. Some people are terrible drivers in their lifetimes, but if you are in tune with the new moon, if you are in tune with everything new, everything flows so beautifully.

*

What is Torah *She'be'al peh*? Torah *She'bichsav* is always the same Torah, but Torah *She'be'al peh* is *mamesh* coming down every second. It's too awesome to think about. Too heartbreaking.

Imagine if we would utilize every second of our lives for the Torah which is coming down every moment. Let's say that this afternoon, at four o'clock, it was meant for me to be *mechadesh* a *gevalt* Torah, but at four o'clock I was reading the fashion section in the newspaper.

When I'm coming up to heaven, they will show me this and say, "*Gevalt*, what you could have only done at four o'clock!"

Now the whole way of sanctifying the new month is based on that one moment when I see the first ray of light.

So Reb Nachman says – Who is the *Beis Din HaGadol*? The high court in *Yerushalayim* was composed of people who can shine into *Yidden* that they should utilize that one moment.

Who are the *Tzaddikim*, the holy righteous people in the world? *Tzaddikim* give you the strength that when this light is shining, you are capable of grabbing it.

*

The first mitzvah G-d gave us when we came out of Egypt is to sanctify the moon. The witnesses had to see just one ray of light. One would think we should celebrate the moon when the moon is full, so why do we celebrate when there is just one ray of light?

I'll tell you something very deep.

Imagine my closest friends go off on a long trip, traveling the world. When I don't hear from them for a long time, my longing to see them grows. Suddenly I get a letter from them and they tell me they are coming back. I'm jumping out of my skin with joy. I'm beyond myself.

Now eventually when they come back, I'm very glad but does it compare to the way I felt when I got this letter? It's something else. The letter was the first ray of light and it hits me so hard.

Before the first ray of the moon, the moon is dark. What have been our darkest moments? Darkness is when G-d forbid, it looks like G-d forgot us. But when I have a new sign that G-d is thinking of me by sending me one ray of light, I'm completely beyond myself.

Here I want you to know the deepest depths.

G-d's carriage has four wheels. One wheel is the holiday of Pesach, the holiday which belongs to Avraham. Another wheel is the holiday of Shavuos which belongs to Yitzchak. And another wheel is Succos which is Ya'akov. And the fourth wheel is *Rosh Chodesh* which belongs to David HaMelech.

Everyone knows that *Mashiach* comes from the line of David HaMelech. I want you to know that there is a place in our hearts where we think G-d forgot us and now treats us like strangers.

But you know something? David HaMelech is the master of sign language. On Pesach G-d took us out of Egypt, and Shavuos is when G-d gave us the Torah. On Succos we are in the Succah. *Rosh Chodesh* is just one ray of light but if you are the master of sign language, you can taste such utmost closeness.

Reb Nachman says that speaking comes from your head. A sign is something you give with your hands. One of the saddest things in the world is when you don't understand G-d's signs anymore.

When are husbands and wives considered close to each other? Our Rabbis teach us that as long as they understand each other through signs, they are still close.

As long as the *Beis HaMikdash* was rebuilt, our relationship with G-d was on the level of talking to us, but today all we have are the stones, and the stones are just signs.

What's a broken stone? Just a sign. When I would come to *Yerushalayim* and see the Holy Temple, everything would be very clear to me. But all you see by the Holy Wall now is brokenness, but what the broken stones are telling us is the deepest.

When it comes to learning, who is considered a good learner? You don't have to be such a great scholar to translate the words of the Torah, but if every word is giving you a sign, it's something so much deeper.

Let's say you are learning the Rambam, and the Rashba says the same thing. If you think they are saying the same thing, you are missing something. When you translate it, it might really be saying the same thing, but when you learn it, *gevalt* does it open worlds for you, because every word they said is sending a different sign to every *Yiddele* in the world.

Now let's go one step further.

The Tree of Knowledge does not believe in signs. Something is either good or bad. A person is either beautiful or ugly. But do you know what a sign is? I can do what looks like the most terrible thing in the world, but what do you know is beneath it all? Do you know what I'm thinking? You *mamesh* don't know.

When it comes to a sign, you cannot say it is either good or bad. When I speak, I can either use good words or bad words. I can talk classy and elegant or I can speak very vulgar. Signs have nothing to do with all of this.

Take a *Yid* with a *shtreimel* who is walking through B'nei Brak with his seven children on Shabbos. And here there is a *Yiddele* in a car. He stops and takes a look at this *Yid* with a *shtreimel* and begins to cry. "*Ribbono shel Olam,* why can't it be my seven children and me? I have no Shabbos, no Yom Tov. I have nothing."

So at this moment, whose Shabbos is bigger?

You see, the *Yid* who keeps Shabbos and is walking with seven children is Torah *She'bichsav.* It's written to keep Shabbos and he is doing it. When this *Yiddele* in the car is crying, for one minute he is giving a sign to G-d. Under his breath he is saying, "Master of the World, if I would have had a different upbringing, if I would have a different world . . . *gevalt,* who I could have been!"

So every *Rosh Chodesh* we are fixing the Tree of Knowledge.

One sign from above, one ray of light, and I'm already busy sanctifying.

*

What is the specialty of us Jewish people?

When we are down to the lowest and can't go any lower, how long does it take us to get on top again? One split second. We were slaves for two hundred and ten years. How long did it take us to reach the highest level, to be the highest human beings, the highest Jews in the world? One night. One *Seder* night.

Yosef HaTzaddik was a prisoner but how long did it take him to become a king of Egypt? One dream.

So we say, "*M'kimi mei'afar dal, mei'ashpot yarim evyon*" – "He lifts the pauper up from the dust, from the ashes He raises up the needy." (Tehillim 113:7)

When we start Seder night, *Am Yisrael* screams "*Kadesh!*" "Sanctify!"

Am Yisrael who just rose from the dust, is saying, "G-d, we are ready for anything holy."

"*Hachodesh hazeh lachem.*" The first thing that a Jew needs to learn is to be a master of time. So after we rise from the dust of slavery, how long do we have to prepare for *Mashiach*'s coming? Someone might come to me and say, "You are a sinner. Who knows what you have done? You need a lot of years to fix yourself."

But this is not the truth. You know what I need? I just need to open all the gates of my heart. To open the opening.

ONLY IN YERUSHALAYIM

And they shall eat the flesh on this night . . . (Sh'mos 12:8)

I WANT YOU TO OPEN YOUR HEARTS FROM HERE TO eternity.

The Mishnah says (*Zevachim* 56b) that you are not permitted to eat the paschal lamb outside of the holy city *Yerushalayim*. So that night when we left Egypt, we were eating the paschal lamb in our houses in Egypt. So how could we have eaten it outside of *Yerushalayim*?

The answer is very simple. A cloud came to every Jewish house, picked up the whole house and brought it to *Yerushalayim*.

I want you to know that every year a little cloud is coming and it takes our house and takes us and our children, and it carries us back to *Yerushalayim*. Can we celebrate Pesach anywhere else other than at the Holy Wall in *Yerushalayim*?

We should be blessed to be privileged that while we eat matzah, we are in the Holy Temple. We can't be anywhere else.

FAST PACE

. . . And you shall eat it in haste . . . (*Sh'mos 12:11*)

EVERYONE WANTS TO BE FREE BUT HOW DO I START believing that I could become free? How do I get my mind out of Egypt?

The Zohar HaKadosh says that a baby does not know who its father or mother are until it eats bread. That means that bread gives strength to my mind to be connected to those who love me. Only after I eat bread do I know what life is all about . . . do I know who my father and mother are.

Now listen to something even deeper.

Matzah gives my mind strength too, but it's working from a different side. Eating matzah gives me strength to be connected to myself and to all who are important to me, but this connection is done without my thinking about it.

How so?

Reb Nachman says there are two kinds of minds. There is a slave mind and a free mind. A slave mind always has ten thousand excuses to not get out of something.

Everybody is drowning in something. Egypt is all about getting out of what you drowned in. Everyone is tied to something, chained to something. We need to have serious compassion on our souls to just get out of it.

You see what it is, it's just like it was in Egypt. We all go through the plagues, witnessing tremendous miracles, but so many of us are still in Egypt.

To really leave the things you are tied to, to leave all the things you had excuses for, is the greatest test in the world. Everyone talks about how beautiful it would be if they could set themselves free from whatever is holding them back, but unfortunately most people can't let go.

How do you get out of Egypt?

"*B'chipazon,* "in haste." (Sh'mos 12:11) You have to get out fast. How do you run out of Egypt?

Reb Nachman says something unbelievably deep. How fast can I walk while I am thinking? Very slowly. When you are talking to someone and are engrossed in conversation, you walk very slowly.

But if you want to run, you have to stop thinking.

I must remember that I am not my mind. I am stronger. I have to stop my mind. So therefore, Reb Nachman says that matzah is called the bread of poverty. We are not necessarily talking about poor people who can't afford bread. We are talking about poverty of the mind and meaning that in a good way . . . I have no mind.

The Gemara says, "*Ein ani ella be'da'as*" – "A poor man is someone who doesn't think." (*Nedarim* 21:1) But on Pesach I flip this concept over. On Pesach I am so strong and I say to myself, "I want to be poor. I have to get out of Egypt fast!" If I stop thinking, I become poor, I have no mind. I might be poor, but this is the sign of utmost strength.

What's the sign of having a strong mind? When my mind says to me, "Stop thinking! Right now there is no time for thinking. Just do it." What does matzah do to my mind? Matzah causes my mind to tell me, "Let go, let go. It's okay. I know what to do."

You see what it is, I need an absolutely strong mind in order to see the clear truth that the only reason I was in Egypt was because of my excuses. They might be valid excuses, but they are still excuses. Matzah gives me such a strong mind. It gives me a super mind not only to understand but to believe that I can start running and get out of Egypt right this minute, and nobody is stopping me. It is only this type of light which instills faith in me to stop thinking and this can get me out of Egypt.

This is matzah.

Everyone needs something to hold onto. Everybody has something little they hold on to. What is the utmost we are holding onto? We usually hold onto a little piece of bread because at the end of the day, everybody really needs bread.

The holiness of leaving Egypt is that we walked out of Egypt without bread. We walked out into the desert and we had nothing to hold onto. You know how strong my mind has to be in order to leave that place of minimum comfort?

I can leave my job and get another job. I can leave one little habit and have another little habit. Everybody needs something small to hold onto. But here, I come out of Egypt and I am not taking anything with me. This is absolute freedom. But it has to be fast. It has to be that night because if I wait more than that night, it's G-d forbid too late.

So Reb Nachman says (based on *Likutei Halachos,* Hilchos Pesach, 9:9–10) that the greatest cleverness is to be able to not think, to be clever enough to choose to stop thinking. Therefore he says that Pesach is the celebration of believing. Matzah is called the bread of believing because it takes a lot of believing to realize that this is what I have to do, to stop thinking.

This is the greatest freedom in the world.

You know what a slave is?

A slave is not a bad person. In fact, a slave can serve G-d as well. He can get married and have children. The problem is you can't run anywhere.

Freedom means there are absolutely no boundaries. No boundaries. Not the past, not the present, not the future. Nothing in the world.

The two greatest G-d revelations in the world are the night of the Seder and Shavuos. On Shavuos we stood on Mount Sinai and G-d gave us the Torah and G-d told us what we have to do. But this is not the beginning. The beginning is Pesach when it's clear to me that there is nothing I cannot do.

*

Reb Tzadok HaKohen says that there are two great redemptions – the redemption of Egypt and the redemption when *Mashiach* is coming. The redemption out of Egypt was fast – "*Ki b'chipazon yatzasem*" – "Because you left in haste." (*Sh'mos Rabbah* 19:6)

Everything about Pesach is fast. Matzah is fast. You take a little water and flour and throw it in the oven. Seder night, when we ate the Paschal Lamb in Egypt, we had our shoes on, we had our staff in our hand and we were ready to move.

So leaving Egypt is fast, but the redemption of *Mashiach* is the slowest thing in the world. (*Tzidkas HaTzaddik* 1:1)

You know friends, when I meet a rich miser, and suddenly he says, "Okay, I will give you a million dollars," you better have him write the check at that moment, because if you'll wait till tomorrow, he won't do it.

When I know a *Yid* is always giving money, and he says, "I'll give you tomorrow," I trust him. But for us, whenever we have an awakening to do something, you cannot afford to wait. Who knows how it will be tomorrow?

Imagine a *Yiddele* has an awakening and he says, "*Gevalt,* I want to move to Israel!" He'd better go out and buy a ticket right away because if he waits too long he will cool off.

There are many people who are not yet married who might have had an awakening at a certain moment. They met someone they loved, but they waited too long. There are certain things you simply have to do fast. Egypt was fast because our insides weren't a hundred percent purified yet.

Whenever I have an awakening, I have to act on it quickly because you don't know what will happen a second later.

Going out of Egypt is fast, but then to receive the Torah is a slow process of forty-nine days. When it comes to learning, it is always a slow process. You don't push a button and suddenly you know the Torah. It is a long and slow process and yet there is something so deep.

Sometimes you meet people who never opened a holy book before and yet they know so much. You see, when we came out of Egypt, what did G-d shine into us that made us run so fast? It was the revelation that there really is one G-d.

And here I want you to know something.

To know there is one G-d, you don't learn slowly. It's not like studying theology. I read a few articles about religion and slowly, slowly I learn there is one G-d. It doesn't go this way.

It happens in one second, when it's suddenly so clear to me there is one G-d. The moment it's clear to me there is one G-d, I realize I am a free person. No one has dominion over me.

When we came out of Egypt, it wasn't that G-d showed me that Pharaoh isn't really anything. We already knew that before. But there was nothing we could have done because he still had a pistol in his hand.

What became clear to us when we came out of Egypt was that G-d is our only Master.

This is basically what Avraham Avinu brought down to the world. When he was three years old, he knew there is one G-d and he spent the rest of his life refining this knowledge. What's the whole thing of learning Torah, learning Kabbalah, learning Chassidus? It's to *mamesh* know it better, to know it stronger, to know it deeper. Deeper and deeper.

But the journey from not knowing to knowing doesn't go slowly. "Head" learning takes time. First I learn the letters and then I learn the words. Then I learn ideas and then I learn more and more and more. The more I learn, the more I know.

But then there is *neshama* learning, soul learning. It has nothing do with my head or with time.

I want you to know something.

What are you learning when you come to the Holy Wall? A great light shines into you. You don't learn words. It's so much deeper.

So Pesach is the holiday of Avraham Avinu. G-d says to him, "Your children will be slaves in a land that is not theirs . . ." (Bereishis 15:13)

On the other hand, everybody knows that Egypt is a preparation for the Torah. Pesach is Avraham and Shavuos is Yitzchak.

You see what it is, there are certain things which you get because you work so hard for them. And then there are certain things which are given to you as a gift when you are born. The *Yiddishkeit* of Avraham is that he *mamesh* worked so hard. He walked through fire for G-d and went through all the tests. But Yitzchak was born a *Yid.*

You can live for two thousand years in this world, serve G-d for two million years, and never know the Torah because the Torah is a gift from heaven. It is not from this world.

All religions are very beautiful, but they don't reach where a human being can reach after serving G-d. Some are *mamesh* serving G-d. But they only reach where a human being can reach on his own. After that – that's it.

The Torah begins where a human being cannot reach.

Here I want you to know something very deep.

What is the whole idea of doing something fast? If you would tell me now, "Hey, Shloime, can you please go to the supermarket and get me a tuna sandwich?" Would I jump up, run out and get it and come back? I wouldn't. I'll get up, then slowly, slowly go there. Finally, I will get there, ask for a tuna sandwich and bring it back.

What happens if someone will come in and say, "Someone is drowning in the Hudson!" You will be out the door in a second because when someone is drowning there are no two ways about it.

But when someone asks me for a tuna sandwich, I'm not jumping and running out the door, because I'm not so clear that they really need a tuna sandwich. I think maybe he should go himself.

You know what Pesach is all about? It's about the first ray of light which is so clear. Do you know how much light I need to leave Egypt? It's deeper than just the light to answer a *Tosafos* or a Rambam. To leave the whole world and become a servant of G-d, one has to be strong.

Who was the first person who paved the way for doing things fast?

When G-d says to Avraham Avinu to leave everything behind, Avraham Avinu leaves everything behind and starts walking to the Holy Land right away.

*

Sometimes our children ask us questions and we take our time answering them. But there are times where, if we take our time in answering them, we will lose them. Reb Nachman says that if our children ask for advice regarding what they should do in life and what career they should have, I can say, "Let's talk about it."

But if they ask us if there is one G-d and we say, "Let's talk it over," we've lost them. If they ask, "Are you a Jew?" and if you have to think about it, that's not good.

So Reb Nachman says that on Seder night when our children ask us, "Is there one G-d?" our answer has to be right away. Don't take any time.

I once read a book written by one of the outstanding Jewish leaders of the other religions. This outstanding leader writes in the foreword to his book that when he was a little boy he once asked a Rabbi if there is one G-d. The Rabbi said, "Come to my house and we'll discuss it."

The Rabbi started quoting from here and quoting from there. The boy said, "I'm just asking one question – is there a G-d or not?" He couldn't get an answer out of him. The next week, he met a Swami and asked him, "Is there one G-d?" The Swami said, "Yes, there is."

Seder night is when I tell my children there is one G-d. There is one Torah. There is *Eretz Yisrael*. I have no time to answer with long answers. It has to be fast.

Do you know why *Mashiach* didn't come yet?

Because we waited . . . we waited so long. How did Moshe Rabbeinu get us out of Egypt? Right now is the time – "*Bachatzi halayla*" – "in the middle of the night." (Sh'mos 12:29) Right now! Don't think!

When I see somebody drowning, where do they grasp me? They touch the deepest depths of my understanding, which triggers something so holy.

So Seder night, everything is fast.

But although everything is fast, it's so clear and it's so good.

*

Sweetest friends, why is it that certain friendships come to an end?

It all depends on certain moments. There are moments when we really need each other. You could be my friend for sixty years but there was one moment when I needed you and you weren't there. What's one moment compared to a hundred years?

But you see, G-d needs us for special moments.

Getting out of Egypt takes place in one moment, and this is what Pesach is really all about. The difference between a slave and a free person is that a free person takes the opportunity of that moment.

Every person is living on two levels: One level of life is where I act like everyone else. I wake up in the morning, I breathe, I put on clothes . . . just like every person in the world.

Then there is something so special that has to do with my personal Exodus out of Egypt. And it's just one moment. This is basically the difference between bread and matzah.

When it comes to the education of children, we focus on what they have to do every day, but do we give them strength to do what they have to do with "great moments"? When the "great moment" comes, are they ready?

When it comes to the holiness of the Torah, what are you teaching your children first? The first thing that you teach them gives them strength for that moment.

Why is there no peace in the world?

Do you really think that in all those thousands of years there weren't moments that we could have brought peace to the world? But when the moment came, we said, "We'll do it tomorrow."

When G-d spoke to us on Mount Sinai, do you think He spoke to us for ten hours? G-d spoke to us for exactly one second, one-billionth of a second. According to our Kabbalistic tradition, G-d didn't even utter a word. He only uttered one letter, because G-d can say with one letter everything there is to say.

I want you to know the deepest depths.

According to Kabbalistic tradition, there are two ways of educating. You can teach children or you can "give over" to them. I can take out a book and teach my baby that when you see a poor man, you give him a dollar. That's teaching. When I'm walking with my baby on the street and she sees me giving a dollar, I wasn't teaching her. I was giving over to her what charity is.

Teaching can take years but giving over can happen in a moment.

TASTING CLARITY

For seven days you shall eat matzahs . . . (Sh'mos 12:15)

YOU CAN BE THE BIGGEST GENIUS IN THE WORLD, but you might be eating yourself up with doubts.

One of the famous stories of Reb Nachman is the story of the fool and the wise man.

There were two friends – a wise man and a fool. The wise man was not really wise, but he was what the world called wise. He was thrown out of every school he went to, moved from town to town and went through so many changes.

First he wanted to be a doctor, then a lawyer and then he decided to be an accountant. After that he wanted to be a jeweler, but then decided to go into politics. He changed his mind every minute because whatever he did was plagued with doubts.

He never got married because he was never sure who the right girl was and he would say, "I don't like her nose, I don't like her ears, I don't like her attitude, I don't like her mother." He was always able to find something wrong.

Now listen to this.

The fool met a girl he loved and married her. Now the fool was really poor, but he knew what life is all about. He didn't operate from his head. He operated from a much higher place.

The wise man had a lot of money. Every night he would go to another restaurant and each time, he had a fight with the waitress. The soup was never good, the beef was not cooked right, the water tasted off. This wise man spent his nights being disgusted with life and everything there was.

By contrast, all the fool had at home was a little bit of water and some stale bread. But listen to this. Every night when he would come home, he would say to his wife, "My sweetest most beautiful wife, what did you prepare for me?"

And she would say, "I prepared for you the most unbelievable champagne and the most unbelievable steak."

She would then bring him a small cup of water and a stale piece of bread.

Reb Nachman says there is no champagne in the world which tasted like that water. There is no steak in the world that tasted like the bread she gave him.

Now let me ask you in all honesty.

Matzah should have no taste at all, but *gevalt,* does matzah taste good. It's like the fool's steak. Do you know what we taste on Seder night when we eat the matzah? There is no French or Chinese restaurant in the world that could compare.

Do you know why there is no time when it comes to making matzah? Because when something is clear to you, what do you need more time for?

On Seder night everything is clear to me.

WHOSE SIDE ARE YOU ON?

. . . And G-d smote every first born in the land of Egypt . . . (Sh'mos 12:29)

WHAT WAS THE FINAL BREAKING POINT BEtween us and the Egyptians?

Here Moshe Rabbeinu is telling Pharaoh that on a certain night, exactly at midnight, all the first-born Egyptian children will die. (Sh'mos 12:29)

Let me ask you – what should the whole nation of Egypt have done? What should Pharaoh have said? They should have begun protesting in the strongest way, "It's true that for the economy of our country we need these slaves to work for us for free, but the lives of our children are more important." But what does Pharaoh say? "I couldn't care less."

The holiness of us *Yidden* is that our whole lives center around children.

What makes us Jewish people holy?

We know the holiness of children.

What do we do the first night we are free?

Do we go out on the street and celebrate?

Do we say, "I was a slave for two hundred and ten years and whipped and tortured on a daily basis. So the first night of my freedom I would like to go out to the street and have a good time? I'd like to be a little bit free, go for a little bit of dancing, find a good disco and just have a good time."

So the holy Ishbitzer says that every Seder night, a person has to look deep into his own hearts and ask himself, "Which side am I on? Does my life center around my children, or am I one of those Egyptians? Children are cute, but what happens if they get in the way of my work?"

You'd be surprised how many people sit by the Seder but basically, they are really Egyptians.

It's time to take a good look into the eyes of our children and get out of Egypt. Once and for all.

BEYOND DREAMS

It was on this very day that all the legions of HaShem left the land of Egypt. (Sh'mos 12:41)

THERE'S A PASSAGE THAT SAYS, *"BA'ASOSCHA nora'os lo nekaveh"* – "Master of the World, we never dared to hope for the wonders you ended up doing for us." (*Yishayahu* 64:2)

There are certain dreams I have which I hope will come true, but there is something even deeper. Deep down inside, I'm hoping for something to happen which I never even dreamed about. Little me, what do I know what G-d wants to do? Do I know what kind of miracles G-d wants to perform?

Imagine I want to go to Israel, but I don't have money. So I can hope and pray that somebody will come and give me money, which would be amazing. But this is not the most amazing thing. I can simply know that I'll get there while not having the faintest idea as to how I'll get there.

It's up to G-d how I'll get there. There is nothing higher than this.

It's especially true about children. Did you ever hear anyone say, "I know my baby. She'll end up being this, being that, and being a few things more." What do you know? Maybe she'll be something you never dreamed about.

So the Ishbitzer says that when G-d set us free, it does not only mean that I'm no longer a slave. Freedom means my relationship to G-d is on the level of freedom.

If I have plans for that which G-d will do for me, it's sweet but then I'm making G-d a slave. I'm telling G-d what to do. To be on the level of freedom with G-d means that I never need to know what G-d will end up doing.

You see, while we were in Egypt we hoped we would be free, but the night we got out of Egypt something happened which we never dreamed about . . . something we never dared to dream about.

So this is what the Ishbitzer says. If I wake up in the morning and I say, "Today is going to be a good day," it's sweet but it has to be more than that. You have to be ready every second for unbelievable miracles which you never even dared to dream of.

THE NIGHT OF LEARNING PATIENCE

It is a night of guarding for HaShem . . . (Sh'mos 12:42)

THE NIGHT OF PESACH IS CALLED, *"LEYL Shimurim"* – "the night of guarding, the night of watching." (Sh'mos 12:42)

According to our mystical tradition, G-d is giving back to us all the things we thought we had lost, all the holy moments we had in our lives and were sure they were gone. All the great prayers, all the beautiful moments that we thought we had lost. On that holy night, we suddenly know that G-d was guarding them and now they are right here in front of us.

You know what it is? When you put a little seed in the soil you might think it's lost. It seems that nothing is happening. If you could possibly look right through the soil and see that it's completely disintegrating, you would think you wasted your time. But wait one second! A tree is growing.

So since according to us, the spiritual and the physical of the Divine is all one, the springtime is the time when G-d is showing us that He is guarding this little seed. G-d is guarding it. Even while the seed was disintegrating, G-d watched over it even more.

When you meet people who are completely disintegrating, don't give up on them. They are actually just growing.

OUR FIRST

Sanctify to me every first born . . . (Sh'mos 13:2)

THE ZOHAR HAKADOSH SAYS SOMETHING VERY deep (Krach 1, Bereishis). After one, comes two. After the first comes nothing. First means there is no second.

I want you to open your hearts. If you will wake me up in the middle of the night and say to me, "Tell me fast – who is the first person you loved?" And then you ask, "Who is the second?" It's not the same thing. After the first, that's it. First has no second. Certain things are so deep that if it's not the first, forget about it.

A slave is someone who has given up on that first. They don't have that first anymore. They lost it and became a slave. A slave is always second. Someone tells him what to do. So the Ishbitzer says that on Pesach G-d has given me back that which is first by me.

You know friends, our lives are always based on seconds. We are constantly compromising, giving up and giving in. We don't really do what we want to do. We always do what has become our second choice. We never do what we want as our first choice. We are living in a whole world where everybody cuts down our first.

Now listen to this.

The *Medrash* says that G-d is called first, Israel is called first and the Holy Temple is called first. (*Midrash Rabbah Bereishis* 1:4; *Midrash Rabbah Vayikra* 36:4) G-d cannot be second. If G-d is second, it's not G-d you are talking about. If you will, so to speak, ask G-d, "Who's your first?"

G-d will say *"Yidden."* If you ask *Yidden,* "Who's your first?" they will say "G-d."

If the Holy Temple is second, it's a cute building, but it's not the Holy Temple you are talking about. The Holy Temple is that place which connects you to that first. The destruction of the Holy Temple means that our first is a little bit destroyed.

What has exile done to us? In exile we can't get together with our first. Some forgot it, some lost it.

The *Medrash* says that twice a year we are redeeming our first. Pesach is called, *"Bayom harishon"* (Sh'mos 12:15) and Succos is called *"U-le'kachtem lachem bayom harishon"* – "And you should take for yourselves on the first day." (Vayikra 23:40) On Pesach, G-d takes me out of slavery and when this happens, G-d gives me back my first.

And here I want you to open your hearts in the deepest way.

Do you know how special it is to meet people who hold on to their first? *Gevalt,* is it special! Children . . . they know they are first. Even if they have no words for it yet, they know what they want.

Heartbreakingly, the way we answer our children's questions . . . we are taking away their first.

Imagine if my child would say to me, "I'd love to be a great musician," but I want her to be a doctor. Imagine she asks me how you become a musician. The way I answer her is that I make being a musician so ugly that she gives up her first.

On Seder night we are making peace between us and our children. How so? We are answering their questions about their first in the most beautiful way.

By the Seder we welcome Elijah the Prophet, who is the one who connects the first of the parents to the first of the children, to the first of the world.

And here I want you to blow your mind.

People who fight are people who lost their first and their lives are so empty. The first is the relationship with G-d and when people hold onto their first, my first and your first always love each other.

On Seder night, G-d gives us back our first. I'm sitting with my wife and children. I'm sitting with the whole world and I'm opening the door and I say, "Please, anyone who is hungry, come and eat." What's the world hungriest for? They lost their first. They don't know what to do with themselves anymore.

G-d is first – *"Ani rishon va'ani acharon"* – "I'm the first and I'm the last." (*Yishayahu* 44:6) Imagine I say, "G-d is my first choice and if not G-d, I'll take somebody else." G-d is not number one as opposed to being number two. He is the first. The first does not come from thinking.

The first comes from beyond this world. It comes from the deepest depths of my heart. And when G-d gives this back to me, I know again what I want from myself.

You know, friends, what does it mean to be in exile? When we come out of Egypt, G-d says to Moshe, *"hachodesh hazeh"* – "this new month." *"Rishon hu lachem"* – "Let it be first unto you." (Sh'mos 12:2)

It has millions of meanings, but I want to share one with you. The question is very simple. Is there anything in your life which is first? Is there anything in your life that is so important that it is first? If you don't have a first, you're in the lowest exile.

You might be doing everything right but is there something so deep inside of you which is first? It's beautiful to have four hundred close friends but is there one person who is first by you? You have two million books. Do you have one book that is first? If you don't have it, you have exile . . . the lowest exile.

And here I want to share something very deep with you.

All year long, when we celebrate all the holidays, it's beautiful if our children are at the table. But if they're not at the table, it's not the end of the world. The way I celebrate my freedom on Pesach night is that I am sitting with my children at my table and they have to ask me the deepest questions in the world.

These questions are the deepest secrets of the world, but the deepest secrets are always hidden under many garments/layers of clothing, so they all seems like simple questions. When do we eat matzah? When do we eat chametz? What kind of vegetables are we eating tonight?

If you are not in tune with the deepest secrets of the world, you think these are shallow questions, but they truly are the deepest questions of the world.

Everybody knows that the deeper something is the more simple it sounds. Have you ever met people who use big words but they say nothing?

If you say something strong, you cannot say it with way-out words. You have to say it as simple as it is. If it takes two hours, fifteen accents and fifteen kinds of formulas to tell a girl that you want to marry her, she will say, "When you're finished, call me." Who has the strength to listen to all that?

Anything which is earth-shattering is just one sentence, just a few words.

But here I want you to know something and I want you to open your hearts. If I have something to share from my heart which is *mamesh* first, then my children can connect to me because children are always first.

Children only connect to a person who has this holiness of first. I'm sure you share my feelings. I have seen people like this. I am invited to someone's home. As we sit there and we talk, the door opens and in walks a little boy, and a little girl. We say "Hi,"and then the door opens and the president of the Synagogue walks in. Suddenly the father of these children really gets up and gives full attention. I'd rather eat dinner on the street than in that house.

First. Your child comes first.

There was once a very wealthy person who was on the Moshav for Shabbos and he *mamesh* liked it. He was dancing like mad with one of our top *chevre* on the Moshav, with Zusha. Zusha had polio when he was a boy, so it's very hard for him to walk. You cannot dance acrobatic dancing with him, only soul dancing.

This millionaire danced with Zusha and was really turned on by the whole thing. I went to visit with him and wanted to know if he wants to support the Moshav. He didn't take his eyes off the stocks which were on his screen in front of him the whole time I was talking to him. So I said to him, "I don't want to waste your time and I don't want to waste my time. Just tell me straight – does Israel interest you?"

"Not a bit," he says.

"I thought you went to the Moshav and liked what you saw there."

"Yeah, I liked it, but it doesn't interest me."

"Does it interest you to bring thousands of kids back to *Yiddishkeit*?"

"I don't care, I don't like taking sides."

Suddenly he gets a call from his little girl of nine. Sweet as sugar. She was on the Moshav that Friday night as well.

"I told you not to disturb me when I'm in the office." He slams the phone down, while not taking his eyes off the screen for one second.

Suddenly he gets a call from Russia because he makes billions on shipping wheat to Russia. You should see how he shaped up. He took his eyes off the screen, started to smile and speak a few words of Russian.

What a nebachdika first. Wheat to Russia! And his child is number one hundred and fifteen. Heartbreaking! Imagine how much fixing this person needs? But you know what's so heartbreaking? From the way the girl was talking to him, I realized that he is still first by his little girl. Can you imagine how sad it is when this little girl will grow up and she will realize, "I'm only number one hundred and fifteen?"

There is something very special about our generation. People want to go back to their first. Why do we hate schools? They are not connecting us to our first. I want somebody to give me my first. I don't want a religion that teaches me that G-d is number six hundred and eighty-five. I want to go into a house of prayer where G-d is First.

Now listen to this.

Every person has a first. The question is – what is your first? Are holy things first, are important things first? Is the stock market first? Is your beauty parlor first?

You can do everything right, keep every law in the world, but if the stock market is first by you, *gevalt* are you in exile. You can have your own 747 and travel around the world with millions in your pocket, but if you don't have this first, you're the lowest slave, you're the lowest of the low.

Let's not kid ourselves. In order to answer our children, we must have clear prophecy. Not the prophecy we usually think of, but prophecy which we receive in the merit of our relationship with the real First.

Do you know exactly when to yell at your children? Do you know when to be sweet? When a child tells you, "I did wrong," do you know when to get angry, do you know when to say, "Don't worry, it's okay. You will fix it tomorrow." Unless you have this inside first, you won't make it.

You know why children are so angry with us? Because sadly enough, children have become second and third. They may even be number one on your list, but children are not number one. Children are first.

When do children stop asking their parents questions? When they sense when they are not first in their parents' eyes anymore.

Imagine if we can reestablish this kind of relationship, to have a real relationship between parents and children the way G-d wants parents and children to relate to each other. Do you know how fast redemption will come to the world?

*

Now listen to me, my sweetest friends.

What is the deepest sign that you are connected to your first? It's that you begin to grow again. Second and third don't grow. First? *Gevalt,* does it grow!

When something grows in the field, it's "*Reishis bikurei admas'cha*" – "The first fruits of your land." (Sh'mos 34:26) Everything in the Torah talks about first because the first sign of growing means it's connected to the first.

Friends, we are living in a world where, thank G-d, you cannot prove anything.

At a certain point in history, everyone was talking about proving. Christianity came out proving there is one G-d, so some holy Rabbi also had to write something about it. Moshe Rabbeinu did not put anything into the Bible proving there is one G-d because we Jewish People are not into proving the oneness of G-d.

What kind of G-d is it that can be proven? What's there to prove? Anything that is real cannot be proven. I can prove to you that this is one bagel, this is one lox, this is butter. Outside stuff can be proven, not inside stuff.

Can I prove to you this melody is stupid and this melody is beautiful? Can I prove to you that Beethoven was a great composer? When something is so exalted, it cannot be proven.

Unless you are connected to your first, you are left in doubt. Anything which by me is first is clear to me. Divinely clear.

*

Friends, I'm sure you know that to meet people who have this first is so beautiful. People who have this first are never old because they are always meeting you for the first time. Every word is for the first time, every day is for the first time.

Toward the end of his life, the Frierdiker Rebbe was paralyzed and his tongue was paralyzed. For him to utter a word was incredible. You had to be very close to him to hear what he says.

He was *nebach* in Siberia, and they beat him up so much that suddenly there was no more strength in his nerves. He was not paralyzed out of sickness. It's just that his nerves gave up from all the beating.

When you would walk in to see him, you would write down a long note. Let's say you had five questions to ask the Rebbe. He would never read the note, but just place his fingers over it.

He would always answer the first question first, the second second, the third third, the fourth fourth, and the fifth fifth. One time someone asked him if his father, the Rebbe Rashab, had clear prophecy. He said, "No, but my father had the *Miskal Risho'n*. He had this holiness of first. He was so much in tune with you. He would say one word, but it included everything."

Friends, when it comes to the most important things in life, you cannot answer from number two. It has to be from the first.

*

Man is constantly in search of truth. We used to think that Western civilization is real and now we are realizing that Western civilization is not so real. We thought people who wage war in the name of G-d must be something real, but we see now that this is not where it's at either.

Before *Mashiach* is coming, there is a great sifting taking place in the world. The sifting taking place in the world is always through the first-born. The question parents are asked before *Mashiach* is coming is, "Why do you want children? How are you preparing the world for your children to come into?"

Just look at civilization. Everyone talks about loving kids and being connected with the real you, but what has really changed? For the most part, it's just talk. G-d is sifting through the world to see who is *mamesh* for real. This sifting has been going on since the night we left Egypt and it will go on until *Mashiach* is coming.

So the Ishbitzer says like this – the moment a first-born comes into the world there is a little glimpse of the great day to come. Each time a little baby is born, something so blissful takes place.

Now when we left Egypt, the first-born were the ones who were chosen to serve in the Tabernacle but something happened and the priests took over.

What happened? Until we made the Golden Calf the service was done by the first born. After we made the Golden Calf, G-d took this privilege away and gave it to the priests and this is how it will be until *Mashiach* is coming.

The Gemara says that we made the Golden Calf from all the gold and silver we got from the Egyptians. G-d says, "If I wouldn't have given you so much gold and silver, you wouldn't have made a Golden Calf."

In other words, the first-born lost their right because of money. Therefore today, when a little baby is born, the Kohen comes to the parents and says, "Tell me the truth, what's more important to you – the baby or money?"

The only way of correcting it is by saying, "I don't care about money. I just care about my child." The moment you made the Golden Calf and you made a god out of gold and silver, you lost the holiness of what it is to be the first-born.

You see what it is, the first-born lost the holiness when it began bowing down to money. Therefore, each time a little first born is born you have to correct the sin of the Golden Calf.

Everyone knows that the whole fight between Eisav and Ya'akov is over the *bechora*, the first-born's rights. This fight over who and what is important is still taking place today.

Evil says to goodness, "I don't want to wipe you out. I understand you run a little charity on the side and you like doing some mitzvahs, but are these the most important things?

There are other things. First fill yourself with some pleasure." But our *Heilige* Ya'akov Avinu says, "No, the most important thing is the service of G-d." This tension will go on until *Mashiach* is coming.

Each time a little boy is born, the priest comes to the father and asks him, "Who's the first-born by you, Eisav or Ya'akov?" So the parents say, "My child is more important than money. In fact, I'd give up all the money I have."

When a baby is born, it's a glimpse of *Mashiach* coming, but this is too strong for the world to bear. Therefore, after thirty days, the holiness of the Kohen takes over because the holiness of the Kohen is already established.

The holiness of the priest is a holiness which the world can bear. But the world cannot yet bear the holiness of the first born because it's just too strong.

If you really care for the world, then you want children to exist because the strongest way for the world to be is to have children in the world. The night we left Egypt, a tremendous light was shining. If you would X-ray an Egyptian heart, you would see that the parents couldn't care less about their children. Therefore, they couldn't exist in the world on that night.

This comes out via your first-born. The world is simply not ready yet for the real holiness of the first born . . . of really wanting the world to exist. Only when *Mashiach* is coming will we be on the level that we really want the world to exist.

Right now, G-d is still sifting through, looking at each set of parents and asking them, “What kind of a world do you want your children to come into?”

CHILDREN'S SAFETY

And it shall be when your son will ask you . . . (Sh'mos 13:14)

WHEN DO CHILDREN BEGIN TO CLOSE UP TO their parents?

When I sit with my child and it is clear to me that I have no dominion over my child, they feel safe enough to open up and ask me any question in the world. Seder night is the first time we are sitting with our children without having dominion over them.

I want you to know – people don't ask questions of a slave driver. A slave driver gives orders. He doesn't respond to questions. When children stop asking their parents deep questions, it's because the parents live under the illusion that their children are their slaves.

Do you know who a good teacher is? A good teacher is telling me all the holy information in the world but they are telling it to me in such a humble way. It's clear that all they are doing is bringing me a message from G-d.

Imagine if I could be in a classroom without ever telling the students, "Do this, don't do this." *Gevalt,* how they would learn from me! But even if I give them the highest information, it's still not enough.

For many students, they feel that just like their teacher told them to sit up straight, they also told them there is one G-d. My teacher told me, "Don't go to the bathroom for another half an hour," and he also told me that G-d spoke to us on Mount Sinai. So it's all the same thing.

Imagine if someday we will have schools where you teach children by giving them information without making them into little slaves. I don't know how to do it myself, to tell you the truth. Maybe we won't have such a school until *Mashiach* is coming.

Before we are even going out of Egypt we are sitting with our children. The greatest test is always how are you sitting with your children.

If you know how to sit with your children, then you are a free man. If you know how to sit with your children, then the next morning you can walk out of Egypt.

בשלח

BESHALACH

בשלח

לעילוי נשמת

Dedicated to the blessed memory of my dearest Ima

BLOSSOM SELMA MILLER

שרה בלה בת מאיר צבי ויטא ז"ל

Left this world י"ג אלול תשע"ט –
just shy of her 90th birthday.

Mames farshteyen vos kinder zogen nisht

Mothers understand what their children cannot say.

DAVID YISRAEL

WE COULD HAVE BROUGHT *MASHIACH*

EVERYONE KNOWS THAT THE WORD *"VAYEHI"* ALways alludes to something sad. So, sadly, it came to pass that Pharaoh let the Jewish people go. All the commentaries ask why the word *"Vayehi"* is used here? Leaving Egypt was the greatest joy in the world.

There are two million answers, but the *Divrei Bina* of Biala says like this:

There are moments when we have the opportunity to receive everything in the world, but sadly enough, at that moment we are satisfied with much less.

Do you know how much G-d wanted to give us the night we came out of Egypt? On that night we could have brought redemption to the world. We could have brought the Messiah. But, sadly enough, we were happy just to get out of Egypt.

Sometimes we want something so badly and then when it happens, we are so happy it happens, but we don't realize that at that exact moment we can do thousands of more things.

I want you to know an unbelievable story.

Reb Nachman of Breslov was named after his grandfather, Reb Nachman of Horodenka, who was one of the Baal Shem Tov's greatest pupils. Reb Nachman Horodenka was always telling the Baal Shem Tov that he wanted to marry someone special.

In the meantime, there was a young lady, and she was also always coming to the Baal Shem Tov with the same request. So the Baal shem Tov says to her, "I have someone very special – this Reb Nachman is my highest *Chassid,* but he is a little bit out of this world. You must promise me that if you have any complaints, you will come and tell me."

They get married, but the craziest thing happened – Reb Nachman Horodenka doesn't come home after the wedding. He only comes home the next day for lunch, eats a little bit and leaves. He comes back the next day for lunch and then leaves again. The next day he comes for breakfast.

So his wife went to the holy Baal Shem Tov to let him know what is going on. The holy Baal Shem Tov then went to Reb Nachman Horodenka and said, "Nachman, what's going on? Why don't you go home?" So he says "Rebbe, you know and I know that sadly enough, it's decreed for my wife to die in childbirth. I don't want her to die so young."

So the Baal Shem Tov says, "Let me tell you something. Why don't you just talk straight to your wife?"

So he goes home and says to her, "I want you to know . . . I love you so much. The reason I'm not coming home is because I know what's decreed in heaven and I don't want you to die."

So she says to him, "Is the way I am living now any better? I would rather have one good year with you than live like this forever."

That year she had a baby. At the moment the baby was born, she cried out, "*Ribbono shel Olam,* I can't leave like this. I carried this baby in my womb for nine months, and I won't even get to see it? *Ribbono shel Olam,* let me live for four more weeks."

So she lived for four weeks and then she *nebach* died. This baby was named Simcha and this Simcha is the father of Reb Nachman of Breslov.

Now listen to this.

When Reb Nachman Horodenka came to the Baal Shem Tov to tell him what happened, the Baal Shem Tov screamed out, "Oy, don't you know that at that moment all the gates were open for her? She could have asked G-d to stay alive forever."

Everyone knows we were in three different exiles after Egypt – Babylon, Persia, and Rome. The moment G-d took us out of Egypt, we could have eliminated everything. We could have said, "*Ribbono shel Olam,* please bring the great day for the whole world."

The moment the gates are open, don't limit yourself to something. Don't limit yourself to anything.

*

It says that the lowest person in the world had a higher vision than Ezekiel the prophet when we crossed the Red Sea (*Mechilta D'shira 3,* Ze Keili.) All the gates were open for us. Suddenly all of Israel and Moshe had the same vision. "*Az yashir Moshe u-ve'nei Yisrael. . . .*" (Sh'mos 15:1.)

Moshe and three million Jews were all singing. For one moment, they all had the same vision as Moshe, and were ready to receive the absolute highest light.

And here I want you to know a mind-blowing teaching from the *Ne'os Desheh.*

On Pesach, you have to bring a *korban chatas,* a sin offering. Even if you are an expert on sinning – on the last night before we got out of Egypt, how much sinning time do you have to do by Seder night? The next morning you already have to bring a sin offering?

So he says the deepest Torah in the world.

We could have brought *Mashiach* the night we got out of Egypt. The gates were open. But we were just so happy to get out of Egypt, and we didn't ask for more.

During the Six Day War, when we came back to *Yerushalayim,* we could have asked the *Ribbono shel Olam,* "Bring *Mashiach!*" At that moment, the gates were open. We were just so happy to go out and blow the shofar by the Holy Wall . . . and that's it.

Why didn't we ask for more?

Imagine you want to raise some funds for your school or Synagogue, and you finally have an interview with Rothschild. Rothschild says, "I'm very much impressed with your work. What can I give you?"

You start thinking to yourself, "I don't want to be a pig . . . what should I ask for?"

You say, "We need fifty thousand dollars."

Rothschild says, "Strange, I wanted to give you two million."

You see what it is, on Yom Kippur I'm giving G-d a clear detailed account of everything. You know why I have to tell Him exactly what I want? Because the doors are not that much open. It's still a supermarket. You tell G-d, "I want this, I want that."

G-d says, "Let's open your account and see how much credit you have."

Seder night is a completely different story. On Seder night, the gates of heaven are so open. G-d wants to give you everything, so why don't you take it?

The Frierdiker Rebbe of Lubavitch says that we are always coming to G-d like beggars. What's a beggar on the street asking for? For a quarter, a dollar. If he has *gevalt chutzpa,* he asks for five dollars.

The Rebbe told us that we are not beggars. We are not homeless people. So why don't you ask G-d for everything? Can you imagine the son of Rothschild standing on a street corner, begging for a quarter?

The *Ribbono shel Olam* wants to give us everything. Why are we so small in our own eyes?

DIFFERENT EXPECTATIONS

SOME COUPLES ARE BRIDE AND GROOM FOREVER. And then there are some couples who stop being bride and groom once they get married. How could this be? This is an unbelievable *Midrash.*

The passage says, *"Vayehi be'shalach Par'oh es ha'am"* – "And it was when Pharaoh sent the people out." (Sh'mos 13:17)

And everyone asks the same question: Why does the Torah use the word *"Vayehi,"* which always alludes to something sad, when it comes to describing the exodus out of Egypt?

Do you know what the saddest thing in the world is?

Most of the things in the world are never as beautiful as we hoped they would be. The *Midrash* says that even when we left Egypt it wasn't as beautiful as we thought it would be.

Why wasn't it as beautiful?

What happened was that on that night we could have asked for the *Mashiach* to come. We could have brought redemption to the world, but we were just so happy to get out of Egypt that we forgot the rest. We could have prayed for the generations to come, but we didn't. And so, we felt something was missing . . . it wasn't complete.

But you know something?

G-d in His infinite compassion gave us a little vision of the *Mashiach* while we were crossing the waters. While we were crossing the Sea,

G-d was letting each and every one of us know – "Even if he hasn't come yet, from time to time you should have the vision when you get too desperate."

G-d gives you a little vision to keep you going. When *Mashiach* comes, it says, *"hayinu ke'cholmim,"* – "it will be the way we were hoping and dreaming it would be." (*Tehillim* 126:1)

What a world it is when each couple that gets married realizes that it is even higher and more beautiful than whatever they thought life with each other was going to be like.

REDEMPTION FROM FEAR

It happened when Pharaoh sent out the people . . . (Sh'mos 13:17)

AS MUCH AS WE GOT OUT FROM THE SLAVERY OF Egypt, there was something in us that was still afraid of the Egyptians. When we came out of Egypt, we didn't have to work for the Egyptians anymore, but we were still afraid of them.

What happened to us when we crossed the Red Sea?

I want you to know something awesome.

There was never a storm on the ocean like that night when we crossed the Red Sea. It was the biggest storm in the history of the world. At that moment there was a voice in heaven saying, "Nachshon, one of your children, who is not afraid of anything, will be the Messiah."

Nachshon's great-grandson was King David, who at nine years old was fighting Goliath. Goliath was not just a bit bigger than him – there was nobody who could fight him.

But King David, at nine years old, comes and knocks him off.

So when we crossed the Red Sea, it was the first time we had a little taste of what *Mashiach* is all about. We realized that for the first time, we were not afraid of the world. We were not afraid of the storm on the ocean. But even deeper than that, we stopped being afraid of our own shortcomings.

Do you know what instills the greatest fears in us? It is yesterday's failures. The holy Baal Shem Tov says that the greatest slave driver is our own yesterdays. This is *mamesh* paralyzing.

On Yom Kippur, we are already half paralyzed, as Amalek comes and says, "You already promised G-d so many things last year . . . why bother going to Shul?"

The Chasam Sofer says, "I'm not afraid of G-d. I stand in awe before G-d, but I am really afraid of somebody who is not afraid of G-d."

*

What's the first sign that someone's a slave? It's that he or she has no self-confidence.

Why isn't *Mashiach* coming?

Because we're still a little afraid of it actually happening. On the first day of Pesach a sin offering is brought to ask G-d to forgive us for not bringing *Mashiach* sooner. We might have, but we were afraid to.

Reb Nachman says that you can't taste the hidden light of the world unless you first get rid of fear, because fear can physically and mentally paralyze you. At the Red Sea we learned not to be afraid and to trust G-d in the deepest way.

What else are we afraid of?

To love people can terrify us. The only ones who aren't afraid are our children. Seder night is the fixing of fear.

How do we do it? We make children the center.

When we get out of Egypt, Pharaoh is still there. There is still some evil left in the world. If I know that there is still evil left in the world, how can I sing? But when we crossed over the Red Sea, there was no evil in our world.

In order to sing you must be free. The slaves from Africa used to sing all the time . . . to let each other know that no matter how much people tried to enslave them, they were still free.

Singing comes from the world of freedom. When you sing, you are telling evil, "You have no dominion over me. None at all."

TAKE ONE MORE LOOK

. . . Return and encamp before Pi Hachirot . . . (Sh'mos 14:2)

AT THE END OF LAST WEEK'S PORTION, PHARAOH comes to Moshe in the middle of the night and says, "Please leave." The strangest thing is that when we were leaving, it says that G-d gave us *Yiddelach* favor in the eyes of the Egyptians. (Sh'mos 12:36.)

The Egyptians really despised the Jews to the utmost. They were taught that the Jews were second-rate citizens. But the greatest miracle happened that night. Something shifted in the Egyptians' eyes.

How did we leave Egypt? *"U-v'nei Yisrael yotzim be'yad ramah"* – "We walked out with great pride, with holy pride." (Sh'mos 14:8) We walked by our Egyptian neighbors and said, "I just want to say goodbye. I'm leaving." After two hundred and ten years of being slaves, we became free.

What should we have done? A little bit of stealing, a little bit of killing, a little bit of beating up Egyptians? But not one Jew uttered one bad word. It was tremendous. The Egyptians looked at us and realized that these people in front of them had really been free people the whole time.

On the one hand, this was very beautiful. But on the other hand, it was very bad for us.

And here I want you to open your hearts.

What's so holy about the children of Avraham, Yitzchak, and Ya'akov? We want the world to be good so much, that we forget so fast how bad the Egyptians really were. We walked out of Egypt and all we remembered was the way the Egyptians were waving at us, saying goodbye as we were leaving.

We forgot about all the years of torture. We began thinking that maybe they are not such bad people.

At this point, we were not really free yet. We were not ready yet to receive the Torah on Mount Sinai.

Three days later, Pharaoh regrets that he sent us out and is running after us, trying to get us back. Everything is forgotten in three days. G-d's plagues and all the miracles they came with . . . all forgotten in three days.

Do you know why? Because the Egyptian economy was based on slaves, and when we left Egypt, we took all the slaves of Egypt out with us. The whole country of Egypt was based on slaves. Every person had a slave whom he could kill or do whatever he wanted with. Suddenly there was no domestic help, so the whole country began going crazy.

But you see what it is.

As long as you think that Pharaoh wasn't so bad, Egyptian civilization might not seem so bad. *"Ve'yashuvu"* – G-d tells us to turn back. We *Yiddelach* had to see the real Egyptians once more. Otherwise we can never get to Mount Sinai.

In order to become emotionally free, divinely free and mentally free, we needed to take one more look.

*

We still need to cross the Red Sea.

When we walked out of Egypt, the Egyptians were not wiped out.

You see what it is, sometimes you get away from evil but it still exists somewhere. However, when we crossed the Red Sea, the Egyptians *mamesh* drowned. There was nothing left. This means that this also took place on the inside. Inside they were really wiped out.

Look friends, we came out of Auschwitz and hatred is still alive in the world. People are still hating. I'm not only talking about the world, I'm talking about *Yidden.*

All the fighting in Israel – this one is *frum,* this one is not *frum,* Ashkenaz, Sefard . . . it's all left over from Auschwitz. We might have gotten out of Egypt, but we didn't cross the Red Sea yet.

*

G-d only does what is utmostly necessary. If the world can be good without G-d talking to us, G-d doesn't have to talk to us. But until we hear from G-d himself, "Don't kill," you can kill. Until we hear from G-d himself, "I am the Lord your G-d," you don't believe in G-d. Until I hear from G-d, "Keep the Shabbos holy," I don't know what Shabbos is.

We had to go back once more.

The most ridiculous thing in the world is that Pharaoh had a favorite idol. Its name was "Freedom." This little idol was placed by the Red Sea, by the borders of Egypt.

Here I want you to know something amazing.

When Yosef HaTzaddik was Pharaoh's right-hand man, he collected billions of pieces of gold.

How so? During the famine, everyone bought food from Egypt. Yosef divided it into three parts. One part belonged to Pharaoh and the other two parts were hid by Yosef.

One part was found by Korach, which explains how rich Korach was. One part we never found yet, and one part was made into the idol "Freedom." There were soldiers there, guarding this great treasure. The night G-d killed all the first born, all idols were completely destroyed as well, except one.

The only idol which G-d did not destroy was the idol called "Freedom," because G-d always leaves us a little bit of free choice. So Pharaoh began thinking to himself, "Their G-d is pretty strong, but my little idol 'Freedom' seems to be stronger."

Now when G-d says to the *Yiddelach* who are walking out of Egypt, that it's "time to go back" – they couldn't believe it. But Moshe was saying to them, "You have got to go back. You have got to meet Pharaoh once more."

When they start returning back they meet up with the Egyptians right by the idol 'Freedom,' right by the Red Sea. *Pi Hachirot* – the mouth of Freedom. Here the Egyptians are coming and the Jews have no weapons.

Pharaoh comes with a tremendous army. Pharaoh thought that his little idol will take them down. He thinks, "They are sitting there by *Pi Hachirot,* by my idol 'Freedom.' We will come to the Red Sea and they have no weapons. They have no way out."

That night miraculously, all the wild animals came from the desert and they were standing there. We couldn't go through them either. So one side is where Pharaoh was coming from and one side were the wild animals, and behind them was the Red Sea.

We had nowhere to go. The only place you can go is into the Red Sea.

Now everyone knows that we never crossed the Red Sea completely. We came out on the same side that we walked in from. We didn't have to get to the other side of the Red Sea. We just kept on walking toward the land of Israel on the same side.

When the Red Sea split right open, we walked through and the waters split into twelve tunnels, one for each tribe, and we came out to the other side – which was the same side we went in from.

The moment Pharaoh saw that the Sea split and that there were twelve tunnels, he should have said, "How can I fight them? G-d is with them."

No, Pharaoh will never learn, Pharaoh will never learn. The non-Mount

Sinai people will never learn. Those who don't want to hear from G-d will never learn. They can see all the miracles, but it doesn't matter to them.

The only way is that you have to go to Mount Sinai and hear from G-d Himself.

The vision we had that night was greater than all the prophetic visions in the world. That night we *mamesh* knew that there really is one G-d.

Unless you know that there is one G-d, nothing will change you. Nothing will get through to you.

Strange . . . look at the world. After six million Jews are murdered, we come back to the Holy Land. Then there was the Six Day War, the Yom Kippur War and so much more.

G-d has done the greatest miracles in the world, but it just doesn't touch the world one bit. After the Six Day War, G-d showed the world that He is opening up the Holy Land for the *Yidden.* Can G-d show Himself in a more open way than this?

The Prophets told us for two thousand years that we will come back, and we did.

But the world says, "No, we got to fight again, got to make war again." They think they are waiting for a sign from G-d, but G-d is giving signs all the time. They just don't want to see these signs.

Now our portion begins, *"Vayehi beshalach Par'oh."*

"Ein vayehi ella lashon tza'ar." "Vayehi" is always a language of sadness. What are we so sad about? The sadness was that we were not free from Egypt.

How so? With Pharaoh walking out with us and saying goodbye, we thought maybe he really isn't so bad. Maybe we should give him one more chance. The whole point of the Red Sea came about from this, because it really was not necessary for us to cross the Red Sea on our way to the Holy Land. We came out of the water to the same side we went in from. It was only because we were not free from Egypt yet.

So in order to be free, you have to walk on the Sea . . . not on dry land. The Sfas Emes says (Sfas Emes Pesach 1836) that in order to be completely free, G-d has to turn over the earth, which is what happened with the ten plagues.

On the way, He also turns over the ocean. We come to Mount Sinai and G-d turns over heaven and earth. Only after you see the turning of all three, are you ready to hear G-d's voice.

Everybody has a little bit of earth when they walk, they have a little bit of ocean, and they even have a little bit of heaven . . . but even heaven has to be turned over. My heaven isn't good enough. I think I'm spiritual but do you think that is good enough for Mount Sinai?

Let's turn over heaven, let's turn over the ocean and let's turn over the dry land.

BELIEVING IN OUR OWN *NUSACH*

EVERY SLAVE WANTS TO BE FREE AND EVERY POOR man wants to be rich. But the question is – how much does it mean to you? What is important enough for you that you would change for it?

For two hundred and ten years we were slaves. Eventually we became free, but when did we actually change? This was only once we stood by the Red Sea.

Now listen to the deepest depths.

What does it mean that man was created in G-d's image? It means that whatever we are doing, nature is doing too.

Why do you think the water suddenly changed to dry land? It's very simple – it's because we changed. When we came out of Egypt, we thought it was a beautiful thing to be free. It was great, but it didn't necessarily change who we were.

There are a lot of things we find beautiful, but we don't become them. When we stood by the Red Sea, there was no way of getting away from the Egyptians. We said "*Ribbono shel Olam,* freedom really is so important for us. We would do anything for it . . . anything in the world."

So what is it that we ended up doing that made us change for it?

Everyone knows that when we crossed the Red Sea, there were twelve tunnels. Every tribe had its own tunnel. These tunnels were, so to speak, made out of glass, and the tribes could see each other.

Imagine, Reuven goes through a tunnel and, instead of wondering the whole time if Shimon and the others are drowning, they could see that everyone was taken care of. More importantly, each tribe could see that the others were finding their way. Every tribe had a different way of going through the water.

So the question is – why couldn't all the *Yidden* go in one tunnel? Why separate?

You know what it is, everybody is learning Torah, everyone is putting on *tefillin,* everybody is hopefully keeping Shabbos.

When do you become an individual? In order to become an individual, you have to cross the Red Sea.

And here I want you to know something so deep.

At one point I met someone who used to have a lot of money and then lost it all. He asked me what he should do to get out of his situation. So, I said to him, "Promise G-d that when He gives you money again, you will do something you never did before."

So now open your hearts.

Reb Nachman says that whenever you are at the end, you have to say to G-d, "Obviously everything I did so far did not prevent me from getting to this place. That means that You want something from me which I never did before."

And here I want you to know something so special.

When we came out of Egypt, we didn't promise G-d that we will build the *Beis Hamikdash.* We thought we would be *Yidden.* We would be *frum* . . . we would be cute and sweet and start going to Israel.

But when we got to the Red Sea, there was nowhere to go. We were at the end, so you know what we said to ourselves? There is one thing that we never thought of doing, and that is to build a *Beis HaMikdash* . . .

that there should *mamesh* be one place that is so untouched. Not just a physical *Beis Hamikdash,* but a temple in our hearts.

When we crossed the Red Sea, we each took upon ourselves something we had never done before. We took on individuality. When we came out of Egypt, we all came out of Egypt but it was not personal yet. Crossing the Red Sea was the first time that the revelation was that everyone has to go through their own tunnel.

The Gemara says that to find your soul mate is like crossing the Red Sea. (*Sanhedrin* 22:1.)

What do I do when I can't find my soul mate? I might say, "Listen, G-d, when You help me find my soul mate, I will donate ten dollars to Israel."

G-d says, "Please, you can do that without finding your soul mate."

You know what I have to do? I have to promise G-d I will build a little *Beis HaMikdash.* I have to promise G-d my house will be one little holy place. It's so hard to find another person who is going through the same tunnel as you.

The question is if you would turn back the clock to the tunnels at the Red Sea, do you think your soul mate would go down the same tunnel as you?

Meaning to say, when it comes to the most important things in life, on an individual level, does she really want the same thing as you do? I'm not talking about which carpet you want in the dining room and which tile you want in the bedroom.

I'm talking about the depths of life.

What was one of the main revelations the Baal Shem Tov brought down to the world? It's that one person finds his tunnel in Belz, one in Lubavitch, one in Breslov. Why can't everyone be Belz? Why can't everyone be Lubavitch?

In the town of Sanz, when someone would come for Shabbos, you had to say "Good Shabbos!" on Friday afternoon to check in, to be there for Shabbos. Then the holy Sanzer might say, "Your *neshama* is not part of my *neshama.* You are wasting your time. I am not your Rebbe," but he would not say where to go to.

In Komarna it was so strong. The *Heilige* Komarner would not only say, "I'm not your Rebbe," but he would also say, "You have to go Sadiger, to Ziditchov, or Dzhikov." But today everybody wants to grab every *Yid.*

This is what *Kriyas Yam Suf* is all about. What the Baal Shem Tov brought down before *Mashiach* is coming, is not only to be *frum* and to serve G-d, but that you have to serve G-d in your way.

Gevalt, do you have to believe that you yourself have your own *nusach,* your own style!

G-D'S TIME

THERE IS NO QUESTION IN OUR MINDS THAT WE will always be in Israel and we will always be in *Yerushalayim*. We will also always be *Yidden,* but we are always wondering, "G-d, why are you making it so hard on us?"

Is there anybody who understood the way G-d is running the world more than Moshe Rabbeinu? Yet at the end of the portion of Sh'mos, we see that Moshe Rabbeinu could not understand how G-d was taking us out from Egypt.

Do you know what that means?

Reb Leibe'le says this means that G-d's plan is coming from the most exalted place in the world. It is coming from such a deep place that not even Moshe Rabbeinu can grasp it.

Moshe Rabbeinu never asked G-d anything for himself his whole life except for one time. He would only ask on behalf of the *Yidden*. The only time where Moshe Rabbeinu asks something for himself is when he says to G-d, "Let me see the Holy Land."

The *Midrash* is so heartbreaking. The *Midrash* says that Moshe Rabbeinu says to G-d, "I don't mind being just a bird. Make me into a bird and I will fly into *Yerushalayim.* I just want to be able to see the holy city."

How much can you ask?

And G-d says, "No." Do you know what that means? It means that

G-d's plan is coming from such a deep place that even Moshe can't understand it.

But you know something?

Forget about then. What about now? Can anybody understand what is happening today? Anyone who says, "I understand what is happening today" has no idea what they are talking about.

I want you to know the deepest depths.

Sometimes G-d is leading us in a very clear way. Sometimes G-d is leading us and we know what He wants. When G-d says, "Keep Shabbos," I know what He wants. He wants me to keep Shabbos. When G-d says "Put on *tefillin,*" I know what He wants.

What G-d wants of us today reaches so deep, because we don't know what He wants, but *gevalt,* are we believing in G-d in the deepest, most passionate way.

The question is – did we ever understand anything? When we came out of Egypt, we were waiting for G-d to redeem us. G-d fulfills His promise and He redeems us and takes us out of Egypt. That much we understood. But when we come to the Red Sea, Pharaoh is running after us again.

Imagine I would interview a *Yiddele* five minutes before the splitting of the Red Sea. On one side is the sea, on one side is the Egyptian army, and on both sides are wild animals. I would ask him, "Can you explain to me what is going on here?

G-d took you out of Egypt. He took care of you with the ten plagues. What does he want now? It just doesn't make sense . . . He just brings you here to the Red Sea for Pharaoh to kill you? He could have done it before, so what's going on?"

So you see what this is – this struggle is about Moshe Rabbeinu saying to G-d, *"Lama ha-rei'osa?"* – "I don't understand this whole thing."

(Sh'mos 5:22) Therefore, G-d says, *"Ata tir'eh"* – "Now you will see . . . Moshe Rabbeinu, you will see what I am all about." (Sh'mos 6:1)

And here I want you to open your hearts in the deepest way.

Why do we recite the portion of the crossing of the Red Sea every morning? Because a Jew never forgets. A Jew is someone who never forgets that G-d is doing miracles for us all the time.

And even five minutes before the miracle is happening, you absolutely don't understand what's going on.

Just wait . . . wait a few minutes.

There is one more very important ingredient.

This *parsha* always comes together with *Chamisha Assar B'Shvat,* the 15th day of the month of *Shvat – Tu B'Shvat,* the New Year of the Trees. What is the connection between crossing the Red Sea and *Chamisha Assar B'Shvat*?

Do you know what *Chamisha Assar B'Shvat* is?

Reb Leibe'le Eiger says that on that day it is clear to the tree that unless new sustenance is coming up from the roots, the tree will die. It will completely dry out.

When does the tree receive this new energy? One second before the tree dies . . . not a second before. Do you know when G-d opens the sea? At the last moment.

There is a passage that says *"Ve'ata nosein lahem es ochlam be'ito"* – "You feed everyone in their time." (*Tehillim* 145:15) G-d is doing miracles in His time . . . *mamesh* in His time. If the miracles we need didn't happen yet, it means it still isn't the right time.

To believe in G-d is not only to believe in G-d at this moment. To believe in G-d means – how much do you remember the miracles of yesterday? Do you remember how much G-d took care of you all your life? Do you realize how often you had to leave Egypt? Are you aware of how many Red Seas you crossed?

Let's go one step deeper.

Moshe Rabbeinu says to Pharaoh that we will be leaving Egypt "*kachatzos*" – "at about midnight." (Sh'mos 11:4) And everybody is asking why doesn't he just say "midnight?" Why does he say "at about midnight?"

Reb Nachman says the deepest depths.

There is a passage in Tehillim where King David says "*chatzos layla akum*" – "I'm waking up at 'exactly at midnight.'" (*Tehillim* 119:62.) It doesn't make sense. Moshe Rabbeinu didn't know exactly when midnight is, but King David did?

The answer is like this: When it comes to the redemption from Egypt, we were not that much in touch with G-d's clock. So therefore, Moshe Rabbeinu said it will happen "at about midnight."

But *Mashiach* comes from the line of King David. On the great day, we will know exactly when it will happen.

*

When did the crossing of the sea begin?

At the very last second. That means that if the sea would have split open one second later, we would have been so close to Pharaoh that he could kill us from afar. If we would have stayed there one more day we would have been lost forever.

So G-d took us out in the last second.

You see what it is – the whole story of leaving Egypt is all about the last moment. In the last moment G-d always helps. Not only does G-d help in the last moment, but G-d doesn't help until you *mamesh* need it.

If I wait for something and G-d didn't help me yet, you can't be angry with G-d. It simply wasn't time yet.

Who knows the time better than G-d?

And here is the story.

At one point the Yid HaKodesh didn't have food in the house for three days. His son, the *Heilige* Reb Yerachmiel was crying so much. So the Yid Hakodesh says to him, "You know something? If you would be as hungry as you cry, we would have food."

At that moment, the Yid Hakodesh saw a piece of gold under the table. He looks over to his Yerachmiel and says, "Please forgive me . . . you really are as hungry as you cry."

I'll tell you an unbelievable story.

I once went for a treatment on a Sunday morning, and stupidly, I put on my *Shabbosdika* pants. So I didn't have any money on me. I said to this woman, "I'm really so sorry. I don't have money, but one way or the other, I will send it to you."

When I walked away, I completely forgot that she gave me the treatment, and only a few weeks later did I realize that I still have to pay her. The only thing was that I didn't remember her address. I didn't even remember her name. It really hurt me a lot.

Listen to this unbelievable thing.

Three years later, I'm coming out from a restaurant in Manhattan and there she is. I say to her, "Did you know I'm looking for you all over the universe because I owe you some money. I lost your address. I love you but I forgot your name."

Listen to what she says: "Rabbi, let me tell you – there is one G-d. Last night I was robbed and I don't have a single penny in my pocket. And here I'm walking up and down 72nd Street for two hours, looking to see if there is anyone I know who I could ask for some money." Unbelievable.

The *Ribbono shel Olam* made me forget her name and her address two years before, so I'd meet her when she *mamesh* needed it.

I want you to know something so strong.

We read of the crossing of the Red Sea always around *Chamisha Asar B'Shvat.* What is *Chamisha Assar B'Shvat* all about? It means that whenever you think you are really at the end, this is when it happens.

And now we have to go one step higher.

It says, *"Vachamushim alu ve'nei Yisrael."* (Sh'mos 13:18) The way it's translated is that we had weapons as we were leaving Egypt. But the Zohar HaKadosh points us to the word, *"chamishim,"* – "fifty."

The Zohar says that if G-d would have waited one more second, we would have sunk into the fiftieth gate of impurity. Everyone knows that there is no coming out of the fiftieth gate. It's forever. By the fiftieth gate you don't have choice anymore.

So vachamushim alu ve'nei Yisrael means that since Pharaoh wanted to push us down to the fiftieth gate of impurity, the reward was that when we crossed the Red Sea, we tasted the fiftieth gate of eternity.

*

When we came out of Egypt, we thought the Exodus was over. But seeing Pharaoh and the Egyptians chasing us put so much fear and confusion into us. Only when the Egyptians drowned did we realize that G-d gave us freedom forever.

And here I want you to know something very deep.

When we came out of Egypt, we didn't have the concept of *Mashiach* coming. We didn't know that one day there will be the redemption for the whole world. But that changed while we were crossing the waters.

When we crossed the Red Sea, we start speaking of the great day to come. *"Mikdash HaShem konenu Yadecha"* – "the Temple which will be built by G-d's hands." (Sh'mos 15:17)

Everyone knows that there are three holy temples. The first two were built by us human beings and the third, when *Mashiach* is coming, will be built by G-d.

We will open our eyes and it will be there.

RED SEA SOUL MATES

Finding your soul mate is as difficult as crossing the Red Sea. (Sanhedrin 22:1)

BEFORE YOU FIND YOUR SOUL MATE, YOU THINK there is absolutely no way. All the people you meet just don't fit. Misfits are all over the place.

This is exactly what was happening as we left Egypt. On one side were the Egyptians, on another side were wild animals. And you think, "*Ribbono shel Olam,* you sent me down at the wrong time." Then, at that exact moment, G-d opens the gates.

Before the Second World War, there were very sweet *Yiddische* parents who didn't let their children cross the Red Sea. They said, "We are doing it for you, and we will tell you who to marry."

You know what's happening to the world today?

G-d is taking the whole thing in His hands again. G-d is saying to parents, "You are cute and sweet, but when it comes to soul mates let Me decide." *Baruch HaShem,* we are living in a world where G-d is taking the whole thing into His own hands.

G-d lets you find your own soul mate.

A RELATIONSHIP OF BEAUTY

. . . And I will make Him more beautiful . . . (Sh'mos 15:2)

WHEN WE CROSSED THE RED SEA, WE WERE singing, *"Zeh kayli ve'anvayhu,"* – "this is my G-d and I make Him more beautiful" – *"Elokei avi,"* – "the G-d of my father" – *"va'aromemenhu,"* – "and I will make him high." (Sh'mos 15:2)

What is it that we were singing? What do these words mean?

It's a very high thing to believe in the G-d of your father, but it's not necessarily beautiful. Beauty is when you really find G-d on your own, and right after that you connect to the G-d of your father. Once that happens, it's high and beautiful.

*

When they call out in heaven, forty days before a person is born, the male and female souls say, "Can you show me the other one?" They are shown the pure souls, but down here, in this world, they don't recognize each other. They say, "This is not my Yankele! This is not my Chanele!"

Here is an unbelievable, heartbreaking story. A true story. An awesome story.

There was a young *Chassidic* man in Cracow who was engaged. When the Germans came, he was taken away and he didn't know where his bride was.

In Auschwitz, the men and women were separated, but somehow, from afar, they could see each other. Sometimes they broke through the gates.

One night, close to the end of the war, suddenly he saw his bride on the women's side. Unbelievable. They were blessing each other, "Hold out! The end is near. Please, hold out until the end." One way or another, they sent food to each other. When the Russians came and freed them, somehow they met, and they went off together.

Everything was bombed. Finally, they found one house and they were alone for the first time. They were so happy to be alone. He had not seen himself in a mirror for years. He didn't know what he looked like. He had no hair, no *peyos* – sidecurls. He was full of scars and covered with blood.

But even more heartbreaking, she was clean-shaven. She had no hair. She had no teeth. Her face was full of scars.

They had not seen themselves for so long. They came into the house and suddenly, they looked into a mirror. They were shocked, especially the girl. She said: "This is the way I look! Not even the Angel of Death looks so bad." And then she asked him, "Tell me two things. How did you recognize me? And, how can you love somebody who looks like I look?"

You know what he said to her? "You never looked more beautiful to me than right at this moment."

This means that there is some kind of beauty that is produced in heaven.

Do you know when we tasted this kind of beauty?

When we crossed the Red Sea, we said, "This is my G-d, and I will glorify Him." We suddenly saw that there are two kinds of beauty in the world.

There is one beauty that comes down from heaven and another one that is made by man. The *Ribbono shel Olam* makes us love each other so much that behind all the brokenness, behind all that we go through, we recognize each other . . . we see how beautiful we are.

A WOMAN'S BELIEF

REB NACHMAN SAYS THE WHOLE WORLD IS OPERating on the basis of belief.

A child goes to school, the teacher teaches him the alphabet, and the child completely believes the teacher.

Imagine if the child would be an intellectual and he would start asking, "How do you know that this A is an A and this B is a B?" Thank G-d we teach kids the alphabet while they still believe. The whole world is based on alphabets.

The Rambam says (*Guide to the Perplexed* 3:51) that G-d's Providence is on you as much as you are aware of G-d. What does this mean? G-d's Providence is all over the world, but the more you are aware of G-d, the more His Providence is particularly evident in your life.

For instance, there were *Tzaddikim* who would open to the exact page they wanted every time they opened a book, because they were so aware of G-d that He was guarding every step of their lives.

Our Sages teach us that in the merit of righteous women we were redeemed from Egypt. (*Yalkut Shimoni, Tehillim* 68)

The Jewish women were so holy that while we were slaves in Egypt, not one Egyptian man was able to get close to a Jewish woman. The Jewish men believed in G-d as well, but not on this level of the women . . . the level of miracles.

The *Midrash* says that women can't usually give birth on their own. But since the women were afraid to have their babies in the cities, they went out into the fields, and they had faith that G-d would take care of them and their babies.

The *Midrash* further says that G-d Himself was helping the babies to be born and then angels would come and bring food for the mothers. Everything would happen in the fields, and they would stay there until the baby wasn't crying much anymore.

While we crossed the Red Sea, the children of Israel sang, "This is my G-d and I will exalt Him, the G-d of my father and I will make Him great" (Sh'mos 15:2.) The *Midrash* asks, "Who said, 'This is my G-d?' How did you recognize Him?"

You see what it is – if I saw someone before, then I can identify them again. The *Midrash* says that these were the children who were born in Egypt. They saw G-d before, because it was G-d who was really delivering them into the world. This was all in the merit of what their mothers put into them from birth.

HANDS OF STRENGTH

. . . HaShem, Your hands have established Your Sanctuary (Sh'mos 15:17)

WHAT IS THE FUNCTION OF THE HANDS?

When it comes to Eisav and Ya'akov, everyone imagines Eisav to be much stronger than Ya'akov, but the truth is that Ya'akov was a thousand times stronger.

When Yosef wanted to change the position of his father Ya'akov's hands, Ya'akov tells him, "Don't touch my hands. My hands are strong enough to fight Eisav." *Yedei Eisav,* the hands of Eisav, are very strong when it comes to using them for power and force.

But there is one thing they don't know how to do – they don't know how to hold onto something. Before Ya'akov Avinu met Rachel, he saw a large stone upon the mouth of a well. The people there told him that it takes all the shepherds of the area to push away the stone.

Right after Ya'akov saw Rachel, it says *"vayagel es ha'even mei'al pi habe'eir"* – "he rolled the stone off the mouth of the well." (Bereishis 29:10)

So I want to say a *gevalt* Torah.

Do you know what it means to meet your soul mate? It means you have someone to hold onto, and when you have someone to hold onto, your hands become so strong. *"Mikdash HaShem konenu Yadecha"* – *"HaShem,* Your hands have established Your Sanctuary." (Sh'mos 15:17)

Why are G-d's hands so strong? Because humanly speaking, He is holding onto us. The more we are holding onto G-d's hands, the more the *Ribbono shel Olam* can build the *Beis HaMikdash.*

I want you to know something so deep.

As long as we were afraid of Pharaoh, we weren't really holding onto G-d's hands. When did we begin to *mamesh* hold onto G-d's hands? Not when we left Egypt . . . but only when we crossed the Red Sea.

On Shabbos I'm not doing anything with my hands, because on Shabbos I'm just holding onto G-d. The Mishnah on Shabbos begins with the hands, "*yado bifnim, yado bachutz*" – "his hand is inside, his hand is outside." (Mishnah *Shabbos* 1:1) Shabbos is all about hands.

You see what it is – a slave is someone who needs his hands for working. A free person is someone whose hands are for holding onto someone else.

As long as children are holding onto their parents, they feel close enough to ask them all the questions in the world. But the moment children can't hold onto their parents anymore, they stop asking them questions because they are not close enough. The first sign of freedom from slavery is on Seder night, when our children come and ask us all the questions,

Our holy Rabbis teach us that G-d created the world with one hand, and he will build the *Beis HaMikdash* with both hands. Strong hands, double hands. (Rashi, Sh'mos 15:17)

Now open your hearts.

The hands with which G-d built the world are pretty strong, but there can still be war in the world. However, "*Mikdash HaShem konenu Yadecha*" – when we *Yidden* hold onto G-d's hands, humanly speaking, G-d's hands become so strong. They can build a Holy Temple.

I want you to know the deepest depths.

The Gemara says (*Ta'anis* 29a) that while the *Beis HaMikdash* was burning, the priests didn't want to leave and the High Priest was holding onto the keys of the Holy Temple. At the last moment he threw the keys up to heaven, and a hand came down and caught them.

You know what the hand was telling us? It was saying, "Hold onto G-d's hand."

G-d's last message was to simply hold on. *Mikdash HaShem konenu Yadecha* – the hands which will build the *Beis HaMikdash* are the key to everything.

It doesn't take that much pain to learn how to be a carpenter or a jeweler, but it takes so long to learn with whom to hold hands, and whom to hold onto. We *Yidden* have to go through so much pain until we learn how to hold onto the Torah.

It says that when we left Egypt, we left *"be'yad ramah,"* – "with an exalted hand." (Sh'mos 14:8) Onkelos says it means that we left *"bege'usa,"* with pride.

I want you to know something.

When it comes to saying hello to someone, I can say hello to anyone. I can say hello to the Queen of England, but I can't sit there and hold hands with her.

You have got to be very close in order to hold someone's hand. You can always talk to G-d, but to hold hands?

Bege'usa? With pride? This is *mamesh* something else. I can shake hands with someone I hate, but I can't hold hands with them. Holding hands is only with someone I love very much. If you want to know how much you are holding onto the Torah, see how much you can hold hands with every *Yid* in the world.

You know friends, if you start walking around with the Gemara like a it's a book of physics, you are not holding onto the Torah anymore.

Sometimes late at night on the subway you can see a little boy with *peyalach,* side locks, and a yarmulke, coming to the subway holding onto his Gemara.

Gevalt, is it holy! Heartbreakingly holy. Then somebody walks in with a book of psychology in their hands. It's sweet, but it's not holy.

Do you know how you end up making a Golden Calf?

This happens when you stop holding onto the Torah. The fixing is to build the *Mishkan* with your hands. Everyone was working for the *Mishkan* with their hands.

Let's go one step deeper.

Does Moshe Rabbeinu need to bring down the tablets with his hands? G-d could have given it to him down here. Obviously, the tablets were heavy. And even more so, G-d was holding them from one side by six handbreadths, and Moshe by six handbreadths from the other.

You know what that means?

Holding onto the Torah is not from this world – it's from heaven. Unless your connection to the Torah is heavenly, you don't hold hands.

In heaven, forty days before you are born, they call out whom you will end up marrying. How come? Any man and woman can live in the same house and live for a hundred years. But holding each other's hands is something else . . . it's from heaven.

The *Heilige* Reb Yitzchak Vorker says that, if we would all hold hands, our hand would be so long . . . it would reach heaven.

When I hold up the Torah, I say, "*Vezos haTorah asher sahm Moshe*" – "this is the Torah which Moshe placed before us." Shouldn't I say this when I'm reading from the Torah? But I don't say it then. I'm saying that the real Torah is when I'm holding it up.

I want you to know the deepest Torah in the world.

The *Heilige* Chortkover didn't eat and didn't sleep. He was just from another world. In Chortkov it was a tradition that the Rebbe would get *hagbah* on Simchas Torah – the Rebbe would be the one to lift the Torah.

The Torah scroll he was about to pick up was incredibly heavy, but when the *Heilige* Chortkover went up for *hagbah,* he *mamesh* lifted up the Torah with such ease.

So the *Chassidim* asked him, "Rebbe, how did you do it?"

So he said, "If you know that the Torah carries you, you can do anything."

CONDITIONS OF CHANGE

. . . The sea returned to its strength by dawn . . . (Sh'mos 14:27)

AFTER WE CROSSED THE RED SEA, THERE IS A PASsage that says, "the sea returned to its strength by dawn." (Sh'mos 14:27) The Gemara says – do not read it as "strength," but as "condition – meaning that the Red Sea returned to its original condition.

What condition are we talking about?

When G-d created the Red Sea, he made a condition with it that on the seventh night of Pesach, when we *Yidden* would be by the shores of the Red Sea, the sea should split open and allow us to pass through.

Now open your hearts like mad.

G-d makes conditions, and not only with the Sea. G-d makes a condition with every person in the world. G-d tells each person at the time of his or her creation, "There will be one moment in your life when you can save someone else's life. There will be a moment when you can do the greatest thing, which I created you for, but you have to be ready to be something else.

You have to be ready to completely turn yourself over – like from water to become dry land. To become anything in the world.

The deepest secret of life is that I always have to be what I am, but there are moments when I have to not be what I am also."

What's going on today with our establishment?

According to their schedule, the way the world is today doesn't fit in.

So they just ignore what's really going on. In the Sixties we lost thousands of kids to drugs. The establishment didn't talk about it because it was not on their agenda.

What's going on in *Eretz Yisrael* now? They all talk about the Arabs. What about on the inside? We are losing our kids, thousands of kids, but it's not on their agenda.

How about changing from an ocean to become dry land? Be something else!

True, a Rabbi has an office. Why doesn't he go outside sometimes? Out on to the street?

How do you know if you really love somebody? Are you ready to change for that person? Even for just a moment?

The Gemara says that finding your soul mate is like crossing the Red Sea. And everybody asks – why does G-d call out, forty days before a person is born, who a person's soul mate is? Because, for two people to find each other and live together, everybody living on their own schedule all the time, they will never make it.

I am me, and you are you. Unless they are like the Red Sea. At the time that G-d created the Red Sea, He put in the condition that there will come a moment that it will have to stop being a sea and become dry land. But this is a heavenly power.

Change is the hardest thing in the world. The kind of change we are talking about is not from this world. It's as deep as when G-d created the world.

Now I want to go one step deeper.

Why does the Torah say that the Red Sea went back to its original condition? And here is the deepest Torah in the world. What happens to you if you refuse to change?

You might say: "Okay, at least I am what I am." But really, you are nothing. You know what the Torah says? When was the Red Sea really a sea? After it was ready to change. When are you really what you are? Only if you can be anything for somebody you love.

When the sea returned to its original condition, suddenly it was really a sea. A real sea. Now its water was really water. When *Mashiach* is coming, it says, "*kamayim layam mechasim*" – "as water covers the sea." (*Yishayahu* 1:19) Which waters are we talking about? They are the waters of the Red Sea – waters that are ready to change to save people's lives.

Who was the first person that did something awesome for somebody else? It was our holy mother, Rachel. Imagine if Rachel would have called up a group of Rabbis and said, "Listen, my father, Lavan, is putting my sister Leah under the *chuppah* instead of me. What should I do? Should I give her the signs or not?" They would answer, "Are you crazy? *Chas v'shalom,* G-d forbid!"

Rachel and Leah – together they established the family of Israel.

Everybody knows that when they carried the casket of Yosef HaTzaddik to the Red Sea, the sea split . . . because of Yosef. Yosef, the son of Rachel. But I think it was also because of Rachel herself.

When Yosef came to the Sea, he said, "Do you know how much my mother changed for her sister? She gave up everything. And you don't want to give up being a sea for a few minutes?"

The *Midrash* says that the moment that the casket of Yosef came, "*hayam ra-ah vayanos,*" – "the sea saw and fled." What did it see? It saw the casket of Yosef. (*Midrash Tehillim* 114:9)

When Yosef HaTzaddik made peace with his brothers, can you imagine how much he changed himself not to be angry?

Our great Rabbis say that the greatest thing Yosef the Tzaddik did was that he withstood the test of Potiphar's wife. He didn't give in to that temptation. But you know what is even greater? The greatest thing Yosef the Tzaddik ever did was to forgive his brothers.

So everybody asks – wasn't it when the Sea split open and became dry land that it went back to its original condition – when it fulfilled the condition G-d made with it – and not when it became water again?

Open your hearts, friends.

What happens to most of us when we have a *gevalt* moment? We go back to where we were before we had it. We go to Shul on Yom Kippur and have a wonderful experience. But then we go back to the way we were before Yom Kippur.

"The Sea returned to its original strength." Where did the Sea return to? Not to where it was before it split. It went back to the splitting all the time. The Sea was still connected every second, to its splitting.

All of us have moments when we give up everything, but we forget them so fast. Do you know why? Because they are not connected to our daily life. This condition that G-d makes with us, of the splitting of the Red Sea, has to be every second in our lives. Every minute, every second.

Everybody knows that the Temple was destroyed because we hated one another. When we crossed the Red Sea, the Jews saw a vision of the Third Temple, of *Mashiach*.

If only every *Yiddele* would say, "I'm ready to be something else, for the sake of another Jew."

Okay, everybody knows that the children were the first to say, "This is my G-d, and I will glorify Him." At the splitting of the Red Sea, the children were the highest.

My theory is that as much as parents think we love our children the most, they are the ones who really love us the most. Because we may give up on our children so fast, but they never give up on us.

We may be the biggest creeps in the world, and they still love us. Little children believe that their parents are the best people in the world. For our children, we are willing to turn ourselves over a thousand times.

The Gemara says that finding your soul mate is like crossing the Red Sea, because to find your soul mate, means to have children, and you cannot have children unless you are ready to turn over a thousand times for them. For my children, there is nothing in the world I will not do.

I'll be water, I'll be dry land, I'll be anything.

There is nobody in the world more ready to be anything than children. They have no set formula. They are not yet water. They are not yet dry land. So when we crossed the Red Sea, the children felt most at home. Suddenly, when they crossed the Red Sea, they saw that all the Jews were like children. No set form, no schedule. That's why they felt at home.

I want to make it so clear that, unless you are ready to cross the Red Sea for every Jew in the world, you cannot have a *Mashiach* vision.

Rav Aharon Karliner says a beautiful Torah.

When G-d said to the Red Sea, "You are going to split open for the Jews," the Sea said to G-d, "Can You show me the Jews that I'll be splitting open for?"

G-d showed it the way the Jews looked in heaven. They looked so holy and beautiful and clean. Then when the Sea saw the Jews standing before it, looking so tired and so broken, it said, "These are not the people I am supposed to split open for!" It was so hard to convince the Sea that those were the people.

*

What happens to you when you *mamesh* have an infinite experience? What do you do when something happens to you that is beyond anything you ever knew?

You either carry this moment with you forever or forget it ever happened.

Everybody knows that when G-d created the ocean he made a condition with the ocean, saying, "On the seventh night of Pesach there will be three million *Yidden* standing by your shores, and you have to split open to let them through."

"*Vayashav hayam lifnos boker le'eisano.*" (Sh'mos 14:27) The *Midrash* says after the Sea split, it went back to the original deal it had with G-d (*Bereishis Rabbah* 5:5, *Sh'mos Rabbah* 21:6, Zohar 2 198b.)

So, our holy Rabbis ask – why do we say that the sea fulfilled its deal when it went back to being water? Surely it fulfilled its deal when it split open. For the ocean to flow was nothing new . . . that's the way G-d created it.

So what's going on here?

You know what kind of a deal G-d made with the ocean? *Vayashav hayam lifnos boker le'eisano*. How do you know that what you are doing is what G-d created you for?

You go back and you are *mamesh* yourself again. But even more than that . . . only then do you really know what you are here for. The ocean never knew what it was created for.

After the ocean returned to being an ocean, it was clear to it that G-d created it to be an ocean only in order to split and become dry land and then become an ocean again. To show the world that there is one G-d.

When I leave Egypt, I feel that I, as a human being, can be infinite. But by the time I get to the crossing of the sea, it's clear to me that not only I, the human being, am infinite . . . even nature is infinite.

An ocean can be dry and dry land can be ocean. A tree can be a flower and a flower can be a tree. Everything is infinite . . . the whole world is infinite.

There is nothing in my way.

Why is it that spiritually, in most Synagogues, nothing is happening? It's because if too much is happening, we won't want to go to our own house. What are we going to do there? If it's too much, we can't handle it. So it's better if nothing is happening.

But you know something? A real G-d experience is that when you go back home, you realize this is what life is all about . . . it's so much deeper.

Wherever we go, whenever we talk to people, G-d should bless us to lift them up to the highest level. And also give them strength that, when they come home, they should know how much they are *mamesh* capable of doing in this world.

Why are people afraid to *mamesh* pour out their hearts to daven? This is because I wouldn't know how to handle it five minutes later. I've seen a lot of people who really love each other and for one moment there is a feeling of, "Maybe we should really tell each other everything and pour out our hearts." But then they are so afraid, and they ask themselves, "What are we going to do five minutes later? Let's just play it cool."

You know what *kriyas Yam Suf* is?

"*Tafsu omanus avoseihem beyadeihem*" – we grabbed the art of our fathers (*Midrash Tanchuma Beshalach* 9.) We said, "Let's storm the heavens with prayer."

Can you imagine how much the *Yidden* turned over their hearts and souls before G-d? When the ocean saw this, the ocean said, "If they can do it, I can do it too. If they can change for G-d a thousand times, I can also change from water to dry land."

And here I want you to open your hearts.

The Gemara says that finding your soul mate is as hard as crossing the Red Sea (*Sanhedrin* 22:1), which has millions of meanings. But my favorite one is when you love somebody a little and you say, "I want you to know, I'm getting up at 7:30 in the morning. Then I have my coffee and then I have my orange juice. Then at 9 o'clock I'm going to my office. I'm coming home at 6:30, and I want my schnitzel. Then I go to sleep and that's it."

Does this sound like the most passionate love story in the world? To love a person means that for you I can be water, for you I can be dry land. For you, I can be anything in the world.

People always think that when two people love each other, they fit into each other's schedules. On the contrary – when you love somebody very much, it's *mamesh* like *kriyas Yam Suf*. I'll be anything in the world for you.

When we crossed the Red Sea, the Gemara says our children were the first ones who started to sing. Do you know why? Because children have no trouble being anything in the world.

We older people are already so established. I'm a Rabbi, I'm a doctor. I'm this and I'm that. I'm *frum,* I'm not *frum.* I eat meat, I'm a vegetarian. Everyone has their own self-establishment.

Children have none of this . . . they can be anything in the world.

A *YID* REMEMBERS

IF YOU WERE TO ASK ME WHO SHOULD BE THE FIRST one to drown in the sea, who would I say should be the first? Pharaoh of course!

The one who enslaved the Jews for all those years. The one who tortured parents and children. The one who gave orders to throw newborns into the water.

The craziest thing is that all the Egyptians drowned besides for one person – Pharaoh. The holy of holiest, Moshe Rabbeinu, held out his hand and pulled him out from the ocean.

How could this be? It's very simple. A *Yid* doesn't forget. With all the bad things, Pharaoh had been a father figure to Moshe – he was good to him when Moshe was a little boy. Is there a better time to pay him back than when he is really in trouble?

You know what that means?

The holiness of a *Yid* is that he doesn't forget for one second when someone did a favor to him, even if it's the most rotten person in the world.

You see friends – crossing the Red Sea is not only to remember what G-d did for you, but how much do you remember what other people did for you? How much do you remember what good friends are?

SUSTENANCE

Receiving sustenance is like crossing the Red Sea. (Pesachim 118:1)

WHEN WE CROSSED THE RED SEA, WE CAME out on the same side we went in from. In order to get to Eretz Yisrael, we didn't have to cross the Red Sea. You go through the desert and you come to Israel. When we went into the Red Sea, we basically made a U-turn.

So why did we have to go into the water to begin with?

So here is a teaching from Reb Mendele Vizhnitzer and I want you to know the deepest depths.

Sometimes G-d gives you a gift, but it only becomes yours when you are ready to die for it. It's not a test – it simply is what it is. We came out of Egypt, but how much is freedom worth to us?

When we crossed the Red Sea, we were *mamesh* ready to die for it, and at that moment, freedom became ours. But here the Vizhnitzer reaches even deeper. The Vizhnitzer says that a person is only ready to die for something that they cannot live without. If I can live without it, then I'm not going to die for it.

We have no idea with how little we can live. We also have no idea how much we can suffer and yet still stay alive. One time the *Heilige* Apter began crying and simply didn't stop.

For days and days, he was crying. Everyone came to talk to him, but no one knew why he was crying. Finally, the Rebbe, Reb Zusha, came to visit and asked why he was crying uncontrollably. At that time nobody knew what the Apter meant when he answered, but now we unfortunately understand.

He said, "I'll tell you why I'm crying. I see that the Jewish people have to go through such tremendous suffering, and I can't bear seeing it."

So the Rebbe, Reb Zusha, says to the Apter, "Yes, but don't you know G-d only gives you as much pain as you can bear?"

"Exactly," says the Apter, "We are able to bear so much pain . . . so very much pain."

You are not going to die for something you can live without. This is the ultimate. Can you live without G-d? Can you live without *Yiddishkeit?* Can you live without the Torah?

Will you jump into the Red Sea for a bagel? I like bagels and lox, but I'm not going to jump into the Red Sea for it. I'm not even jumping in for a hundred thousand dollars.

The greatest storm in the history of the world took place that night. The waves of the Red Sea were stronger than ever. So here the Jewish people were walking into the ocean while the waves were storming their way up to heaven.

Do you know when I'm going into those waters? When I can't live without it. So imagine G-d forbid, that someone who I love the most will drown. Sure, for them I'll jump in.

So the Vizhnitzer says like this – when the Gemara says that receiving sustenance is like crossing the Red Sea (*Pesachim* 118:1), we are not talking here about finding a job for a hundred dollars a day. We are clearly talking about something else.

The question is – what keeps you alive? What sustains you? Of course, we have to eat, but what sustains us is not the bread we eat. That which sustains us is something so much deeper. Therefore, the Gemara says that finding your soulmate is as hard as crossing the Red Sea.

How many people marry each other and they absolutely don't sustain each other? Heartbreaking.

How many people get married and tear each other apart? Heartbreaking.

The deepest relationship is when I find somebody who *mamesh* sustains me, or if I find somebody for whom I'm ready to jump into the ocean.

When I have the privilege of marrying people off – before I even decide if I want to marry them off, I ask them if they can live without each other. If you can live without each other, don't bother getting married. Even if you cannot live without each other, it's already a gamble. But if you are able to live without each other, don't bother.

I want to share with you a very cute story.

Many years ago I received a call at 4 am. A *Yiddele* from New Jersey is on the phone. "Rabbi," he says. "My wife and I always fight. Tonight we had a terrible fight, and we decided to finally break up. So, I said we need to talk to a Rabbi. Let's talk to the Rabbi whose records we listen to."

I said, "For you, brother, come tomorrow morning at 10 o'clock." They were the cutest couple I ever saw. They were both seventy-five years old and were married for forty years.

So I asked him, "Do you love her?"

He says, "Could I love somebody as dumb as she is." *Gevalt* answer.

I asked her, "Do you love him?"

She says, "This idiot, this disgusting piece of garbage?"

Don't ask me why, but for some reason, it struck me that they really do belong together. There was something there. So I made a deal with them and I said. "I don't know what you really think of each other, but let me ask of you the following. For five minutes every day, can you say good things to each other? Just for five minutes? Before you go to sleep at night, *mamesh* say good things to each other, and call me back in a few weeks."

Two weeks later they call me back, and *Baruch HaShem*, things were good. He says to me, "Rabbi, I want to see you again, but we don't have to come back because of fighting. Things are so good between us. I never knew you have to say good things to another person. I always thought I could knock my wife all the time." And then she gets on the phone and says, "It's true – for some reason I thought it was okay to call my husband an idiot."

You see what it is – after everything, they realized that they *mamesh* sustain each other.

HOW LONG WILL IT LAST?

And Amalek came . . . (Sh'mos 17:8)

WHEN DOES AMALEK COME AND ATTACK US? *"Vayavo Amalek vayilachem im Yisrael be'Refidim"* – "and Amalek fought with us in the city of Refidim." (Sh'mos 17:8)

So the *Midrash* says (*Yalkut Sh'mos* 23) that this place of battle was called Refidim because *"she'rafu ye'deihem midivrei Torah."* The simple translation is that we weren't learning as much as we could have, but it's obviously much deeper than this. We were learning, but something was holding us back.

The Beis Ya'akov asks (*Beis Ya'akov Beshalach* 110) – why is it that it was only Amalek who came to attack us? What did he know? It's because Amalek comes from Eisav, and Eisav is Ya'akov's twin.

Don't kid yourself – he is very close to Ya'akov. The rest of the world may not know when Ya'akov has cooled off a little bit from *Yiddishkeit,* but Amalek smells it right away.

When I'm not serving G-d with so much enthusiasm, Amalek smells it. He is right there, and he says, "Brother, you can tell me the truth. I know you are going through changes now. Why are you hanging on to the old tradition?"

Now open your hearts in the deepest depths.

How strong are my vessels on Yom Kippur? How much *Yiddishkeit* can I take in on Yom Kippur? On Yom Kippur I'm taking in *Yiddishkeit* that is a little bit removed from the world.

On Yom Kippur I'm not eating, I'm sitting in Shul, and I have all the vessels to receive the Torah. The question is – what am I doing when I walk out from Shul? On Mount Sinai I have very strong vessels to receive the Torah. I see the voices. I hear the shofar. I'm at the highest level in the world.

The thing is that today we are in a different world. How many vessels do you have left? We would love to, we want to . . . but in reality, our vessels are not strong enough to take in the *Ribbono shel Olam* in the same way that we do on Yom Kippur.

This is exactly when Amalek comes and says to you, "Brother, I know you dream about being holy. You'd love to be holy, but face it – you don't have vessels for it."

In all honesty, if I were to ask you if we have vessels today for the coming of the *Mashiach,* what would you say? As much as I'm hoping for *Mashiach* to come, I have no vessels for it.

So Amalek says, "You don't have vessels for it . . . just forget it." Our problem is always that, whenever there is an opening in heaven to give us the greatest thing in the world, we flake out. We always think, "We can't handle it, it's too much for us."

Why didn't we fully receive the Torah on Mount Sinai? It's because we were so afraid that we didn't really have the vessels. We thought to ourselves, "Okay, I'm standing on Mount Sinai right now, so of course I'm good, but what will be with me in five minutes?"

I want you to know something so deep.

Anything I want the most – I'm so afraid it won't happen. If I won't buy apples next week, so I won't buy apples. If I won't have my favorite gefilte fish on Shabbos, I'll somehow manage. But when it comes to things I want the most . . . I'm so afraid they won't happen.

And here I want you to open your hearts.

While crossing the Red Sea, we *mamesh* had the vision of *Mashiach*'s coming. But what happened? *"She'rafu ye'deihem midivrei Torah."* We got so afraid because we started to ask ourselves, "What are we going to do afterwards? What are we going to do if it doesn't last?"

These are the vibrations of Amalek. During the war with Amalek, Moshe Rabbeinu was holding up his hands. What was he telling us with his hands? He was saying, *"Yidden,* where do you think you are connected? You are connected to the highest place in heaven. You are connected to the highest place. Even if your head doesn't reach there, it's beyond what you are reaching."

A HEART THAT IS WHOLE

And Aharon and Hur supported his hands . . . (Sh'mos 17:12)

HOW DO WE FIGHT AMALEK?

Do you think Yehoshua had a weak army, so Amalek thought that it would be easy to knock us off? Yehoshua had the best army in the world. Thousands of holy warriors on the battlefield and thousands of holy warriors in prayer.

But you know something? You don't win the war with Amalek unless Moshe Rabbeinu is holding up his hands with Hur and Aharon on each side.

What is Aharon HaKohen all about?

Aharon HaKohen is all about "*Avodah.*" His whole thing was how to serve and work in the Temple. And Reb Leibe'le Eiger says that Hur comes from the word "*chor,*" a hole.

And here I want you to open your hearts.

When someone tells me that something hurts them, does it make a hole in my heart? If someone says to me, "I'm really in trouble," and all I say is, "Okay, I'll try my best to help you," it's really nothing.

What a privilege it is when someone shares their heart with you, and in a certain way they make a hole in your heart.

How healthy is that heart that is full of holes . . . full of holes.

יתרו

YISRO

יתרו

Dedicated to our daughter

HODAYAH TAL LEVANAH SHIRA YAM
הודיה טל לבנה שירה ים

In honor of her bat mitzvah *parsha*
2012 / 5772 – תשע"ב

Quoting, as an 11-year-old preparing her *drash* on the *pasuk*:

וְעַתָּה אִם שָׁמוֹעַ תִּשְׁמְעוּ בְּקֹלִי וּשְׁמַרְתֶּם אֶת בְּרִיתִי וִהְיִיתֶם
לִי סְגֻלָּה מִכָּל הָעַמִּים כִּי לִי כָּל הָאָרֶץ: (שמות יט:ה)

And now if you listen to my voice and keep my covenant you will be a special treasure to me from all the other nations because the land is mine. (19:5)

About the 4th commandment, keeping Shabbos, citing the Gemora stating that if the Jewish people keep two Shabboses the *geula/Mashiach* would come (Shabbos 118a). She says:

"Our Rebbe, Reb Shlomo Carlebach says in the name of the Chernobler Rebbe that these two Shabboses (*Zachor v'Shamor*) are the Shabbos below and the Shabbos above."

From the mouths of babes may we be blessed with

One more Shabbos. . . One more Shabbos. . .
One more Shabbos.

DAVID YISRAEL & BAT SHEVA (Vera) MILLER

THOSE THAT CHANGE, THOSE THAT DON'T

He heard of the splitting of the Red Sea and the war with Amalek. (Rashi on Sh'mos 18:1)

THERE ARE PEOPLE IN THE WORLD WHO NEVER change. You can show them they are wrong but they just don't care. There are those who can see the greatest tragedy in the world and not become one ounce deeper. G-d can also show them the greatest joy in the world, and nothing about their essence is touched or changed.

Then there are people, whatever happens to them touches them so deep, they become different people. I don't mean that you can't recognize them, but something happens to them on the inside.

Rashi says that after Yisro heard of the crossing of the Red Sea and about the war with Amalek, he decided he has to come and be with his son-in-law Moshe. What was it that touched him so deeply?

Yisro heard that there are two kinds of people in the world. Do you know why the waters of the Red Sea changed for us Jewish people? When the water saw that a whole nation is changing their heart and their souls before G-d every second, the water said, "I am changing with you – what do you need me to be right now?"

Then Yisro heard about Amalek. Amalek always hated the Jewish people. Amalek was the one who gave Pharaoh the idea to make slaves out of the Jews. After all the miracles that happened to the Jews, and revelations of the one true G-d, Amalek didn't change one bit.

So Yisro realized, "I got to get close to the people who always change, to the people who are actually touched by what G-d is doing in the world."

There are those who didn't change one bit after the horrors of six million. There are those who see that G-d gave us back the Holy Land and still haven't changed one bit.

Then there are people that whatever happens from G-d *mamesh* reaches them. They change, they wake-up and become deeper. Our young people today are ready to change before G-d every second. As soon as they see a little sign from above, they are willing to do anything for G-d.

Now let's go one step deeper. Everyone is asking, why does the *parsha* of the Ten Commandments begin with the story of Yisro?

Open your hearts wide.

When we go back to the first family in the Torah, we see the only two brothers who existed in the world, and they could not get it together. In a certain deep way, G-d, so to speak, could not come down to Mount Sinai before they made peace with each other. So this *parsha* begins saying that Cain and Abel made peace.

How so?

According to our kabbalists, Yisro was a reincarnation of the soul of Cain and Moshe was the soul of Abel (*Sha'ar Hagilgulim,* Hakdama 36). Now can you imagine what it took out of Yisro to leave behind all that he left and join Am Yisrael?

He was extremely established, he was the priest of the pagan world! He was like the Pope, and he is leaving everything behind him and coming to Moshe!

Now how did Moshe reach beyond himself? Yisro is a Jew for one day, and here he comes and is giving Moshe advice how to run the show?

It's the biggest *chutzpah* in the world! Moshe could have said to him, "Let's face it, you are a pagan. Do you know who I am? I'm talking to G-d all the time. You're a Jew for just one day! Who are you to tell me anything?"

Can you imagine how much Moshe reached beyond himself? It takes a lot of "beyond yourself" to take advice from somebody else, all the more so to take advice from someone who has just stopped being an idol worshipper.

So the beginning of the *parsha* is that both Yisro and Moshe are reaching beyond themselves.

Now what was the duel between Cain and Abel really all about? Abel was bringing sacrifices that G-d accepted, which means that Abel really knew how to serve G-d. So, Cain was really angry – he was asking his brother Abel, "You saw that I also wanted to do something for G-d, but I didn't know how to do it. How do you walk away without teaching me?"

Now what was wrong with Cain? He should have said, "Master of the World, I really don't know how to do it, but I'm so glad I have a brother who knows how to." If Cain really wants to serve G-d, he should have said, "G-d, I'm so glad I have a brother who really knows how to do it."

And there is something wrong with Abel. It was Cain's idea to bring a sacrifice, not Abel's. So why didn't he thank Cain for the idea? Why didn't Abel acknowledge that Cain knows something that he didn't know?

Now listen to this unbelievable fixing. The fixing is that Yisro, who is the *gilgul* reincarnation of Cain, comes to Moshe, who is the *gilgul* of Abel, and is begging him to teach him. The next day, Yisro comes to Moshe and says, "You are doing the whole judging thing wrong. I'll teach you how to do it the right way."

So you see what it is, these two souls, these two brothers, finally reached beyond themselves, and when this happens, only then do we taste what living with G-d's word is all about. What living with the Torah is all about.

*

Every slave wants to be free, every poor man wants to be rich. But the question is, how much does it mean to you? We were slaves and we became free, but that is not when we changed. Do you know when we changed? When we stood by the Red Sea.

Do you know what it means that man is created in G-d's image? Whatever we are doing, nature is doing. Why do you think the water suddenly changed to dry land? Because we changed.

When we came out of Egypt, we thought it was beautiful to be free. We stood by the Red Sea. There was no way of getting away from the Egyptians. We said, "*Ribbono shel Olam,* we would do anything for this, anything in the world."

I want you to know, sweetest friends, do you think the water suddenly became dry land? The water stayed water, but do you know what the water said? *Ribbono shel Olam,* in order to save people, I'm ready to become dry land.

For somebody else . . . to do somebody a favor, I would do anything in the world. But again, you don't have to change, on the contrary. You can do it the way you are, the question is how much are you ready?

Listen to this. Yisro was told that we crossed the Red Sea and Amalek attacked us. Do you know what he heard? Can you imagine how much he had to change, from the top pagan man to suddenly become a Jew? Can you imagine how much he was ready to change? I'm sure he was so afraid. Nobody wants to suddenly be somebody else.

But he heard of the crossing of the Red Sea. He heard that when you really change, you are still the same. The great miracle is, whenever it means so much to you, that you want to change, in the last second

G-d says, "You don't need to change, do it the way you are," because obviously G-d created you into something, you're not somebody else.

So Yisro heard that in order to be a servant of G-d you have to be ready to change, but when you are really a servant of G-d it's the same.

Then Yisro heard of Amalek. Amalek comes and says, "You will never change, I know you too well. You mean to tell me that yesterday you didn't keep Shabbos, and today you will keep Shabbos? You can do something today that you didn't do all your life? Amalek comes and cools you off.

"Don't kid yourself, you will never be able to do it." Amalek says, "Yes, one time in history there was crossing of the Red Sea. One time in your life you had a little Jewish attack and you changed, but face it. Do you think you will do it all the time? You are crazy."

What is the greatest evil in the world?

The greatest evil is when someone comes and tells you, "You won't make it anyway, forget it. Even if you did it once, it doesn't mean you will do it twice." Evil comes to you and says to do something wrong, that's not too terrible yet. Okay, I'm a human being, I do something wrong; tomorrow I will do something good.

Reb Nachman says to take away someone's self-confidence is murder, *mamesh* murder.

I was once invited to somebody's house, there was a girl of twelve who came home with a report card. She was so happy, it was all "A"s.

Leave it up to her *yenta* mother to *mamesh* damage her. Her mother says to her, "Don't let it go to your head. You think because you have all "A"s this one time, you will have it again?" She can have a *sheitel* from here to heaven, but she has not one ounce of *Yiddishkeit.*

*

The Ishbitzer says something awesome.

How much did it take out of Yisro to stop being the greatest personality in the field of idol worship and suddenly become a *"pashut Yid,"* a simple Jew? He had to turn himself over from one corner in his heart to the other.

It is heartbreakingly sad when some of us *Yiddelach* think that since we were born Jewish, therefore we are Jewish. You might be a Jew, but to hear G-d's voice is something else.

To be on Mount Sinai you have to turn yourself over from one corner of the world to the other.

CONQUERING PROCRASTINATION

EVERYONE WANTS TO CHANGE, BUT EVERYONE has so many questions before changing:

How long does it take to really change? How much does it hurt? Will I be someone else when I change?

All it takes is to open our ears, and to properly listen to what we say every day. We say *"HaShem Echad"* – "G-d is one" a hundred times a day. But you've never heard it yet. You see, if you *mamesh* hear it – you have no problem changing.

Now something even deeper, if you think it's a change, then you are an outsider to it.

Reb Leibe'le says the *parsha* begins, *"Vayishma Yisro"* – "And Yisro heard," to let you know that you can be so far away. From being the head of the pagan world to Mount Sinai is a far shot.

How long did it take Yisro? Not only did he become a Jew and a servant of G-d, he comes to Moshe the next day and his words are written in the Torah. In one day he *mamesh* reached the highest level in the world.

I want to share something very deep with you.

Do you know what the fixing of the soul is? Imagine I'm traveling to New York, so if I'm in San Francisco I have to go east. If I want to go to Hawaii I am going west. Now imagine I am sitting on a plane going east and I think I am going to Hawaii. Suddenly, while I am sitting on the plane, talking to people, telling them I am so glad I am going to

Hawaii, people start to say, "You are crazy, you are going east, you have to go west."

But you know what I have to do? First, I have to go back to San Francisco where I began, change planes, and begin to go toward Hawaii.

Imagine I go wrong on a spiritual level, and I'm going the wrong direction. Do I have to first go back to where I began, and change planes? No. The moment I realize I am in the wrong direction, I am already there. I don't even have to turn around. It's always right there, but it takes so much strength to realize this.

You know what it is, friends? We feel much better when we feel we could be more guilty. We always feel better if we are able to feel like *shleppers* and *kvetchers*. If someone were to tell us that it really doesn't take any time to turn the tables, we wouldn't know what to do with them.

We want someone to tell us how sick we are. We want someone to tell us that we have to walk barefoot from Israel to India and from there to China. And then for ten years you have to sit on a mountain and do nothing, and then for twenty years you have to pull out your hair. Then and only then will your soul be fixed.

But if someone tells you, you don't have to do anything, you just have to open your eyes and ears – we just don't know what to do with ourselves.

The holiness of Mount Sinai is that when you hear G-d's word, you feel the power to change right away.

It's such a strange world. For someone to tell me that life is bad, you don't need G-d to tell you it's bad. But to hear a message that life is really good, this can really only come from heaven because, somehow, we are not conditioned to hear good things.

On Mount Sinai, we *mamesh* heard from G-d, "I am G-d who took you out of Egypt. I'm still around."

FINITE AND INFINITE

WHAT IS THE SPECIALTY OF US JEWS, AND what is the specialty of the non-Jewish world?

G-d created the world with unbelievable borders. There is day, there is night; there is fire, there is water. There is winter and there is summer. But within all this, there is something beyond time and space.

We Jewish people represent the world beyond time and space. Why does the world have so much trouble accepting that we have a land? They are not idiots, it's deeper than just foolish hatred. You know what it is? They know we don't fit into the world because they know we are beyond time and space. How is it naturally possible that after two thousand years, we suddenly come back to our land?

On the other hand, we are also part of time and space. Imagine a person who says that since they are beyond time and space, they keep Shabbos on Wednesday. Yom Kippur comes out in the fall, but you know something? It doesn't fit into my schedule; I'd rather have Yom Kippur in the winter when it's shorter.

It just doesn't go like this. Imagine you are supposed to light the Shabbos candles by 4:48, but because we are beyond time and space, I will light the candles at midnight. Why not?

You know what it is, a *Yid* has to *mamesh* be infinite and also has to be finite.

The problem is that some people are absolutely slaves to their watches.

Therefore, before we went out of Egypt, G-d says to Moshe, "Tell the *Yidden* to sanctify the new moon." *Hachodesh hazeh lachem*." (Sh'mos 12:2)

Tell the *Yidden,* a person who is coming out of Egypt is not a slave to time. We *Yidden* are not slaves to time. What does it mean that you have to learn day and night? The Torah is not a slave to time.

Everything other than the Torah that the world is learning has to do with time. I learn for five months at a time in the university, and then I go on vacation. Then I go back to learning for another semester, and then I have vacation again. Everything has to do with time because time is a great slave driver.

But since the Torah is what connects us to being beyond time and space, how could I ever stop learning? There is no vacation from learning.

I want to share with you something that *mamesh* reached me so deeply.

When I was a little boy, my father was very close to the Telzer Rav. He was a *ga'on olam,* a world genius. In the summer, the Telzer Rav would travel to a city near Danzig, and they had a house by the ocean. At one time, my father asked him, "What do you do on your vacation?"

So he says like this: "I'll tell you, when I'm in Telz I'm the rabbi in Telz. I spend so much time with people and with the community's needs. When I'm on vacation my greatest pleasure is that I can learn for eighteen hours. I get myself a chair and a table right on the sand of the beach and I'm learning eighteen hours."

Is there any science in the world where people learn *mamesh* day and night? Can you imagine coming to a university on a Thursday night and all the students are sitting there, *shuckeling* away and learning?

So, on the one hand the Torah is beyond time and space; on the other hand, the Torah is so finite. Do you know how finite the laws of slaughtering a cow are? *Gevalt,* is it finite. There are an infinite amount of finite laws pertaining to the knife, the animal, and the ritual slaughterer.

So, what are we working on, being finite or being infinite? I want you to open your heart from here to eternity.

The deepest secret in life is to know when to be finite and when to be infinite. Sometimes I watch married couples. On a finite level, they connect in a very good way, but when it comes to being a little bit beyond time and space – they are not connected.

And sometimes it's the other way around. When it comes to being beyond time and space, they are connected, but on a "this world" level – they are not.

The deepest connection is if there is connection on both levels. And it's the same with G-d's commandments. Do you know how deep Shabbos is? Shabbos is both. It begins at 5:28 and is over at 6:20, but Shabbos itself is infinite, it simply wears the *l'vushim* – garments – of the finite world.

So here begins the Torah of the *Heilige* Ishbitzer.

You know something, a Jew is a Jew, a non-Jew is a non-Jew. A Chinaman is a Chinaman. A Hindu is a Hindu. With all these borders, how could we ever bring peace into the world? Let's face it, I'm a Jew and he is a Hindu. But this is only what the world thinks.

The craziest thing in the world happened by the Red Sea. Water suddenly changed into dry land. You mean to say that at a certain moment, when it's important, you can change?

This is what Yisro saw.

He saw that beyond all the defining borders there is something infinite in the world because if G-d created the world, and water can become dry land, it must be that within everything which G-d created there is still the possibility of going beyond borders.

When do you feel absolutely G-dly? When you are privileged to save someone's life. In order to save someone's life, you will become anything in the world. To love somebody means that I can do anything in the world for them, anything in the world.

Yom Kippur by the Seer of Lublin was *mamesh* awesome with heavenly fire coming down from above. One year, after Yom Kippur was over, the *Heilige* Lubliner gathered his holy pupils and said, "Today the davening was very special. I want everyone to tell me what they did today."

The pupils began sharing how deep their intentions were during the prayers. Then came the turn of the *Heilige* Ziditchover to share, and this is what he said. "Rebbe, I'll tell you the truth, I didn't have time to daven at all because someone was sick and the doctor told him he needs some hot water and hot soup throughout the night and day. So I didn't have time to daven, I was busy making a fire. I had to run into the forest to chop wood."

The Lubliner looked him in the heart and said, "I want you to know, while you were preparing the fire for the sick person, you were putting fire into all our prayers."

So the Beis Ya'akov says like this:

When G-d created the world, he really created the world with borders. Just look at the way the sun and the moon operate. The Gemara says the way the sun and the moon and the stars operate is precisely exactly one with G-d's time.

Why do we start Shabbos eighteen minutes earlier than when it really begins? Because for us human beings, we cannot fathom this split billionth of a second when Shabbos begins. We have no words for the way G-d is precisely operating in nature.

And here I want to go one step deeper.

Sometimes G-d is called *Elokim,* sometimes G-d is called *Yud Key Vav Key*. When G-d is called *Elokim* it alludes to finite power. The name

Elokim always refers to judgment, to things being exact. *Yud Key Vav Key* means infinite.

So it says that "Yisro heard that which *Elokim* did to Moshe and Israel," that He took them out of Egypt. One of the things Yisro heard was that the sea had split. From this he understood that with all the finiteness of the world, the world is ultimately infinite.

You know what paganism is? Making G-d into a finite creature. A pagan relationship is when all I do is ask G-d for money, for health, for agriculture. This is a very finite relationship with G-d, but us *Yidden* are all about how G-d is everywhere.

In life itself you need to be finite and infinite.

If I want to give my daughter a real Jewish education, I'll tell her, "I want you to know that you are completely beyond time and space. Sleep during the day and study throughout the night." Someone came to the old Lubavitcher Rebbe and said, "Rebbe, I would like to be up all night, studying. I'll be a different person the next day."

The Frierdiker Rebbe was *mamesh* sharp like a knife. He says to him, "I'm sure you will be different; everyone will be up and you will be sleeping." So I have to tell my children that morning is morning, and evening is evening. But if I'm only telling them this, I'm cutting them off from the most important part of life.

So here comes the Torah of the Ishbitzer.

What is your heart most open to? Is your heart open to the finiteness of the world, or is your heart more open to the infiniteness of the world?

The Mishnah asks (*Avos* 5:19), "What was the difference between the pupils of Avraham Avinu and the pupils of Bil'am?" In those days they had gold coins and copper coins. When you bought something, and let's say you gave a gold piece, they have to give you back copper coins. So the students of Bil'am would stand there and count the copper coins;

the students of Avraham wouldn't count. Are you going to argue over two pennies?

You see what it is, G-d wants the roots of my *neshama* to be connected to the infinite, but at the same time I should have no trouble relating to the world because I'm also finite. The roots of my *neshama* are connected to the place in heaven that is infinite. The world understands there are times to be infinite, but sustenance comes from the finite world.

G-d divided the world into two departments. The whole world receives their sustenance via their department. But a person has a right to say to G-d, "I want You to be the one who gives it to me."

What did Ya'akov Avinu mean when he prayed, "If G-d will give me bread to eat and a shirt to wear?" (Bereishis 28:20)

Of course, bread is to eat and a shirt is to wear, but Ya'akov Avinu was saying something so mind-blowingly deep. "Not only do I want You to give me bread, I want You to be the one who feeds me. Not only do I want You to give me a shirt, I want You to be the one who puts it on me."

This is infinite. How do you know if a parent loves their children finitely or infinitely? When a child needs a suit, how important is to for them to be the ones who not only buy the suit, but put it on them as well?

Now let me ask you, why didn't Amalek attack us before we crossed the Red Sea? He is our archenemy; he should have come and attack the second we left Egypt.

So the Ishbitzer says the deepest depths.

When we came out of Egypt, we sent a message to the world that you shouldn't be slaves. Amalek doesn't mind that, but when we crossed the Red Sea we told the world that you can change, and this is what threatened Amalek in the deepest depths.

You see what it is, a lot of people think that in order to become religious, you have to become someone else. Don't ever become somebody else. G-d created you the way you are. Change doesn't mean to become someone else; change means to become a little bit more infinite. Change means receiving your sustenance from the infiniteness of the world.

Here I want you to know something very deep. *Chamisha Assar B'Shvat,* the 15th day of the month of *Shvat,* always comes out around the time we read about crossing the Red Sea and Yisro coming to see Moshe.

What's the connection? *Tu B'Shvat* is when suddenly the tree realizes what it needs the most. The tree understands that besides earth and dew, it needs to be sustained by its roots.

So here comes the deepest depths.

Why is it that one apple tree produces good apples, one has mediocre apples, and one has no taste at all? It depends from where the tree is receiving its sustenance.

If the tree is really getting its sustenance from the deepest depths of its own roots, then it tastes so good. But if it is sustained from something else, it might be sweet, but it doesn't last.

Without saying anything bad, I once had a private audience with Ram Dass. I said to him, "Brother, I don't understand you. You are a Jew, you know you are a Jew, that means when G-d made you as a Jew . . . he wants you to serve him as a Jew. Why are you doing everything else?"

So he says, "I know you are right, give me two years." The craziest thing is exactly two years later – at that time I lived on 91st St – I was going to a very good chiropractor, and who is sitting there? Brother Ram Dass, exactly two years later. At that time, he was involved with a woman on the east side who acted as a medium. He was sitting in the waiting room with a book covering his face. *Nebech,* he didn't want me to see him. So I pretended not to see him either.

Basically, before we go to Mount Sinai, I have to be absolutely beyond time and space, and I also have to be entirely grounded in time and space. Yisro was the most grounded person in borders because he was worshiping every pagan god.

One of the explanations of the name "Yisro" is that *Yeser* means he added, he added something to the Torah which we needed the most. We needed to also be connected to time and space because the Torah is both. Shabbos begins 5:25, Yom Kippur begins 7:20, and it's over 7:28, everything has to do with time and space.

Israel is really the Land of Israel, *Yerushalayim* is *Yerushalayim*.

But *gevalt*, do you have to taste the infinite beauty in a finite world.

YESER – REACHING "MORE"

WHY IS THE BEGINNING OF THE PORTION where we read the Ten Commandments named after a pagan priest who becomes a Jew? It's beautiful but really, who cares?

What's the saddest thing in the world? If you are born a Jew and you don't want more. I have it, G-d is in my pocket. I have Shabbos, I have a *yarmulke,* I have *tzitzis* – what else do you need?

You see what it is, unless you want more, you don't really have anything. The name Yisro comes from the word *"Yeser,"* which means "more." You see what it is, Yisro went through all pagan worship in the world and realized there has to be more, there is more to G-d than what I have seen.

I have seen people who had moments of *mamesh* reaching "more." In the mid-60s I had the privilege to know a lot of *chevre* in *Yerushalayim.* One of them was an underground juvenile delinquent, *nebech,* he was such an outcast.

When he was with our *chevre* we gave him a little honor, and it made him feel so special. During the six-day war, I'm coming to an airfield to play for the soldiers. I heard that the general of that airfield is a pilot who was one of the pilots who bombed Cairo and saved all of Israel. He *mamesh* had a part of saving three million Jews. Simple as that.

So the army picked me up in a helicopter, and here I'm going to see this general, one of the greatest heroes in Israel. I walk in and who is this general? It is my underground juvenile delinquent. He looked so serious, so dignified. Do you know what happened to him? In one night he reached beyond himself.

One Saturday night after the Yom Kippur war, I was playing for wounded soldiers – it should never happen again, there should only be peace – when they wheel a soldier in on a wheelchair. You know that something is wrong with their feet. When they walk in, it means they have feet but they might not have hands. They might have no eyes or no ears.

In comes walking a little *Sefardishe* boy, eighteen years old. He has no hands, no arms. In the middle of heavy fighting, he saw another soldier who just got wounded, he ran back and picked him up. While he carried him on his shoulders, his own two arms were shot off, but he kept on running with this soldier on his shoulders.

Can you imagine where this person reached that night? I don't know why, but as I was playing, I started talking about our father Abraham. Suddenly this boy says to me, "Have you ever seen our father Abraham?" "I wish I did. Why, have you?" So he says to me, "I want you to know, since the day my two arms were shot off, our father Abraham is sitting on my bed every night and consoling me."

Let me ask you something, how many holy rabbis have ever seen Abraham, and how many ever will? *Gevalt,* did this boy reach beyond himself.

RELIGIOUS HARMONY

WHY DOES THE TORAH PORTION OF THE TEN Commandments begin with the story of Yisro?

On a very simple level, until we understand and welcome back other spiritual seekers, we aren't yet ready to receive the Torah for ourselves.

Thank G-d, the religions are getting more and more together, people are getting together. I don't mean to make gefilte fish out of religions, which, sadly enough, hurts me a little bit. Some people think, let's make a gefilte fish out of all religions. This is not what I am talking about.

If I see that somebody else has a beautiful nose, it doesn't mean that I have to take off his nose and put it on my face. He has his nose and I have my nose. I can just look at his nose and see that it's beautiful.

I have to do what G-d is revealing to me because if I cut myself off from my own revelation, I have nothing and your revelation means nothing to me. People have to realize that every religion is a revelation of G-d. All I can ask is, let me know a little bit of what G-d is revealing to you.

We need something that G-d will reveal to all mankind, beyond everything in the world, deeper than any previous revelation.

Rav Kook says the deepest depths. The religions of the world relate to each other on three levels. Sadly enough, in the beginning all the religions were fighting with each other. The next level is when all religions are coming together and trying to be one. This is a higher level, but not the highest level. Imagine if we all looked alike, thought alike, and sounded alike. The world would be a most boring place in which to live since there would be nothing to learn from one another.

So Rav Kook says something *gevalt;* there is a third level. When *Mashiach* comes, every religion in the world will begin to accept the differences and uniqueness of the other religions.

THE FOOL'S EVENTUAL ENLIGHTENMENT

Based on Mei Hashiloach II, Parshas Yisro (Sh'mos 18:24)

THE ISHBITZER SAYS THAT THERE ARE TWO TYPES of evil in the world. Both are wrong.

One evil is when you believe in everything. Today I believe in this yogi, tomorrow in the next one. Then back to the other one. That's bad, but there is another evil, when I don't believe in anything, when everything is a joke to me.

This is the story of both Yisro and Amalek. In a certain deep way, both are wrong.

Amalek doesn't believe in anything. Do you know to what extent he doesn't believe in anything? He is told that G-d took the Jews out of Egypt, which was the greatest miracle in the world, but to him it's a joke. Then he hears of the crossing of the Red Sea, which is the most unbelievable thing in the world which has ever happened. It doesn't turn him on either because everything is still a joke to him.

Now there is a passage that says, *"Letz takeh ufeti ya'arim"* – "When you strike a scorner, the simple will become prudent." (*Mishlei* 19:25) *"Letz takeh,"* the one who makes fun of everything – you got to get rid of him; *"ufeti,"* the one who believes in everything *"ya'arim,"* you got to make him clever.

Let's take Amalek. Amalek is the one who makes fun of everything. To him everything is a joke. Him you have to fight. *"Ufeti ya'arim"* – "and the fool who believes everything" – you have to make him clever. This is Yisro. Yisro believed in everything, he went through everything, but in the end, something happened. He became so clever and *mamesh* believed in G-d.

So here comes the holy Ishbitzer.

The secret of life is to know what is wrong with me. If nothing is wrong with me I wouldn't be born. I'm here to fix something. Until I am completely aware of what's wrong with me, I'm wasting my time. It is possible to know what's wrong with me and still not fix it, but this is already okay.

If I'm sick I'll go to the doctor and I will get my medicine. If I know, G-d forbid, that my teeth are the problem, I'm already on the way. Sometimes when you have a heart attack, your heart is not what hurts you, your *kishkes* hurt you. You have to know where the sickness is.

So the thing is like this. People who believes everything is so desperate, have to find out what's wrong with themselves. They go from person to person thinking perhaps this one can fix them, maybe that one. But eventually they will be okay because they will find a way to fixing themselves. At the end of the day, they will know there is one G-d.

What about the person who thinks that everything is a joke? What will happen when you will show him what's actually wrong with him? He will laugh in your face. The more you show him, the more he will laugh.

Did you ever notice how people laugh when you really reach their heart of hearts? They have to laugh it off because if it will enter their heart they wouldn't know what to do with themselves. They are so afraid, so they put up the biggest wall in the world.

Each of us has a little bit of this non-believing, this making a joke of things. Sometimes someone comes up to us and tells us the most real and true words, but it is too awesome to be true, so we have to laugh.

This laughing it off is Amalek and needs to be wiped out, *letz takeh*. G-d forbid, again, if you believe what everybody tells you it's also bad, but it's not so bad because eventually you will get there.

We all live in a certain fear, all of us. Deep down in the depth of our souls, we all know there is something wrong with us. We are afraid that maybe someone will really discover what is wrong with us. I'm afraid to tell anybody. Who should I tell?

Reb Elimelech says a good friend is somebody who you can tell what is really wrong with you and they still love you the most, and even more so. But maybe we are afraid to find out if we have such a friend, so we want to hide it all the time.

One time I was the guest on a radio program that was on a really good station with a lot of spiritual people listening. The program was for two hours; it was a *gevalt*. After the official program, they had call-ins for half an hour.

I'll never forget what happened. A woman called and said, "Please pray for me, I suffer so much from compulsive eating." She said that her husband drowned last year, left her with a boy of nine. Four weeks later her parents got into an accident and died. She just doesn't know what to do with herself, and she is eating all the time. She says that at this point she weighs three hundred and fifty pounds – can you imagine?

So she says that she has to go through a bypass operation, a very serious operation. The doctor told her that it's a dangerous operation, but because she is so overweight, there is only a fifty per cent chance she will stay alive. She doesn't know what to do with her little boy of nine.

She told us that she decided to have the operation, because her little boy refuses to eat when she is there, because it's so ugly to look at. This boy is the only thing she has in her life. What this woman must be going through every second is unbearable. So she called us up and asked us to please pray for her.

I said to her, "I don't think you should do the operation. All you need is good friends to give you strength and you will stop eating." She said, "I don't have such good friends." So I told her, "Right here at the radio station, you have about a hundred kids who really love you." She says, "No, I don't think so, I really have to do this operation."

Anyway, the craziest thing happened. One night I went to visit her in the hospital. They gave her such strong drugs, she was asleep. I left my record for her and wrote her a few words. In the meantime, the greatest miracle in the world happened. For whatever reason, the doctor wasn't able to perform the operation.

I had asked my sister and other friends to call her and keep in touch with her. A few weeks later she told me she is feeling strong and she is going to Weight Watchers. She might have only lost two ounces by now but it doesn't matter – she is gaining strength. But you know what is? What do we do when we are afraid of something? We start eating . . . it's a very deep connection.

Now listen to this. Reb Tzadok HaKohen says that food is a very delicate thing because our life depends on food (*Pri Tzaddik Kedoshim* 2; *Balak* 9). "Without eating I am dying; my connection to food is very deep."

Adam and Eve had never eaten in their whole life before. They knew that eventually they would have to eat and this was their first meal. The truth is, the whole story of eating from the tree took place on Friday afternoon. Adam and Eve were supposed to fast until Friday night. The feast of Shabbos was supposed to be the Tree of Life.

It's really heartbreaking – all they were supposed to do was not eat from the Tree of Knowledge for six hours.

So after they sinned, G-d asked Adam and Eve "Where are you?" If they would have known that G-d is a good friend, they should have said, "We have some trouble with the way we relate to food. We saw an apple and we just threw ourselves at it – even though I know it's bad for us."

But instead Adam said, "It's crazy, Eve came over to me with an apple, and I knew I shouldn't have eaten it, but I did." But what does Adam say to G-d? He says, "The moment I heard your voice I got so shook up!"

Adam, who are you talking to? You are talking to G-d! Tell Him the truth.

Now listen to this. This is very deep.

Imagine if I have something wrong with me and I tell everybody about it; it's also wrong. That means I am also not relating to what is really wrong with me.

You see, if I make a joke out of it – it is wrong and if I publicize it, it is wrong. Let's say I'll go to this Baba and tell them everything that is wrong with me, then I go to this holy person and then to this holy person and share with them what is wrong with me – this is not the way of fixing it either.

Yisro went to every Rebbe'le in the world, and said, "Please fix my soul." This is also bad, but Yisro can be fixed.

Now listen to this very deep thing. When Yisro comes to Moshe, Moshe Rabbeinu should say to Yisro, "Since you came here to me to fix your soul, let me tell you everything which is wrong with you." But you see what it is, someone who is really fixing your soul doesn't talk like that. Moshe Rabbeinu starts telling him the story of Am Yisrael. "My dear father-in-law, if you really want me to fix your soul, let me tell you a story about how G-d took us out of Egypt."

I want you to know something very deep.

Every Thursday night, the holy Vorker would learn the portion of the week with the *Medrash*. The *Medrash* is a top commentary. The Kotzker Rebbe said that until *Mashiach* comes, we won't understand what the *Medrash* says, but I'm sure the Vorker knew it.

One Thursday night in walks a little *Yiddele,* and suddenly the *Yiddele* faints. The Vorker goes up to the *Yiddele,* whispers something into his ear, and he gets up again. So the *Yidden* asked this *Yiddele,* "First of all, why did you faint? And second of all, what did the Vorker tell you?"

He says, "I'll tell you, I'm an ordinary sinner man. I walked in here and heard the Vorker learning, but what I was hearing was that he is telling me everything I did wrong. So I thought that everybody else heard what he said, and I was so ashamed in public. But then the Vorker came up to me and says, 'Brother, you are the only one who knew what I meant.' Nobody else knew, so I got up."

You see, the Ishbitzer is saying that this Shabbos of Mount Sinai is the Shabbos of fixing the soul. That part of us which thinks that everything is a joke is bad, and that part of us which tells everybody what's wrong with me is also bad.

It has to be very holy; it has be a secret between you and G-d. For a person who is really fixing, it has to be so holy that it also has to be a secret. He doesn't even have to say anything.

GREETING YISRO

Moshe went out to greet his father-in-law. (Sh'mos 18:7)

YISRO HAD TWO KINDS OF FRIENDS: CROSSING of the sea friends, telling him he can do it, and Amalek friends, telling him he can't. You know what Yisro did? He came to Moshe Rabbeinu.

The Zohar HaKadosh says that a teacher is not someone who can give you information. A real teacher is someone who gives you the strength to believe that you can do it. Yisro came to Moshe and said, "Please come out to greet me."

Do you think he was looking for honor? Did Yisro need a welcoming committee? The Zohar says that Yisro was saying to Moshe, "I need courage, I don't think I'll be able to do it." So Moshe Rabbeinu, the great teacher, came out to give him courage.

*

I want you to know something so deep. For me it's not hard to be a Jew. My father was a Jew, my mother was a Jew, I grew up a Jew and that's it. Can you imagine how Yisro had to reach beyond himself to leave everything behind him and come to Moshe?

Moshe and Aharon, the whole camp of Israel, three million people went to greet him. Sounds pretty strange, no? What's so big about him? He was a pagan, priest of all pagans, and now he wants to become a Jew. Let him come, we will give him a little teacher somewhere, we will send him to an *ulpan* to learn some Hebrew.

But why do Moshe, Aharon and all the *Yidden* go out to greet him? It was clear to them that they were witnessing someone who was reaching beyond himself.

When you meet a person who reaches beyond himself, all the honor in the world is not enough, all the honor in the world is not enough.

EFFECTIVE INREACH

And Moshe told his father-in-law everything HaShem had done to Pharaoh. (Sh'mos 18:8)

THERE ARE SO MANY JEWISH KIDS WHO HAVE been spiritually oriented with all different types of religions. Thank G-d, they have found a way back home, and are coming to the Holy Land.

I cannot walk up to these kids and say, "I want you to know, you have lived the life of a pagan. So far you did nothing. Now it's time for you to do *t'shuvah* and return to G-d." I'd push them so far away. They might end up experiencing G-d in their own way, but it may not be the Jewish way.

Imagine a boy comes with a long ponytail, and a hundred beads hanging on him. Does it really matter if he has long hair? What does it matter if he has fifteen beads or no beads? Do you know how many thousands of kids have been pushed away from yeshivas because the first thing they tell them is, "Get a haircut?"

When Yisro came to Moshe, Moshe Rabbeinu could have told him, "My dear father-in-law, I want you to know, you are the dirtiest pagan, I want you to do *t'shuvah*." Moshe Rabbeinu greeted him with so much joy and honor. You know what Moshe said to Yisro? "I've been waiting for you, we have all been waiting for you, because G-d couldn't speak to us on Mount Sinai until you came."

Imagine if we would greet all the kids who are thinking a little bit about *Yiddishkeit* and say, "G-d wants to reveal to us the deepest secrets. He was just waiting for you to join."

This is how you bring someone to Mount Sinai.

ALL THE GOOD

And Yisro rejoiced over all the good that HaShem had done for Israel. (Sh'mos 18:9)

IF YOU GIVE ME TWO APPLES AND I SAY, "I'M HAPPY with all the apples of the world," why didn't you say that you are happy with two apples? I only gave you two apples. But if you taste how much I put my soul in the apples – how can you say that you are happy with all the apples of the world?

After Moshe told Yisro what happened to us *Yiddelach* in Egypt, it says, *"Vayichad Yisro al kol hatovah"* "Yisro was happy with all the good." (Sh'mos 18:9)

What is "all the good" referring to?

After hearing from Moshe Rabbeinu what G-d had just done for the people of Israel, Yisro was happy with everything that is good in the world. How so? Because Yisro got a little bit of a taste of how G-d blessed us *Yiddelach* with so much love.

WHEN BOTH SIDES STAND TALL

And the people stood by Moshe. (Sh'mos 18:13)

MOSHE RABBEINU WAS THE ONLY JUDGE FOR the people of Israel. We were standing on top of Moshe all day and all night. Can you imagine three million people coming to Moshe with every problem they have between themselves?

So Yisro comes and says, *"Navol tibol"* (Sh'mos 18:18) – You can't live like this, you simply won't last. Moshe Rabbeinu says, you are one hundred percent right, but the way the Torah talks about the relationship between Moshe and the people is beyond awesome.

"Vaya'amod ha'am" – "they were standing."

When two people have a fight and come before a judge, and the judge decides that one of them is right, what happens to the other one? He falls flat on his face. But you see, the most amazing thing happened when you came to be judged before Moshe Rabbeinu. When you were judged by Moshe Rabbeinu, *"Vaya'amod ha'am al Moshe,"* both were standing tall.

You see, it's very easy to give sustenance to a person who was right, but the way Moshe Rabbeinu was judging was so divine. The person who might have been found guilty walked away with dignity.

Therefore, Moshe Rabbeinu says, "I can't let anyone else judge. Yes, I'm sure they will tell them the truth, if they owe a hundred dollars or not, but how will the other person walk away from the ruling?"

MOUNT SINAI

The whole world was invited

AFTER TWO HUNDRED AND TEN YEARS OF SLAVERY, we came out of Egypt, preparing ourselves to stand on Mount Sinai. How does the portion of the revelation of Sinai begin? *"Vayishma Yisro"* – "And Yisro heard." (Sh'mos 18:1)

We start talking about Yisro, who was the head of the pagan world. Suddenly Yisro comes and wants to become a Jew.

How does this sound to you? Is this a good enough reason to name the portion of the receiving of the Torah after him?

Open your hearts.

Imagine I spend so much time preparing myself for a certain occasion. Suddenly, right before it happens, someone comes and says, "I want to join you," and he ends up reaching higher than me and all my preparations. Does it make any sense?

I want you to know something so strong. When we say that G-d invited the whole world to come to Mount Sinai, it was not that G-d sent out invitations to every person. But there was an awakening in the world. The whole world knew that on this day G-d will speak to us on Mount Sinai.

On a national level, we were the only ones who wanted to come. On a private level, a lot of people wanted to come, too. Those private people didn't end up coming because their nation didn't want to come, but their soul was there on Mount Sinai. They are the people who were born later and converted, their souls really were on Mount Sinai.

Sometimes you see somebody who is *mamesh* a refined person. Let it be clear to you, they wanted to be on Mount Sinai.

Yisro came as a delegation of all the non-Jews who wanted to come to Mount Sinai. For one reason or another, some of them didn't make it. Maybe they did in another lifetime, I'm not judging, I have no idea.

But there had to be one non-Jew coming to represent the non-Jewish world.

*

You know friends, there are still some sweet and holy rabbis who think we can live in a world without non-Jews. The truth is, we are living in a world where we have to bring the message to the rest of the world.

The Gemara tells us that before G-d gave us the Torah on Mount Sinai, he asked the whole world to accept the Torah, but no one showed up, just us Jewish people. So the deepest question is, didn't G-d know that the other nations would decline before they actually said to G-d, "No, thank you"? There are thousands of answers, but I want to share this one with you.

Whatever G-d has done – he never stops doing. It's not that before Mount Sinai G-d was begging the world to receive the Torah but eventually he took back that invitation. He is still begging the world to come.

Do you know what this means? When I receive the Torah on Mount Sinai, I become G-d's voice to the world, and I am asking, "Can you please receive the Torah?"

If I received the Torah and I say, "the hell with the world," I didn't hear G-d's voice either. Sadly enough, we never had a chance to really carry out this message.

For two thousand years we Jews were not heard. The world wanted to kill us, they surely didn't want to hear us. Right now, the world wants to hear us, they really want to hear us, but they don't want to come to *shul* and hear about freedom, liberty, or other universal concepts. They can hear that somewhere else.

They want to hear about Pesach, about Shabbos, about Purim.

G-D ONLY DOES WHAT IS NECESSARY

WHY DID G-D TAKE US TO MOUNT SINAI?

If you think that the world can exist without Mount Sinai, Mount Sinai has no meaning.

If the world can be good without G-d talking to us, G-d doesn't have to talk to us.

But don't you see that until we hear from G-d Himself, "Don't kill," we can kill.

And until I hear from G-d Himself, "Keep the Shabbos holy," I don't know what Shabbos is.

Until I hear from G-d Himself, "I am the L-rd your G-d," I don't believe in G-d.

G-d only does what is necessary.

LOCATION OF THE MOUNTAIN

YOU KNOW WHERE MOUNT SINAI IS?

Mount Sinai is where people know that the world is still a desert.

Mount Sinai is wherever people really would like to hear G-d's voice.

Mount Sinai is wherever people are really troubled, asking what am I born for? What am I doing here? – and really wait for the answer.

So, friends, let's get much closer, because we all are troubled by the same thing.

WHY THE DESERT

And they arrived in the Sinai Desert. (Sh'mos 19:2)

G-D COULD HAVE TAKEN US TO THE LAND OF Israel and given us the Torah there, but you know what would have happened? The whole world would have said that it's just a Jewish affair.

According to our tradition, G-d invited the whole world, and He spoke to us in the desert. The desert isn't touched by any civilization, completely untouched. So the first thing I have to do, if I want to hear G-d's words, I have to know that I am still in the desert; I didn't prove myself yet.

*

The Torah was given to us in the desert. The desert has no limitations. In the desert everything is open, completely open.

In the prophets, it says, "*Vayasem midbarah k'eden v'arvasah k'gan HaShem*" – "He will make her wilderness like Eden and her wasteland like a garden of HaShem. . . ." (Isaiah 51:3)

Do you know what it is we are doing to the desert? We're changing the desert to paradise. It's still a desert, it's still completely open. There are no limitations in the desert. So what do us *Yiddelach* do when we feel free? We take the desert and it becomes our paradise.

PREPARING TO HEAR G-D'S VOICE

On this day they arrived at Mount Sinai. (Sh'mos 19:1)

WE ARRIVED AT MOUNT SINAI ON *ROSH Chodesh* the first day of Sivan, and the Gemara says that on the day we got there, G-d didn't say anything. Why? *"Mishum chulsha de'orcha"* – "Because we were knocked out from the way." (*Shabbos* 66b)

On the second day, G-d told them *"Ve'atem tihiyu li mamleches Kohanim"* – "And you should be for me a kingdom of priests." (Sh'mos 19:6) And on the third day he told them about *"mitzvas hagbala"* – "the commandment of limiting" access to Mount Sinai.

Let's go step by step. *Mishum chulsha de'orcha*?

What is *chulsha de'orcha?* The way it's translated is that we were walking in the desert for nearly seven weeks. So G-d says, "Take a rest, I'll talk to you tomorrow." Obviously, it's deeper than that, and here I want you to open your hearts in the deepest way.

If you think very little of yourself, G-d can't talk to you. What good would it be if G-d tells you anything? You wouldn't know what He means anyway; you have no vessels for it. *Mishum chulsha de'orcha* means we were so downhearted because Amalek just came and fought with us.

Amalek is the utmost evil in the world. What does utmost evil do to you? It takes away your self-confidence. The Gemara says that when I embarrass somebody, I have no share in the world to come. (*Bava Metzia* 59a) You can translate this in a million ways.

Reb Nachman says that putting someone to shame is by taking away their *azus dikdusha*. (*Likutei Moharan* 30:8; *Likutei Halachos, Hilchos Halva'ah* 3:4) *Azus dikdusha* is holy self-confidence; it's when someone says, "I don't care, I can do anything in the world."

In former good days we had the greatest rabbis in the world – today it's a little bit *shvach*, a little weak. Do you think we don't have such good heads anymore? Do you think we became dumber?

It's not true. I wouldn't be surprised if we are actually intellectually more advanced, but you know what we don't have? We don't have self-confidence anymore, we don't trust ourselves like we used to.

When you ask somebody today if they want to begin to study the Talmud, they say, "Well, I'll study a page or two, but it might not be for me." They don't even have the self-confidence to just say "Yes." Why can't you learn the whole Talmud? Why can't you be the greatest rabbi in the world?

You see what it is, in a crazy way, on a material level we have a lot of self-confidence. I'll grow up to be a big millionaire, I'll become a big businessman. For that the world gives you self-confidence. But when it comes to a higher level, being a *gevalt* Jew, being a *gevalt* servant of G-d, there is no *azus dikdusha*.

Amalek comes to you and says, "Listen, let's face it, you are trying but you won't make it, you won't last." Imagine you are trying to keep Shabbos. Amalek comes to you after the first Shabbos and says to you, "Shabbos was pretty hard on you, right? I know you."

"Yes, but I think I will do it again next Shabbos."

"Maybe you will do it for two Shabboses, but you won't do it more than that."

Before Amalek came, they asked, *"Hayesh HaShem b'kirbeinu im ayin"* – "Is G-d in our midst, and if so, where is He?" The Zohar HaKadosh says, *"Hayesh HaShem"* – "if G-d is limited;" *"Yesh HaShem?"* means is G-d limited in His relationship with us or *"Im ayin,"* or is G-d completely infinite?

But then, there is another understanding of *chulsha d'urcha,* I *mamesh* want you to open your hearts.

When I talk to my little girl of five, I talk to her like I'm talking to a five-year-old. The garments of my words are in accordance with whatever she can understand.

Now imagine, G-d forbid, there will be a fire in the house, and I have to grab her fast. I will not limit myself to talk to her on the level that she is five, because I have no time. When it comes to life itself there is no time for garmenting words through limitations.

All I say is, "Let's go now, let's jump out the window." Even if have to explain it to her, I will not explain to her like a child of five. I will treat her like my equal, maybe even a little bit higher.

The question is, how does G-d talk to me? Up there in heaven, in the root of all roots, does G-d relate to me on His level? If so, it's completely infinite and He doesn't have to garment His words.

If G-d is relating to me in such a way that His light is coming down and reaching me in this world, then it depends on what I'm doing, and on what level I'm on. In this situation, G-d can only talk to me on my level.

Now listen to the deepest depths. The Zohar HaKadosh says that every person would love to know, how close he or she is to G-d. Sometimes you love somebody very much, and you wish you knew where you are reaching that person.

Is my whole relationship with this person that when I smile they smile back? When I say hello, they say hello back, or is it beyond all this? Am I touching this person on such a deep place, at the root of all roots, the beginning of all beginnings?

So the Ishbitzer says, "If you would only ask G-d, 'Please let me know,'

G-d would be overjoyed to let you know." But you see what it is, we didn't ask G-d, we wanted to test G-d. When you want to test somebody – that's the end.

Testing means I want to catch you. When I do this, I tear myself away from you. It means there is a certain part of me where you don't reach, because if you reach every part of me, how could I ever test you?

So the Ishbitzer says this is what Avraham Avinu was asking all the time. Avraham Avinu wanted to know, "Please G-d, let me know how you rule the world. Does your revelation in the world depend on how the world is reacting to you or does your revelation in the world have nothing to do with the way people are reacting? "*Efshar bira b'lo manhig*?" – "Can there be a capital city without a leader?" (*Bereishis Rabbah* 39:1)

"*Ad sh'heitzis alav ba'al habira.*" – "Until the Master of the capital looked at him." G-d *mamesh* shined into him that, "You, Avraham, you are My headquarters of revelation." What was going on here?

If you ask behind G-d's back how much does G-d love me, that means that when you are in G-d's presence you don't feel it. Let's put it this way. Let's say I have trouble davening; when I pray I don't feel G-d's presence. The question is not if G-d answers your prayers, the question is, do you feel that you are in G-d's presence? Since G-d is all over, it is you who is hiding, you are simply not there.

Now listen to this – *gevalt,* is this deep.

The deepest Torah in the world is the Torah you are learning after a mistake. You know friends, the way G-d opens gates for us after we make a mistake is not to be believed.

Let me ask you something. When do you feel closer to a person, when someone gives you a gift and you say, "Thank you," or after you mistakenly thought someone was your biggest enemy only to realize this person saved your life?

Clearly, after I realize I was wrong; this shakes you up to the core.

So the way the Ishbitzer translates it is so deep. On the first day we got to Mount Sinai, G-d didn't tell us anything. Why? *Mishum chulsha de'orcha.* Because this was the day when they realized how wrong they were.

On that day it was clear to them that G-d is leading the world in the most infinite way. On that day they realized that even when they might be doing wrong, they are infinitely connected. G-d can always reach you.

What are the great moments in our lives? The great moments in our lives are those moments when we are *mamesh* infinite.

What's the difference between bliss and joy, between *sasson* and *simcha*? I feel joy over something. G-d gave me freedom, G-d gave me the Torah, so therefore I feel joy. Shabbos has nothing to do with G-d giving me something. Shabbos is *mamesh* infinite. The gift of Shabbos is that G-d gives me twenty-four hours of *mamesh* being infinite.

Now listen to this; this is even deeper. What happens to me when I realize how much I misjudged G-d? *Gevalt,* how little I know, how little I know about the way G-d is relating to me. That touch is *mamesh* infinite. As much as I feel bad about it, there is a great happiness which begins to grow deep inside once I know this.

So the teaching of the first day is "*Ein adam omed al divrei Torah ela im ken nechshal bahen*" – "A person does not learn the Torah unless they make a mistake." (*Gittin* 33a)

And here is the deepest story.

A simple *Yiddele* came to the Holy Spinker two days after Yom Kippur, and he was *mamesh* beside himself. He said, "I live in the shtetl, and I'm too poor to buy myself a calendar. I thought Yom Kippur is on Tuesday. I woke up Monday morning, we ate all day and at night we drove to the city because I thought Monday night is *Kol Nidrei.*

When I came to shul, they were already by *Neila. Gevalt,* I ate on Yom Kippur, I didn't have Yom Kippur. I stayed another day in shul crying. Please, Rebbe, what should I do? I ate on Yom Kippur!

This *Yiddele*'s tears were *mamesh* reaching heaven. The holy Spinker got up, walked up to the window, and began to sob as well. "You know something?" he told his *chassidim,* "I wish that one time in my life I should taste Yom Kippur the way this *Yiddele* tasted Yom Kippur."

Can you imagine, how much he tasted when he came into *shul* and suddenly he realized that Yom Kippur is over? So the Rebbe says, "I wish one time in my life I would daven on Yom Kippur the way this *Yiddele* was davening the day after Yom Kippur." Then he says "*Ribbono shel Olam,* just for this one *Yiddele* you have to send *Mashiach*."

Here I want you to know something so deep.

The Gemara says (*Baba Basra* 99a) that there was a way for the high priest to know if G-d forgave us. There were images of a little boy and of a little girl in the Holy Temple. When these images were looking at each other it meant G-d forgave us. If G-d forbid, they were looking away from each other, it was a bad scene.

The craziest thing is, at that moment when the Holy Temple was destroyed, the Gemara says the Romans walked in and they saw that the *kruvim,* the cherubim, were *mamesh* looking at each other. Crazy, at that moment, when G-d was most angry with us?

Now everybody knows, why is *Mashiach* coming on *Tisha b'Av*? Why isn't *Mashiach* coming on Yom Kippur? The answer is very simple. On Yom Kippur I'm sorry for my sins. I spoke *lashon hara,* gossiping about others all year long – I promise G-d that I won't do it again. It's not that deep.

But imagine if I was wrong, I made a mistake by completely misjudging you. It's not so much about whether you forgive me or not, it's that my whole being is struck to the core.

Now when we were testing G-d, it's not that we doubted the existence of G-d. We didn't doubt that G-d can do the greatest miracles in the world. We wanted to test G-d to see how He relates to us?

Does G-d shine into me something infinite, or does G-d shine into me which *lukshen kugel* is kosher, how to daven and what to do next? The saddest thing is that we didn't stand before G-d saying, "Please reveal Yourself to me." We tested G-d.

Imagine your children would get together and say, "Lets test our father and see if he loves us." Here you are ready to die for your children a million times, and they are testing you?

So on the first day G-d revealed to them that our relationship with G-d is so deep, but this kind of depth is only after *chulsha de'orcha*. The deepest depths reaches us only after we make a mistake.

So you see what it is, the beginning of my relationship to G-d is G-d shining into me that you *mamesh* don't know what G-d is all about. You don't know what *Yiddishkeit* is all about.

I was once preforming in Colombia. A woman came up to me and said "*Yiddishkeit* is a terrible religion, I studied Judaism very deeply. They only talk about two things in Judaism: The inquisition and the holocaust. There is not one ounce of joy in Judaism."

I asked her, "Do you know one billionth of an ounce of what Simchas Torah is? Do you know what the *Oneg* of Shabbos is? Purim?" She went to two lectures, one about the inquisition, one about the holocaust. So according to her, that's all *Yiddishkeit* has to offer.

Imagine this woman would spend her life in India, and when she is eighty years old, she would somehow pass by Israel on her way back to Colombia. She would walk into a *shul* and it would be Simchas Torah. Suddenly she would realize "*Gevalt,* I could have had this all my life, but I didn't have it!"

This is what the first day was all about.

On the second day, G-d told them, "I want you to be a kingdom of priests." What's the whole thing about a priest? The priest is someone who brings down the most infinite things in a finite way.

On a very simple level, what was wrong with the sixties? It was very holy, but when the first little finiteness came, they didn't know how to handle it. It's beautiful, but it doesn't last.

Now listen to this. The Torah is the utmost finite and the utmost infinite at the same time. The hardest thing in the world is that the finiteness in the Torah should not be cut off from being infinite. What's bugging us about so-called very religious people? They are so finite. Sometimes you meet G-d fearing people and you can't even talk to them, it just smells finite.

I'll tell you something very crazy. Sometimes I tell a *chassidishe* story to so-called *chassidishe Yidden* – and it doesn't blow their mind. Sometimes they don't even hear the story. I'll meet a little hippie on the street and tell him the same story, it will blow his mind. Why? Because he tastes the infinite.

But it's not enough, it has to be finite also. What was the holiness of Moshe? "*Ba moshe vehorida la'aretz*" – "And Moshe came and brought it down to earth." (*Psikta Rabbasi* 5) You know what Moshe Rabbeinu did which nobody else could do? Moshe Rabbeinu could go up to heaven and bring G-d's word down to this world. Moshe Rabbeinu took heaven, he brought down the most infinite revelation of G-d, and *mamesh* put it into vessels.

This was the second day.

On the third day, Moshe Rabbeinu told them about "*mitzvas hagbala*," the constrictions and limitations as to how far you can go on Mount Sinai, but what was it really all about?

Now listen to the deepest depths. The moment it is clear to a person that they are infinite, they might not be able to handle you. The Ishbitzer always talks about *t'kifus*. *T'kifus* means inside strength, solid inside strength.

You know what the hardest thing in the world is? To have inside strength in the most infinite way, but you have to know how to use it; it can get out of hand so easily.

On the one hand I want to serve G-d in the most infinite way, on the other hand I have to know exactly where my borders are. To know what I should or shouldn't do is bringing infiniteness into finiteness.

But then there is something deeper than all this. The question is not what to do or not to do, the question is, do you know that inside strength also has limits? G-d says, "Please, don't go any further, that's it."

I want you to know something very deep. You know what the hardest thing in the world is between people? When people love each other very much, they take away each other's privacy.

Do you know how deep this is? Don't you see, if G-d would have wanted a couple to not be two people but one, he would have created one person, not two people. The deepest secrets between people is always being two, while being one.

You know what G-d was teaching us on mount Sinai? Moshe Rabbeinu could go up to Mount Sinai and know that G-d is G-d and he is just Moshe. You know why I can't go up to Mount Sinai and come back down? Because I'll think that I'm G-d.

There are people who are "G-dding" around today. What's their problem? Their problem is that they are not so low, they really are high, but they don't have *mitzvas hagbala*. The fact that they are just a human being is not so strong by them, it's as simple as it is.

Do you know what *mitzvas hagbala* means? Please don't think you are cut off from G-d because now that you are *mamesh* on Mount Sinai you have to be finite.

If you want to know how much somebody loves you, do they do the smallest thing in the same way they are saving your life? When I love somebody very much and they ask me for a handkerchief, I do it with the same joy like I'm saving their life, because the smallest thing is so special.

The big Rebbes would die a thousand times for the smallest thing in *Yiddishkeit.* And here I want you to know something very deep. Everyone is ready to be the Ba'al Shem Tov, everyone is ready to be Avraham Avinu. The question is: Are you ready to serve G-d as you are?

Do you know what happened during those three days? People got ready for G-d to speak to them.

What does it mean when you hear G-d's voice? When you hear G-d's voice there is nothing left on your insides that is not touched by Him. A lot of times we hear beautiful things and it touches only a little bit.

The question is: Is there anything left which is not touched? If there is anything left, then you were not on Mount Sinai.

And here let's go one step deeper. If there is anything in your life which doesn't connect to that which you hear from G-d, then it was not G-d's voice you were hearing. When a human being tells me something and I connect it to a few things, it works, it's interesting, but it doesn't have to apply to everything.

In a nutshell, on the first day G-d gave them a taste of how little they know about G-d, but not just how much they misjudged G-d, can you imagine how many people misjudged each other?

On the first day, G-d opened the gates for all those who misjudged G-d to get a taste of how much they misjudge other people. There is no room for this on Mount Sinai, on Mount Sinai we had to be one.

On the second day we were told to become a nation of priests. A *kohen* is a priest who *mamesh* knows G-d's infiniteness but is able to put it into the most finite thing into the world.

A lot of people walk around thinking "the Torah is so limiting, so not universal." What do you know about the Torah, what do you know about *Yiddishkeit*? They are not tasting the infiniteness within the finiteness of the Torah.

You know, friends, if I have a feeling that I am *mamesh* infinite, I can't do anything finite. I can call up Baron Rothschild and ask him for ten million dollars for a new hospital in Israel. I cannot call up Rothschild when I just arrived at the airport in Paris, and tell him I'm short on cash, and ask him for one hundred dollars for me to find a hotel for the night.

Chutzpa. I say, "Listen, last week I spoke to you about ten million dollars, why can't I ask you for a hundred dollars?" "*Chutzpa,* a hundred dollars from me, Rothschild?" I can only ask him infinitely.

I'll tell you something very deep. At one time I was a little bit sick, and I *mamesh* couldn't bend down to tie my shoes, so I needed someone to do it for me. The craziest thing was that I was able to sense to whom I was close enough to ask them to please tie my shoes. You've got to be very close, very close.

Gevalt, the third day is so deep. After I know what it is to put the infiniteness into the finite, I reach something much deeper. I reach such an exalted level that when G-d, so to speak, limits me and tells me, "Don't go any further," it feels so precious and special.

Do you know what G-d was telling us with *mitzvas hagbala*? "*Yidden,* there will be a time I will tell you not to go any further. Can you still serve Me then?"

Between people, the question is not how much do you love each other when you love each other, the ultimate question between husband and wife is always how much do you love each other when you *mamesh* hate each other, when you can't stand each other?

Mitzvas hagbala is G-d saying to you, "Don't move an inch, that's it, you can't get closer to Me, but, *gevalt,* can you serve Me from there."

Imagine I'm standing three feet away from Moishele, and this other *Yiddele* is two miles away from Moishele. Do you think you are closer because you are standing three feet away while this other person is two miles away?

Do you think you are closer to G-d because of three feet? Again, this is after the whole teaching of finite and infinite. Sure, on a finite level you are ten inches closer, but are you still infinite while you taste being finite?

KISS OF THE MOUNTAIN

And Israel encamped there, opposite the mountain. (Sh'mos 19:2)

HOW LONG CAN I SIT WITH MY KIDS AND TRY teaching them? How much patience do they have? Now imagine after the whole learning is over, I teach whatever I could teach, and I give my child a kiss. This kiss contains much more than what I taught. Through this kiss I'm giving over to them everything there is.

When it comes to the giving of the Torah, it says, "*Yishakeini minshikos pihu*" – "Kiss me with the kisses of your mouth." (*Shir Hashirim* 1:2)

G-d gave us the Ten Commandments and He kissed us. G-d gave over to us everything there is. For that, you have to be very close. What does it mean that G-d came down from heaven? G-d is in heaven, I'm on earth, but when G-d gave us the Torah, we were so close that suddenly G-d says, "I want to give you everything I have."

We *Yiddelach* are always wondering, "Why are we so different than the rest of the world?" "Why is my concept of G-d completely different?" "Why is my concept of the world completely different?" Because G-d is so close to us, in a crazy way, our souls *mamesh* know what G-d wants. G-d spoke to me at Mount Sinai and told me what He wants.

Imagine my child knows that I love her the most. She knows it in her head and even in her toes, but how does she know it at that moment when I show her how much I love her? It's a completely different knowledge.

We always knew we were G-d's children, but at that moment when we stood at Mount Sinai, G-d *mamesh* showed it to us.

MOUNT SINAI FRIENDS

As one person in one heart. (Rashi, Sh'mos 19:2)

IS IT POSSIBLE TO LOVE SOMEONE YOU MEET FOR the first time? You've never seen them before, how could you love them? Simple, you stood next to them on Mt Sinai.

Every friendship, every love in the world, comes from that one split second that G-d spoke to us. When a human being speaks to another for a moment the second is over. When G-d speaks to us for a second, it's forever.

There is a passage that says *"kol gadol v'lo yasaf"* – "a great voice which was never to be repeated." (Devarim 5:19) G-d's voice is still there. Maybe we left Mt Sinai, but G-d is still there, still talking to us.

I bless you and me to meet all the people who stood next to us and we should lift each other up and we should remind each other of that moment, that everlasting moment.

WHY WAS MOSHE CHOSEN TO GO UP?

And Moshe ascended to G-d." (Sh'mos 19:3)

WHY WAS MOSHE RABBEINU CHOSEN TO RE-ceive the Torah on Mount Sinai?

There was no one like Moshe Rabbeinu, who knew that you can do everything holy in the world, but to understand one page in the Gemara is *mamesh* a gift.

When I go buy some herring in the grocery store, I am not overwhelmed by emotion. I don't start kissing the grocery man like crazy. Why is it that when someone gives me a small gift, I have the urge to kiss them? Because a gift brings out the depths of a person.

Why don't I kiss a book on physics when I finish studying from it? Because it's not a gift. If I have a good head, I learn the book and receive information.

When I learn one page of the Gemara, I might only understand very little, but I can't stop thanking the Gemara. I can't stop thanking the Torah. Why? Because it's all a gift.

*

Why was Moshe chosen to go up to Mount Sinai? Because from all the people in the world, he was yearning for it the most.

You know how deep this is? We always think Moses was chosen because he was a genius, or because he was a great leader, and had the personality and charisma. Moshe Rabbeinu was chosen because of one thing. He was a *Yiddele* who was yearning to be on Mount Sinai and hear G-d talk.

Reb Nachman says something so deep. We are living in a generation where we have very little, we do very little, and we know very little. But you know something, G-d is giving us a chance right now.

In regard to holy deeds, maybe we have already done pretty good,but we haven't done so good when it comes to our holy yearning. So before *Mashiach* is coming we have to correct this holy yearning. This is what is left for us right now.

On the one hand, G-d makes it a little bit easier on us, because we know so little, but the "knowing" is not supposed to limit our yearning. On the other hand, it's very hard because everybody tells us to give up. So we got to be strong like never before.

EAGLE'S WINGS

"I have borne you on the wings of eagles" (Sh'mos 19:4)

THERE ARE CERTAIN QUESTIONS ONE CANNOT ignore.

Imagine we would stop for one moment and honestly ask ourselves, "What do I really know about G-d?" I know He created the world, and I know He is around, so therefore . . . what do I know?

What do I know about the holiness of Israel? I know we went through Egypt, I know we were on Mount Sinai. I know that six million were killed and that we came back to Israel, but what do I really know?

What do I know about my own soul, what do I know about my own holiness? What do I know about the world? What does G-d want of me? Why did he bring me here in the first place?

The Torah says, "When I took you out Egypt, I carried you on wings of eagles." (Sh'mos 19:4)

Do you know what G-d did to us when He gave us the Torah? He lifted us up so high, but not the kind of high we are used to. The world always talks about how everyone wants to be high, but what do they know about high? They judge their highness in comparison to the world's lowness, but to be high on eagles' wings is not in comparison to anyone or anything.

Take the highest high anyone ever experienced through drugs and compare it to one moment with the Kotzker Rebbe on a Friday night. Mentioning these two things in the same sentence is a joke. What's to compare?

What is the height that an eagle can soar? Open your hearts like mad.

As much as birds fly high, an eagle can fly the highest. We are talking about the kind of high which is absolutely beyond my concept of being high.

You see what it is, any high which I can still fathom with my head is not what we are talking about here. When it comes to all forms of highness in the world, even if I have a concept that I think is really high – it's still not as high as the eagle flies. An eagle reaches this type of high which is beyond comparison, and this is what G-d took us out of Egypt for.

Then it says *"va'avi eschem Eilai"* "And I brought you unto Me." Do you know what that means? The *Ribbono shel Olam* brought us close to him in order to be a gate through which the word of G-d can spread all over the world.

We are the gates.

King David says, *"Aromimcha, HaShem, ki dilisani."* (*Tehillim* 30:2). The regular translation is that "G-d, I will make you big because you draw me up," but let's go deeper. "G-d, I will make you high because *dilisani,* you made me into a door."

Do you know what the greatest thing in the world is? If I could be a door, I could be that opening through which people can walk to get higher.

Let's put it this way. Do you know what we would look like if we would be that which G-d has dreamt for us since Mount Sinai? Every *Yiddele* would have such a presence, when we would walk down the street, whenever anyone sees us, we would cause such a yearning for G-d in the most unbelievable way.

G-d wants it to be that whenever someone see a *Yiddele* walking down the street, that person should have such a yearning for G-d, such a yearning for this highness. When I see someone with this *"kanfei nesharim"* wings of eagles look, I think to myself, "Wow, what I wouldn't do to be like that." When Avraham Avinu was walking down the street, people were running after him because everybody wanted to be like him.

Let's go one step further.

Any religion that guarantees you something is not real. I can only tell you, "Become a servant of G-d," but I cannot guarantee anything. Even on the holiest level. If someone tells you that if you meditate every morning and do this and that, you will be in tune and you are safe . . . it's sweet, but it doesn't reach where I want to be.

The place G-d wants me to reach is so high, so unknown, and so beyond words that nobody can guarantee me anything. This is the zone of the eagle, a place that no one can speak of.

*

A master shows ownership over his slave by making sure he always puts him down. G-d does just the opposite. How does G-d show ownership? He lifts us up.

My uncle, Rabbi Yosef Carlebach, used to say something so true. *Mashiach* can only come when instead of sending children to school we will send the parents to school. You know something, the way parents show ownership over their children is by putting them down. If you want to really show that you're the master like G-d, you lift them up.

When we received the Torah, G-d says "I lifted you up on eagles' wings." (Sh'mos 19:4) Nobody can fly as high as an eagle.

What G-d is telling us is that I lifted you up beyond your dreams, beyond where you thought you could fly. This is the way G-d shows us he is our master.

KINGS WHO LEAD

You shall be to me a Kingdom of Priests (Sh'mos 19:6)

G-D WANTS MANY THINGS FROM US, BUT THE most important thing G-d told us before Mount Sinai was that we have to be a kingdom of priests.

If you stand before G-d like a beggar, it's beautiful, but this is not what G-d wants. G-d wants us to be kings. You know what a king is? A political king is someone who lets you know that he is a king and you are not. A holy king is somebody in whose presence everybody becomes a king! We have to get back to that!

Our king is King David. Everybody knows that Jerusalem belongs to King David, it's his personal property. "*Ir David*" – "the city of David." Why is Jerusalem King David's own property? The answer is very simple. The seven nations that were occupying all of Israel were such strong warriors. While they were conquering *Yerushalayim,* no one was able to get close.

King David decided, "I'm going to take *Yerushalayim* all by myself." King David walked up to *Yerushalayim* and he conquered the whole city. This is a king. A king is not someone who says, "Listen folks, let's go, I want you all to be ready to be killed. Go to the front line while I direct this war from a safe chamber."

The Gemara says "*Rabbanan ikrei melachim*" – "Our teachers are called kings." (*Gittin* 62a)

A real holy teacher is supposed to be a king, and a real holy king is someone who says, "I'm leading the way for you."

THE NIGHT BEFORE

Moshe brought the people from the camp. (Sh'mos 19:17)

THE NIGHT BEFORE WE HEARD G-D'S VOICE, Moshe Rabbeinu went to every Jewish house and personally took them to Mount Sinai.

Sounds strange. We came out of Egypt and walked through the desert from Pesach till Shavuos for that great morning to come. Didn't everybody know that G-d is going to speak to us on that day before dawn? If we knew the schedule, why did Moshe Rabbeinu have to go to every house?

The answer is from the holy Alexanderer. The Rebbe of Alexander says that when you're a pupil of Moshe Rabbeinu, you suddenly see how beautiful everyone else is.

But this level of becoming a pupil of Moshe Rabbeinu only takes place here, by Mount Sinai. What does it mean to become one of Moshe's pupils? When G-d says to Moshe, "I want you to take out the *Yidden* from Egypt," Moshe argued for a whole week. Moshe said "I think Aharon is better," and according to others he said, "Eliyahu HaNavi is better, *Mashiach* is better for the job." He argued, but G-d said, "No, it is you who has to do it."

What was going on here? How could Moshe try to convince G-d that someone else should do the job? Simple. Moshe Rabbeinu was measuring and he realized that there are people who can do the job better than him.

Now the question is, when G-d says to Moshe to come up to Mount

Sinai, so that G-d can give him the Torah, Moshe doesn't argue. Why didn't he start trying to convince G-d to give the Torah through someone else?

I want you to open your hearts to the deepest depths.

What is the first sign of a slave? A slave measures and calculates how much they think they are capable of doing. Exile is all about calculating. You know what a free person is? Freedom does not mean, "I can do what I want to." To be free means that whatever it is I am doing, I don't measure, I don't measure at all.

If someone calls me up and says, "Can you do me a favor?" a slave answers, "Do you really need me to do it? I don't think I can do it, are you sure?" So you say, "Forget it, I'll get someone else." When you ask a free person for a favor they say, "I don't know if I can do it, but who cares, I will do it."

When G-d says to Moshe, "Bring down the Torah from heaven," he didn't measure. Why not? Because we were *mamesh* out of Egypt.

This is the holiness of Moshe Rabbeinu, the holiness of a leader who became free, and this was the last lesson he had to instill within us *Yiddelach* before receiving the Torah. Becoming free happens when I am free to think that not only is everyone around me *Kodesh haKodashim*, Holy of Holies, but I am too. And unless you learn this – don't bother coming to Mount Sinai.

I hate to say bad things, but imagine we would know that next week at dawn there is a broadcast from the Lord and all the holy people are invited. Everybody will push themselves through and think, "Well, of course I should be there."

Then we get there, and when we see another person that we know, and start thinking to ourselves, "The *chutzpa!* What's he doing here, only holy people are invited! I know him for so long, he doesn't belong here."

You know what people did to prepare themselves? Everyone went to sleep because they were convinced that they weren't properly ready. "I know it's not me. I can't even go there to show my face. I better go to sleep, I don't want to be embarrassed."

But the most unbelievable thing happened. Every family thought to themselves, "I'm sure we are not meant to be here, but our neighbors are so holy and special. I'm sure they are ready."

Everyone was convinced that the other one is meant to experience it, but not themselves. So Moshe Rabbeinu had to knock on every door, telling every family, "You thought you are not wanted, you thought it is only everyone else who is on the level. Don't you see, these are the thoughts which *mamesh* bring you to Mount Sinai."

Can you imagine what a holy community was standing at Mount Sinai? Everybody thinking somebody else is so good.

Someday, someday it will be like this again, hopefully.

What a world. We know till *Mashiach* is coming there won't be such a community. When *Mashiach* is coming, everybody will say, "My neighbors are such good people. I wish I would be like them. *Gevalt,* they are my dear and holy friends."

And *Mashiach* will whisper and say, "Until you know you are part of the holiness, too, I can't come and redeem you."

BEYOND ALL LIMITATIONS

And G-d descended upon Mount Sinai (Sh'mos 19:20)

EVERY PERSON IS LIMITED. EVEN THE HIGHEST person in the world is still a little bit limited. There is only so much I can comprehend. Even Moshe Rabbeinu, the most exalted person in the world, has a limit.

Imagine if suddenly I would see the world with G-d's eyes. Until Mount Sinai we're not changing, we're still the same people. We're better people, we're holy people – everything good and sweet. But something changes when I come to Mount Sinai. G-d takes me out of the whole thing. I'm not limited to my own mind anymore; something new is happening to me.

When it comes to receiving the Torah – you have to be somebody else, because if G-d wants to give me something based on my vessels, G-d doesn't have to come down from heaven to give it to me.

What does it mean that G-d came down from heaven? It means that suddenly all earthly limitations were non-existent. How so? On Mount Sinai, G-d gave Himself to us. *Anochi* stands for *"Ana nafshi ksavis yahavis"* – "I placed my soul into these words." (*Shabbos* 105:1) G-d put His G-dliness into us. And when this happens, there are no limitations.

Why didn't G-d speak to us again after Mount Sinai? Because this moment of Mount Sinai continues to carry us forever. This moment reoccurs whenever I'm beyond myself, with no limitations.

When G-d spoke to us at Mount Sinai, he said, "I am the G-d who took you out of Egypt." Why didn't G-d say something even more important – "I'm the G-d who created heaven and earth?" Yes, G-d did create the heaven and the earth. He created me as well, but I still don't know what I'm doing in this world!

The revelation at Mount Sinai is not to let me know that there is one G-d.

The revelation at Mount Sinai is to take me out of my limitations.

HEAVEN AND EARTH

IN PSALMS IT SAYS *"HASHAMAYIM SHAMAYIM LA-HaShem, v'Ha'Aretz nasan li-V'nei Adam"* – "The Heavens are the Heavens for G-d and the Land He gave to Human Beings." (*Tehillim* 115:16) One of the old Breslover *chassidim* explains this passage like this:

Heaven is heaven because G-d made it heaven, but to make heaven out of the earth – this is what G-d gave to us; this is what our mission is all about.

How do we make heaven out of earth? This is why G-d gave us the Torah. The *Medrash* says (*Sh'mos Rabbah Va'era* 12), until G-d gave us the Torah on Mount Sinai, heaven and earth never met, up and down never met, good and bad never met.

But the Torah is heavenly. The Torah brings everything together.

*

One year I was on the Moshav for Simchas Torah, and we went to a city nearby for *Hakafos Shniyos.* The mayor of the city was there, the whole city was there. Thousands of people came to dance with us.

Before everything started, the mayor came up to me and says, "I want to make it very clear, I didn't come here because I am religious. To me Simchas Torah is meaningless, but I like the music." Now they had those big *Sefardishe* Sefer Torahs. They gave one to the rabbi, one to the mayor and one to the *gabbai.*

They were walking around with the Torahs while thousands were coming up, kids jumping up and kissing the Torah. It was absolutely beautiful! After they brought the Torahs back and the singing stopped, the mayor comes up to me and opened his heart.

"Shloime, I want you to know. I changed my mind, I'm not so 'anti' anymore. I teach English at the University of Tel Aviv. I can't imagine walking around the city with a book of Shakespeare and anyone having the urge to kiss the book."

You see what it is, only something from heaven can make you want to kiss it.

A CHILD'S GUARANTEE

(Based on Shir Hashirim Rabbah I)

WHEN WE STOOD ON MOUNT SINAI, G-D ASKED us, "Can you give me a little guarantee that you will keep the Torah?"

We said, "Our parents will take the guarantee," but our parents didn't want to.

We asked our children, and they agreed.

What does this mean?

When G-d asked us, "Who will remind you of Mount Sinai?" We said, "Our parents will remind us." I'm sorry. There will be a lot of generations of parents that will not remind their children of Mount Sinai.

So then we said, "Our children." Children? Yes, children remind me of Mount Sinai. Children remind you of the holiest things in the world.

SPEAK TO US JUST ONCE MORE

And G-d spoke all these words. (Sh'mos 20:1) (Shabbos Musaf prayer)

YOU SPOKE TO US ONCE ON MOUNT SINAI, BUT the whole world did not hear You.

So we are asking You, Almighty, *"v'hu . . . yashmi'einu b'rachamav sheinis."* Speak to us just once more, let us hear your voice just once more. But this time *l'einei kol chai,* let the whole world see it, let the whole world hear it.

And we promise you, *l'hiyos lachem leilokim.*

We promise you that the whole world will know that you are there, that you are our G-d.

ONLY ONCE

OUR PARENTS LOVE US SO MUCH, BUT SOMETIME they get a little bit on our nerves; they are always telling us the same thing. Do this, do that. Do this again and don't forget to do that again.

The greatest parent in the world is G-d. He took us to Mount Sinai, and only once in the history of mankind He told us what He wants us to do. Could you imagine if every morning there would be a voice form heaven, saying, "I'm G-d, honor your parents, keep Shabbos. Don't steal, don't kill?" It would be the end of the world.

The younger generation is getting turned off because *Yiddishkeit* is taught in a poison way. I cannot talk about other religions, but as far as I'm concerned, our father Abraham wanted us to be free, completely free. I really believe that G-d is the free-est thing in the world.

The most free thing is to really be a servant of G-d. But on the highest level, it's something which is beyond freedom and beyond duty. What's the holiest way of serving G-d? When I want so badly to do G-d's will, and as much as it's my will as well – it is also my duty.

It's a "I want to and have to" relationship.

To be on this level is the hardest thing in the world. That every step should be completely free choice, and after the free choice I realize I have no other way, this is really what I have to do.

*

Do you think G-d spoke to us on Mount Sinai, and then He eventually stopped? G-d is talking to everyone who wants to listen.

The way G-d is still telling us His will is unbelievable. It's just a matter of having the courage to believe that G-d talking to us at Mount Sinai never stopped.

You see what it is, it's not enough to believe that there is one G-d.

The question is, do you believe that G-d is dealing with you?

Do you believe that you can ask G-d and He answers?

Do you believe that G-d cares?

REAL COMMUNICATION

IT WOULD BE THE SWEETEST THING IN THE WORLD if we could all be prophets and see with our own eyes what no one else can see.

Imagine people would know exactly what I want to tell them, and I would know exactly what they want to tell me back – it would be tremendous. It's always hard to put things in words, but you know something, a lot of people are prophets with their eyes, but they are not prophets yet with their ears.

You have to see what nobody sees, but you also have to hear what nobody else hears.

The Zohar says something heartbreaking. My heart comes from a higher place than my words. Words come from my mind. A baby feels everything, but his mind isn't developed yet; therefore, he cannot talk, because words come from my mind.

So I have to put into words something from another world. Now the Zohar HaKadosh says that a person can only express ten percent of what they want to say. This is already bad enough, but now comes something even more heartbreaking. The most someone can hear from me is ten percent of what I'm saying.

I'm not talking about someone who isn't paying any attention, I'm talking about someone who actually is paying attention. This is absolutely heartbreaking, yet this is the world of communication.

Now I want you to know something very beautiful.

Moshe Rabbeinu was so much about the truth, he could only utter complete words. Imagine Moshe would want to tell someone, "I like you, I love you." He couldn't utter it, so he would stammer because while he would say the words, he would realize how the words are much too small and far from what he really wants to say. The craziest thing happened to Moshe Rabbeinu. The second he came down from Mount Sinai he didn't stammer anymore.

And here I want you to open your hearts.

When G-d gave us the Torah on Mount Sinai, G-d told us exactly what He wanted to say. Not ten percent, not twenty percent, but everything.

The craziest thing happened to us as well. When we were on Mount Sinai, we heard a hundred percent of what G-d wanted to tell us. You see what it is, the holiness of the Torah is not only that the ideas and concepts are the holiest, but the words themselves are not limiting.

When I hold onto the Torah, I can say one hundred percent of what I want to say. And if you are a good teacher like Moshe Rabbeinu, people begin to hear one hundred percent of what you want to tell them.

There was a time when people were happy with saying ten percent of what they wanted to say. Imagine if I meet someone who I don't love so much and I really want to tell them something, but they really only know ten percent of what I want to say. Who cares? So they only know ten percent of what I think.

When I meet someone I love very much, it is so important to me that they know everything of what I'm saying.

Before *Mashiach* is coming, there will be so much oneness in the world because we are so desperate to communicate with each other. Our children go to school and they are taught words and ideas that are maybe ten percent of the idea. They are given words that the other person only hears ten percent of what they want to say. So how could there be oneness in the world?

If only we could really tell each other exactly what we want to say, if only we could really hear what we are saying to each other.

LEARNING HOW TO LISTEN

THE MAHARAL SAID THAT A DOG KNOWS EXactly how to be a dog. A tree knows how to be a tree.

Wouldn't it be sad to think that G-d created man in His image and wouldn't let man know what it means to be in His image? It just doesn't make sense.

When G-d spoke to us on Mount Sinai, His voice was heard all over the world. The most incredible thing is that He is still talking. He's talking all the time.

The Torah is still telling us how to be in His image, if we would only take all the dirt out of our ears, we'd hear the answers to our deepest questions.

*

Do you know what happened to us on Mount Sinai? When G-d says, "Thou shalt not kill," these words truly reached our souls. It was not that despite the fact that we wanted to kill, we are now not killing. It's that we simply weren't capable of killing anymore.

Sadly enough, I guess we left Mount Sinai and fell back a little bit, and now it's all a question of if you are obeying the law or not. But the truth is, we have to begin obeying a little bit, and hopefully we will work ourselves back up again.

You know friends, if all I want to do all Shabbos is to work, but I don't because I'm not allowed to, it's not really Shabbos that I have. Shabbos means I have nothing I need to do, I have nothing I want to do.

On Shabbos I'm in another world. If I come up to someone and say, "You know something, I really feel the need to kill you, but what can I do, G-d told me I shouldn't" – deep down inside, I'm a murderer.

Now listen to this. Our sages say that all we really heard from G-d was the word *"Anochi,"* the "I" of G-d. When we came back down from mount Sinai to earth, the *Anochi* was in the form of Ten Commandments. But when we were up on Mount Sinai, when we were really up in front with G-d, it was just one word, just one word, and G-d didn't have to say, "Don't kill."

After hearing one word from G-d, how *can* you kill?

*

On Mount Sinai, the holiness was that we saw G-d with our eyes, but before you fix your eyes, you have to fix your ears. *"Vayishma Yisro"* – "And Yisro heard."

On Mount Sinai we finally heard, for the first time. Sometimes we have the greatest revelations after hearing something which might have been spoken to us thousands of times. So what changed? Simple, we never really heard it before.

One of the greatest rabbis before the First World War was the Alter of Novardok, R' Yossel Horowitz. He had thousands of students. How did he become who he became? He was a pious man who prayed and learned every day, but he abstained from money.

One time he went to learn from Reb Yisrael Salanter, who was one of the greatest ever. Reb Yisrael Salanter told a story from the Talmud, and the story goes like this.

It happened that pirates fell upon the ship that a certain Reb Lazer was on. As they were stealing everything on board, they saw Reb Lazer sitting on the deck, laughing. They asked him, "Why are you laughing?" So he said, "Because you simply cannot steal that which I really have." The whole Torah was in his head and in his heart; it was untouchable.

So Reb Yisrael Salanter said that most people waste their whole life on things which can be stolen, but have no time for the one thing which cannot be stolen. There were hundreds of people there, they all listened to R' Yisrael's words, but it was only the Alter who heard it.

He came home and realized how little time and importance he gave toward that which cannot be stolen and began the journey to becoming the Alter of Novardok.

ANOCHI

I am HaShem (Sh'mos 20:2)

JUST ONE WORD.

One time a chassid of the Alter Rebbe came to a gathering where chassidim of the Mitler Rebbe were talking to each other. Chasidim of the Mitler Rebbe were younger chassidim, while chassidim of the Alter Rebbe were a little bit older.

The longest the Alter Rebbe would give over Torah would be maybe twenty minutes. The Mitler Rebbe would say Chassidus six, seven, eight hours non-stop. This older chassid overheard the younger ones saying, "The Alter Rebbe was a gevalt, but how does he compare to his son?"

So the older chassid said to them, "You have no idea how much you are mistaken. Do you know why the Alter Rebbe couldn't talk more than twenty minutes? Because what he wanted to say was so beyond deep, it almost had no space in the world. The Mitler Rebbe is also deep, but he can talk for hours."

You see what it is, anything you are talking about for a long time might be very holy, but it's not able to hit the point.

I want to tell you the most awesome thing in the world. How long was G-d's speech on Mount Sinai? Let's assume G-d said all Ten Commandments. Basically, it's agreed that G-d said the whole Ten Commandments, but according to even deeper kabbalists, G-d only said the letter Aleph of *Anochi*. Let's assume he said the word *Anochi* which included the ten commandments.

The Komarner says that G-d only let out the air within the letter *aleph*. Do you know what that means? G-d is not stingy, he could have said to Yidden on Mount Sinai, "I want you all to sit here for forty days." Do you know why He didn't? Because G-d can give over his point through the air beneath one letter.

Imagine you give a speech for five hours, and after the whole thing is over, someone asks you tell them in one sentence what you just said. If you really know what you said, you can say it in one sentence – unless you really don't know yourself.

As much as the Torah is ten thousand pages, and fifty thousand paragraphs, G-d knew exactly what he had to say so that he was able say it in the word *Anochi*, and this included everything there is.

*

G-d began speaking at Mount Sinai by saying "*Anochi HaShem Elokecha*," – "I am the Lord your G-d," (Sh'mos 20:2) but this is a very poor translation. *Anochi* means "I" but *gevalt*, does it mean so much more, infinitely more.

Let me ask you, would I need a name if I was all alone in the world? I wouldn't. I only need a name for someone who needs to call me. *Anochi* means "I"; G-d is speaking from the "I" of Him which has no other name, because when G-d is alone He doesn't have a name. So G-d says, "*Anochi*," the real "I" – which is beyond names.

I want to share something very deep with you.

Every person has an "I" which is beyond names. The world talks about meditation, but we talk about *hisbodedus*, which I call "holy aloneness," to go out to a field and talk to G-d. When this happens, my "I," my real holy aloneness, meets the holiness of G-d, the holy aloneness.

You can tell how close someone is to you when they call your name. Someone can call you by your name and someone can call you by your "I," which is beyond the actual name they are calling you.

When it comes to davening, it's the same thing. I can pray to G-d because He is the creator of the world, and He has this big department store in heaven. I can pray to Him because He gives life, He has all the goods, like He is the big boss, or I can really pray, *mamesh*, to G-d Himself.

As long as I am asking G-d for favors, I am asking Him as a creator who can do something for me. This is not praying yet; this is asking for things. Praying happens when my "I," which has no names, connects to the "I" of G-d, which has no names, which is beyond everything.

*

When G-d told us, "I am the Lord Your G-d," G-d talked to us in singular, not in plural. Because the truth is that no one can teach me about G-d.

I can read books that teach me everything in the world, but when it comes to the one thing, knowing there is one G-d – it is just G-d and me.

G-DLY OPENING REMARKS

I am the Lord Your G-d who has taken you out of Egypt, from the house of slavery. (Sh'mos 20:2)

INSIDE-OUT.

What is the difference between winter and summer? Winter is when G-d puts so much depth and life into nature, but nature has no vessels for it. So it looks like nature has completely gone dead, because that which G-d is putting into the roots of nature cannot charm the outside. The outside has no vessels for it.

When you tell someone, "I want to tell the deepest depths of my heart," I have to tell it to them according to their size. Imagine if I would have a friend with whom I can share the deepest depths of my heart, exactly the way it is. You could do it for one second, but more than that would be too much.

So the Ishbitzer says, what happened to us when we were slaves in Egypt? On the outside we were slaves, completely dead. Obviously, there's a plan from Mount Sinai. So what was happening to us on the inside?

The way everyone translates, "*Anochi HaShem Elokecha asher hotzeisicha mei'eretz Mitzrayim mi-beis avadim,*" (Sh'mos 20:2) means the G-d who fulfilled the miracle of getting us out of Egypt. But it's much deeper than that. The Ishbitzer says what it really means is, "I'm the G-d that was planting the deepest seeds into the root of your soul while you were slaves in Egypt."

Do you know what happened to us while we were slaves in Egypt? The holiness and the depths which G-d put in our hearts was so awesome. It had nothing to do with our outsides. Outside we were slaves, we were broken, but what every *Yiddele* had inside was so awesome.

Let's put it on a very down-to-earth level. What is a Russian *Yiddele* doing while he is in Siberia? What kind of *Yiddishkeit* does he get? I can learn in the best yeshiva in the world, but will I get a billionth of a taste of what a Jew gets while he's sitting in Siberia and wants to go to Israel?

So this is what the Ishbitzer is saying. When G-d gave us the Torah, He told us, "I gave you something which is the vessel for all the depths which I gave you in Egypt."

CLARITY

IF YOU WANT TO BE ON MOUNT SINAI, YOU NEED TO know what Mount Sinai means.

Anyone can learn holy things, but on Mount Sinai I don't just learn holy teachings. On Mount Sinai it's clear to you that what you heard is really from G-d. When you learn something and it's not clear to you, you might have had a good teacher but you were not on Mount Sinai. To be on Mount Sinai means it's absolutely clear to me.

I can learn everything in the world about G-d and I can still not be sure there is one G-d. When we were on Mount Sinai, we heard G-d's voice saying, "I am the lord your G-d," and it's clear to me that it's *mamesh* true. I can read all the books on Shabbos, but I still have trouble keeping it. When I hear G-d saying, "*Zachor es Yom HaShabbos l'kodsho*" – "Remember the Shabbos to keep it holy," (Sh'mos 20:8) I have no trouble keeping Shabbos.

In order to reach this clarity of love from G-d, I have to turn myself over. I can believe in G-d, I can be a servant and do everything right, but in order to have this Mount Sinai moment, hearing it from G-d directly, I have to completely turn myself over.

The greatest feeling is when I receive one word from G-d directly. It can happen any time. I can open a little holy book and the words are shining right into me. I can have a moment of seeing someone smile at me, but you know something? They are smiling right into me.

At that moment, everything in the world is so clear.

WORDS THAT BRING CLOSENESS

THERE ARE TWO TYPES OF WORDS. SOMETIMES I need words to give over some information. If you ask how much is one and one I tell you two, but after you know it's two you don't need my words anymore.

When it comes to most teachers, why don't we feel close to them, why do we disregard them after growing up a little bit? Because I don't need them anymore; I know it now on my own.

But then there's another kind of word, there is another type of information. When I hold a baby and say, "You're the cutest baby in the whole world," the baby grows up remembering, "My father couldn't stop telling I was the cutest baby." These are very deep words. And those words are living words because you always mean it.

G-d took us out from Egypt, He split the sea, and suddenly He says, "I am the Lord your G-d." Really? Is that it? Didn't G-d want to blow my mind?

You see what it is, the holiness of Mount Sinai was not that G-d taught me there is only one G-d. Avraham, Yitzchak, and Ya'akov knew there was one G-d, but at Mount Sinai I heard G-d saying to me, "I am the Lord your G-d." I actually heard it, and you actually heard it, we heard something that brought us so much closer together.

Why is it, that when you walk into a classroom, people sit far away from each other? Everyone only hears ten percent of what the teacher is saying, so everyone is living in their own little ivory tower.

But imagine if the teacher says something that everyone was able to truly hear, do you know what would happen? It would bring the class together because they would all hear the same thing.

When people come somewhere, and when they walk out feeling connected to each other, it's because they all heard the same thing.

DON'T BE A PAGAN

You shall not recognize the G-d of others. (Sh'mos 20:3)

BEFORE THE GREAT DAY, BEFORE THE MESSIAH IS coming, all the gates of heaven are opening. All the gates of learning and all the secrets of the world are opening to us as well. But what does this actually mean?

I want you to open your hearts.

There is such a thing as loving G-d and there is such a thing as fearing G-d. Loving G-d is not simple, but it's easier to understand. We have trouble knowing what it means to fear G-d. To fear G-d doesn't mean to be afraid, like the way you are afraid under gunfire.

The Ba'al Shem Tov says, fearing G-d means I'm afraid I will lose His light. I'm afraid I'll do something wrong which will create distance.

Let's go deeper. How much do we know about G-d? The truth is we know very little. We know He created the world, we know He spoke to us on Mount Sinai. We know a lot of things, but if someone were to ask me what I really know about G-d, what could I say?

In order to love, we don't have to know so much. But in order to have this fear, to have this awareness and *mamesh* knowing He is there, you need to know how to feel so much closer.

As an example, I can live in America and love someone who is in Australia. That's *Ahava*. I can love G-d even if He's far away, but *Yirah* is something else. *Yirah* means to know He is right here. So why is it that before *Mashiach* is coming, all the walls between man and man, between man and G-d, are breaking down? Simple. The world is becoming more and more aware that G-d is really here.

The great light of this awareness is coming into the world as the great day is coming closer, but the question is – where are these lights?

Rav Kook says the absolute deepest depths. How did being in exile affect us most strongly? In the root of it all, exile caused us to stop believing in ourselves. Most of us simply don't believe that we are worthy of great light, worthy of newness, worthy of G-dly revelations.

Why is this? Why do we have so much trouble believing that the gates of heaven are open and that we are actually capable of knowing the deepest secrets of the world? Rav Kook says that since we don't believe in ourselves anymore, we prefer to live in darkness than to see the great light.

The Ba'al Shem Tov says that my own yesterdays, my own wrongdoings, are my greatest slave drivers. I'm usually a slave to what I did yesterday, which is the greatest pagan worship. On a certain level, as much as it's holy to sit and cry over my sins, it's still a little bit of slavery. You'll ask a *Yiddele,* "How come you're not a prophet?" "Me? A prophet? Do you know what I did yesterday?" What do you care? Are you a servant of your yesterday or are you a servant of G-d?

The strangest thing is that the people who know there is one G-d don't want to hear of the great lights that are coming down. How could this be? Rav Kook says that the people who were taught that there is one G-d were taught of G-d in an exile way. Therefore, the people who might not know there is one G-d because nobody taught them, they are vessels for this great light coming down in the world.

As crazy as it is, those who do not know anything or were not taught anything – are wide open. You see, they were never taught the exile teaching about G-d.

So before *Mashiach* is coming, all the gates of heaven are open. In order to receive this light, don't be a pagan.

And, you see, this takes refinement, refinement, and more refinement. To *mamesh* believe there is one G-d is not so simple. What have we been doing for the past two thousand years? We are refining ourselves, becoming less and less pagan.

Rav Kook says idol worship doesn't mean that I take a little statue and bow down to it; this is kid stuff. "*Avodah Zarah*" means worship that is strange. I can serve G-d in idol worship as well. If I don't really know there is one G-d, I can keep Shabbos and it is idol worship.

The prophet says that one day the whole world will be filled with knowing G-d like the water is covering the ocean. So Rav Kook says, if you know there is one G-d, you are not in exile and no one has power over you. Nothing can knock you off, nothing in the world.

Before *Mashiach* is coming, the gates of heaven are opening and G-d lets us know who He really is. The more you know who He really is, the less pagan you are. Avraham Avinu really knew there is one G-d, and he taught it to us, but we forgot.

It's coming back.

SHABBOS – MORE THAN JUST NOT FORGETTING

Remember the Sabbath day for its holiness. (Sh'mos 20:8)

WHEN DO DREAMS HELP?

Imagine I am very hungry and I'm dreaming that in about two hours from now I am going to this French restaurant where I'm going to pound it in like mad. But in the meantime, I am still hungry like a dog. Dreaming about food doesn't help. My *kishkes* say, "Listen brother, I appreciate your high caliber, that you are dreaming so much about food, but it doesn't help. I want to eat!"

The holiness about Shabbos is that even when you are just dreaming about Shabbos, you are already "*Shabbosing.*"

How do you know if you love somebody? It's very simple. How close do you feel to them when you think of them? Let's say I'm thinking that next week I have to meet this manager who is going to talk to me about a concert. So when I'll meet him I'll see him, that's all there is to it.

Now imagine that yesterday I was in the airport, and I was thinking to myself, "Tomorrow I'll see my baby'le again . . ." – it's something else. With this one second of thinking about my baby, my soul *mames*h tasted what it feels like to be with my baby.

It's not only important to think about Shabbos so that you shouldn't forget about Shabbos; it's that whenever you think about Shabbos something happens to you.

Let's put it this way. Imagine you want to say something bad about another person and you just can't control yourself. Now let's say you decided that each time you want to say something bad about another person you will think of Shabbos. Do you know what will happen?

You simply won't be able to say one bad word because, *gevalt,* are the vibrations of Shabbos so strong.

THE TASTE OF SHABBOS

Those who have tasted it have merited life. (Shabbos morning prayers)

WHEN MY CHILD MAKES A LITTLE DRAWING, and I show it to somebody subjectively, it might not really do anything to them. But when I will look at it, it's the sweetest thing I ever saw. How come? Because I am "tasting" my child in that drawing. I don't see the drawing, I see my baby.

That's what you see, this is what you taste.

Imagine I'm standing outside a wedding hall, and as each person walks out I ask them, "How was the wedding?" One person I ask takes a look at me and says, "Master of the World . . . thank you so much that they got married. Thank you so much that there is such a thing as weddings."

You know what he tasted? Not only did he taste this wedding, but in this one wedding he tasted all the weddings of the world. Wherever there was a love between a man and a woman, he tasted it at this one wedding.

This person is connected not only to this one wedding, he is plugged into the roots of the roots.

Shabbos means to be plugged in to the *all* of everything. The truth is that when I eat fish on Shabbos, what do I taste? I do not taste the fish; I am tasting that G-d created heaven and earth. I eat a little bit of soup – am I tasting the soup? I taste everything there is in heaven and everything there is on earth.

When I make Kiddush I am standing before G-d, being a witness, testifying that G-d created the heavens and the earth. Some people taste the wine and, sadly enough, spend the rest of the night discussing what they prefer, Manischevitz or Kedem wine.

But then there are those *Yiddelach* who are *mamesh* tasting Kiddush. Imagine if someone could taste the taste of all the *Yiddelach* before us and after us who bear witness that G-d created heaven and earth? Can you imagine what a *Kiddush* it would be?

Do you know what we have to do today? It's a very high level to taste my own soul. Sadly enough, some of us have never tasted the flavor of their own soul. But now imagine if I can taste somebody else's soul. Imagine if I could taste the taste of all the souls of my generation. Imagine if I could taste the taste of all the souls from creation until *Mashiach* is coming.

This is what Shabbos is all about.

You see, if the highest place I reach on Shabbos is to taste my own Shabbos – then you don't long to connect with all *Yidden* who might not keep Shabbos yet. When I connect to every Jew, you know what I taste? I taste that until every *Yiddele* has Shabbos, my taste is incomplete.

THE BEAUTY OF "MORE"

HOW DO YOU KNOW HOW MUCH YOU LOVE somebody? If a person will call me up and ask me for a loan of a hundred dollars, I will give them one hundred dollars. If my little girl asks me for ten dollars, I'll give her eleven because I want her to have more than what she asked for.

When you love somebody very much you want to give them more. So Reb Nachman says that the highest level I can reach during the week is that G-d answers my prayer and really gives me what I need.

This is a very high level; I wish we would be on that level. I wish we would be on the level that whenever we pray, G-d really answers us. But do you know where we reach on Shabbos? Not only does G-d answer me, G-d gives me more than I asked for.

This is what Shabbos is all about. On Shabbos we have what's called "*mishneh lechem*" – "two loaves of bread." In Hebrew, "*Mishneh*" doesn't necessarily mean "double." *Mishneh* means "more.: *Mishneh lechem* doesn't mean one more bread, it means "more," more than one.

Here I want you to understand something very deep. What does it mean to have peace with someone? Peace doesn't mean I give you what you ask for; for that you don't need peace. Peace means I want to give you *more* than you asked for.

Imagine someone comes to you and they are broken, destroyed, and sad. If you give them just as much as they need – they will still be sick, they will still be broken. When you asked me for a hundred dollars and

I gave you a hundred dollars and one penny, this one penny brought so much newness into the world.

I have to share this one story with you. Some poor people still have a bit of dignity left. They don't want to say "Give me a hundred dollars because I need it." They come and say "give me a loan," and this is really the test to see if you are a *mensch* or not.

Some people say, "You want a hundred dollars? I need to know exactly when you are giving it back to me." They squeeze out their last ounce of pride. If you're a mensch, you say, "I know you will give it back to me whenever you have it. I'm so glad to help you."

The way the Rebbe of Sadigerer did it was even deeper. A *Yiddele* would come and say, "Can I have a loan of two hundred rubles?" The Sadigerer says, "I'm so glad you came to ask me. I want you to know that this morning I was praying so hard to G-d that I should have the privilege of giving somebody a loan, and here you are, the answer to my prayer."

Can you imagine how good this *Yiddele* felt? It's a different kind of giving. So the Rebbe would open his little safe, take out two hundred rubles and give it to the *Yiddele*. The *Yiddele* would start counting and see that it is more than two hundred. "Rebbe, you gave me too much." The Rebbe says, "I want to give you more." *Chassidim* who tell this story say that because of that extra ruble that the Rebbe gave him, he became very rich.

The Talmud says something unbelievable. Imagine you walking around the streets in Charan where Avraham Avinu lived, and you wanted to find a pupil of Avraham. So the Talmud says that you hang around the grocery store and watch how people pay for their goods.

So they most probably had some currency, and the *Medrash* says let's take it in our terms. Imagine I'm not a pupil of Avraham and I walk into the grocery store and buy something for $5.75. I hand the cashier a $10 bill and he has to give me back $4.25.

Imagine he gives me back the quarter in pennies or in nickels. So I put the four dollars in my pocket, then I concentrate on those pennies and count them. I say, "You know, you only gave me twenty-four cents." "I'm sorry, I'll give you another penny." You are counting pennies? The Talmud says that a follower of Avraham puts whatever he got back in his pocket. Counting? What are you counting?

Do you know when I count? I count if I don't trust you because I know you are a thief. I know from last time that you are a thief so this time I am counting.

Do you know how you can destroy a person when you don't trust them? Do you know how much strength you give them if you do trust them?

I can swear that most of the people who end up being criminals, their downfall began because people didn't trust them when they were younger. I have had the privilege of performing in many prisons. When you walk up to people in prison and you give them honor like they are the best people in the world, you give them back their life and their soul.

So the first thing is that Avraham's pupils don't count. You give me back change . . . most probably you are right. Counting? You cut yourself off from them even more. Maybe G-d wanted to give you back twenty dollars right now, or maybe G-d wanted the other person to have more. What do I know? Is it my money?

So Reb Nachman says like this: To whom do you give honor? You give honor to a person who has more. You give honor to a person who has something "more" about them.

Reb Nachman says if you ever taste the holiness of Shabbos, then it is so easy for you to give honor to every other human being because you know that every person has more, every human being in the world has something more.

And if you never tasted Shabbos you measure people and ask yourself, "Should I give him honor or not?" You end up deciding that you shouldn't because the moment you start measuring – you are already off.

Do you know what happens to me on Shabbos? Suddenly I realize that everything G-d gave me is much more than I thought, so much more than I thought. I never knew how much G-d gave me, and suddenly I begin to taste the "more" in everything I have.

Why is there is so much peace in the house on Shabbos, between friends or between husband and wife? Here is my wife and I know she is beautiful, but on Friday night I look at her and I see there is so much more than that.

When I look at my children, I know they are beautiful, cute and sweet, but on Friday night I realize how there is so much more to them. If the world would look at each other with the eyes of *Lechem Mishneh,* with the eyes of the two breads of Shabbos, what a world . . . what a world . . . what a world.

Now on Shabbos we don't pray for anything in detail, we just pray in general. The Ishbitzer says like this. I want to build this little village in Israel and I meet Baron Rothschild, and he says to me, "Okay, I am ready to sponsor you, how much money should I give you for the village?"

If I am stupid, I say, "Give me a hundred thousand dollars." This is so stupid, he wanted to give me a million. Do I know how much he wanted to give me? Imagine I say a million, but he was ready to give me ten million. So what do I say to him? "Whatever you thought to give, give me double."

So the Ishbitzer says that on Shabbos I am not asking G-d for particulars – how do you know what G-d wants to give you? He wanted to give you double, G-d wants to give you double. On Shabbos I am not asking, I am just asking G-d to fill my heart, fill my soul, and fill my life.

PEACEFUL ISLAND

THERE IS A *MEDRASH* THAT SAYS THERE WAS A ship that was sailing on the water. Suddenly there was a storm. Everybody was panicking and the ship began to sink. There was a little boy lying on deck on a little chair, taking a little sunbath.

So they say to him, "Hey, brother, aren't you afraid?"

He says, "Not at all, my father is the captain."

The world *shuckles* today from the tornadoes, from missiles, from confusion. Unless it's clear to you that your father is the captain, you will think maybe you should jump to the sea and commit suicide.

What is the world coming to? But if you know your father is the captain, you are sure the ship is on the right path to the right island.

Somewhere there is a beautiful island, and that island is untouched by evil, it is untouched by anything unholy, it's untouched by hatred.

If we have the awesome privilege, we can visit this island every Shabbos.

RESPECTING PARENTS

Honor your father and mother. (Sh'mos 20:12)

WHY IS IT THAT A LOT OF PEOPLE DON'T REally respect their parents? Whoever has trouble with respecting their own parents has trouble respecting life itself.

My parents brought me into this world, they gave me life, but for those who don't respect their parents, life itself is a joke. If I'm completely aware of the holiness of life, I know how to honor my parents. If someone gives me a million dollars, I would do anything in the world for them because I know the value of a million dollars, but when it comes to what my parents gave me? Not so much.

Now let me ask you, if I'm drowning in the ocean and someone gets me out, he might be the lowest criminal in the world. Why is it that I thank him with all my heart? Simple, he saved my life.

So if I thank the one that saves my life, why is it so hard to honor the one who gave me life in the first place?

Honoring a father and mother is only if you honor life. I can only do this if I know what life is, if I know the preciousness of life, and that I'm privileged to be in this world. Only then do I realize, *gevalt,* these two people brought me into this world. Even if they are not the sweetest people in the world, they gave me life and brought me into this world.

So the *Shulchan Aruch* says that when it comes to honoring your parents, *"Tzarich lizahayr me'od"* – "One must be very careful." (*Yore De'ah* 240:1)

I want to tell you a Sanzer Torah. *"L'hi-zahayr"* means to be careful, but *"l'hi-zahayr"* also comes from the word *"zohar,"* to shine. When it comes to honoring my father and mother, if it's not a shining affair – it's meaningless. It has to be something which is shining in my life.

*

Whenever the Shinover came to visit his father the Sanzer, he would sit in the *Beis Medrash* for six hours, reading the psalms, praying that he should know exactly how to talk to his father because they disagreed on a lot of things.

The Sanzer was very holy and believed that you have to make things easy for people.

Let's say someone comes to the holy Sanzer and says, "Listen, today is a fast day. Rabbi, should I fast?" The holy Sanzer says, "If you asked me this question, it must mean that *nebech* you don't feel so good, so you're permitted to eat." The Sanzer himself would grab this *Yiddele, shlep* him to the kitchen, and make him eat.

If someone would come to the holy Shinover and ask, "Should I fast?" he would say, "What's the matter? You look strong like a lion. Do you think you'll die when you fast? You better fast."

The Sanzer said something way out, but only he could say such a thing. If someone else would say it, I would say it's the biggest *chutzpah* in the world. The Sanzer said that our holy rabbis in paradise are ashamed that they initiated so many fast days.

Anyway, when the holy Shinover had to talk to his father, the holy Sanzer, the Sanzer told him to come to him at about 3 o'clock this morning.

In Sanz everything happened late at night. The holy Shinover would come to the *Beis Medrash* at 12 o'clock and start saying *Tehillim,* preparing to speak to his father. Suddenly he looks around – it's already five o'clock. The Shinover doesn't look at the clock when he prays.

He knocks on his father's door at five, and his father says, "I already have to go to the mikveh, and then it's time to daven." The Shinover tried again the following night, but this would happen night after night. So finally, the Sanzer says to the Shinover, "Listen to me, stop saying *Tehillim* before you go to talk to me."

You see what it is, the mitzvah of *"kibbud av v'eim"* respecting your mother and father, is not a simple thing. It's hard to honor your parents, but when you agree with them it's a little bit hard. When you absolutely don't agree with them, if your soul is on a different path, then it can be really, really hard.

NOT FORCING THE REWARD

So that your days will be lengthened on the land that HaShem, your G-d, has given you. (Sh'mos 20:12)

HOW WOULD THE HOLY COURT OPERATE?

If someone comes to the holy court, claiming that someone owes me one hundred dollars and hasn't paid me back, what happens? The holy court gets involved.

They send some holy policemen to Moishele's house and begin to sell whatever possessions he has, in order for him to pay back what he owes.

Basically, the holy court gets involved in the whole matter. But when it comes to honoring your father and mother, the holy court does not interfere. They can't force you to obey this commandment. The question is why not?

Here I want you to know the deepest depths.

The Gemara says anything which G-d specified that you'll be rewarded for – no one can force you to do it – it's up to you. When G-d says, "I reward you for it," it means, "I'm leaving it up to you, I'm not going to get involved and force you to do something which I want to reward you for." That means, in a certain way, this commandment comes from a very high place.

We know that G-d will reward us for everything we do, but G-d makes it clear that when it comes to the mitzvah of honoring your parents, he will reward us with long life – it means that G-d wants to take care of it personally.

So the holy court is not interfering – it's between you and G-d.

DON'T EVER IGNORE

Thou shalt not kill. (Sh'mos 20:13)

I WANT YOU TO KNOW THE DEEPEST DEPTHS.

The Zohar HaKadosh says that when G-d says, "Don't kill," some people heard, "Don't take a knife and kill someone." The higher people heard, "Don't be angry at anyone," but the real holy people heard, "Don't ever ignore anyone."

Reb Yochanan said that in his whole life, it never happened that any human being passed by him without him saying hello first. That means he was so eager to see another human being that nobody could ever say hello to him first.

ROBBING YOURSELF

Thou shalt not steal. (Sh'mos 20:13)

IN KOTZK THEY SAY THAT WASTING SOMEBODY'S time is *mamesh* stealing. What does this mean?

Every person has something to do in this world. Imagine if Einstein would have become a shoe shiner instead of becoming a great scientist. What would he have done? He would have stolen from the whole world.

This is true regarding every person, on their own level. If I'm not on the level I can be on, what am I doing? I'm basically stealing from the world.

Deep down we are all thieves. I steal from myself, I steal from others.

We have to go back to Mount Sinai and hear G-d say, *"Lo tignov,"* – "stop stealing." Be everything that you are meant to be.

SYNESTHESIA

The entire people saw the thunder. (Sh'mos 20:15)

WHAT DOES IT MEAN THAT ON MOUNT SINAI we saw voices? Listen to the deepest depths.

On Mount Sinai we reached the level of oneness, complete oneness.

When I say my body is one, it's not the same oneness as the oneness of my soul. My body can be one while my feet look different from my hands, and my hands look different from my ears.

The oneness of my body is that it's one body, but each part is still separated a little bit. When it comes to my soul it's something else, it really is one.

So what happened on Mount Sinai? On Mount Sinai we reached the level of oneness between body and soul.

And when this happens, I can hear with my eyes and see with my ears.

WE ARE PEOPLE OF SOUL

The entire people saw the thunder and the flames,
and the sound of the shofar. (Sh'mos 20:15)

WHEN WE STOOD BY MOUNT SINAI IT SAYS, *"V'chol ha'am ro'im es hakolos"* – "everyone saw the voices;" *"es halapidim"* – they saw the fire coming out, "the torches;" *"v'es kol hashofar"* – "and they saw the blowing of the trumpet." (Sh'mos 20:14)

Do you know what happened to us? *"V'chol ha'am ro'im es hakolos"* – "we saw the voice," on Mount Sinai, *"v'es halapidim"* – "we saw the fire" of Auschwitz – we saw every fire we have gone through – *"v'es kol hashofar"* – and we saw the blowing of the trumpet" on the great day.

Do you know what this means? If you are a Mount Sinai person, you have to see the whole picture. The moment you want to be a Jew, you have to connect yourself to the past, present, and future picture.

You have to hear G-d's voice, you have to have a taste of all the fires we have gone through. But ultimately, you also have to hear the blowing of the trumpet; otherwise, you don't quite understand what's going on.

Let's put it this way. Sadly enough, I see a lot of holy Jews plugged in to hear G-d's voice on Mount Sinai, but they are absolutely not plugged in to hear the blowing of the great trumpet.

Sadly enough, a lot of kids are walking around college campuses and are plugged into hearing the great trumpet, but you know something? They cry over Hiroshima, but they are not crying over the six million; they are not plugged into the fire of Auschwitz.

With all due respect, take all the folk singers in America. Did any of the folk singers ever make a song for the six million? It's heartbreaking. These kids are holy souls, they are plugged into the blowing of the trumpet, but it's heartbreaking how much they are not plugged into seeing G-d's voice on Mount Sinai, nor to the pain and tears of their grandparents.

The Sfas Emes says, "*V'chol ha'am ro'im es hakolos*" means that "*the all of you*" has to hear it. It's not enough just to be a part-time Jew, *the all of you* has to be a Jew. When *the all of you* is a Jew, your children are plugged in.

ALTAR OF EARTH

Make for me an altar of Earth. (Sh'mos 20:21)

DON'T MAKE ME AN ALTAR OF SILVER AND DON'T make me an altar of gold but make an altar out of earth. *"Mizbach adama ta'aseh-li"* – "Make me an altar out of earth." (Sh'mos 20:21)

I want you to know, this is one of the top passages. The Ishbitzer takes these words to the deepest depths. (*Mei Hashiloach* I, *Parshas Yisro*)

A person is made of two things. A person can have a lot of yearning for that which he hasn't acquired yet, but there is something even deeper than yearning, and that is to be connected to what I really am right now. Not what I'm yearning for, but who I really am right now.

The passage says that when you build an altar before G-d, don't build it only out of yearning. Why not? What could be higher? Yearning is very holy, but this isn't it yet.

Don't build it out of the gold and silver you might have acquired or long to acquire. Make it out of the earth, that part of you which is really the most down-to-earth in you, which is deeper than anything in the word. This is where you build your altar, this is where you serve G-d.

Someone can teach me how to yearn, someone can teach me how to gain something, but this holy "altar of earth" can't be taught by someone. It's between me and G-d.

*

Imagine I have to go to the market place to buy apples, and I don't know which pound of apples to buy. Finally, I decide from which stand I would like to buy the apples.

Let me ask you, from which deep place in my heart does this decision come? It doesn't need to come from such a deep place. If I need to buy a shirt and I don't know which shirt to buy, it's the same thing.

But then imagine, I'm standing on a cliff and I have to jump down to save someone's life, I see death right in front of me. That decision to jump is even deeper because it's a question of life and death right this minute.

Now listen to this. To love and to fear G-d comes from a very deep place, but there is something in my heart which is deeper than loving and fearing. It's deeper than anything in the world because it's deeper than emotions. It is deeper than feeling, and it is deeper than knowing. We have no words for it, but this is where my soul really is.

When I love something, the question is, does it only reach the place where love is coming from, or does it reach that place which is even deeper than love? Is it even deeper than believing?

So this is an unbelievable Torah'le from the holy Ishbitzer. Open your hearts from here to eternity.

When Moshe Rabbeinu comes down from Mount Sinai, we were on a pretty high level. The passage says, "Don't make a G-d of silver, don't make a G-d of gold, but build me an altar of earth." Moshe Rabbeinu doesn't have to tell the *Yiddelach,* "Don't take a little piece of gold and bow down to it." We just spoke to G-d on Mount Sinai; we know there is one G-d.

So what is going on here?

The Zohar HaKadosh says that silver, *kesef,* comes from the word *lichsof,* to yearn for something, to want it so much. This is silver. Gold is always a sign of being aware of the presence of something. So when I know G-d is really there, it means I'm serving G-d on the level of gold.

Here G-d says to us, "Don't serve me on the level of silver, don't even serve me on the level of gold, just make me an altar of earth." Earth is the most simple thing in the world. Not simple in the basic sense of the word, but simple meaning the utmost essence of something.

It's as simple as it gets. You can find earth all over; it has no colors. Do you know how deep it is to say, "I love you" to someone for absolutely no reason other than being real? If I really love them, it's like earth. It's not like silver, it's not like gold, no colors. It's not painted at all, it's just as simple as can be.

So the Ishbitzer says that a lot of people serve G-d on the level of silver, of loving G-d, but it's not real. If you pretend to love G-d more than you do, it's paganism. If when you serve G-d it's one ounce more than how you really feel – if it's not coming from all the honesty in your heart – it's idol worship.

If I say, "I'm aware of G-d's presence," and I'll start shivering here like a milkshake, I'm lying. I wish I would be like that, but I'm not on that level.

I'll tell you something very sad. I met one *Yiddele,* he is sweet and holy but really simple. Whenever he mentions G-d's name in a *bracha, "Baruch atah HaShem,"* he starts shivering like a lulav. You can see he is not on the level to shiver before G-d.

Automatically, when he says *"Baruch atah HaShem,"* he starts shaking like crazy. The Ishbitzer says that idol worship is when you want to serve G-d when it's not a billion percent real. G-d says, "do you want to make a G-d of silver?" "Do you want to serve Me with love? I don't need that. You know what I need? A little bit of earth, a little altar made out of earth. No colors, don't paint yourself. Don't love me, don't fear me, simply serve me with a little bit of earth."

Adama, the earth, means the way it really is, the way you really are. Earth alludes to the deepest depths of you, where you really are.

Most of the time we don't know where we are, but if for one minute we could know where we are and just serve G-d from that sweet little place, it would be the most special thing in the world. I might not be full of love, and I still have to learn how to truly fear G-d, but if this is what I am right now, then this is the holiest thing I can be for G-d.

This is the holiest worship there is, simply because it's real.

משפטים

MISHPATIM

משפטים

With gratitude to Reb Shlomo *z"tl,* who continues to open our hearts to the guidance and wisdom of Torah.

May we, our children and grandchildren all be nourished and nurtured by the ongoing gift of deepening our understanding of the essential truths that continue to sustain us.

Rabbi Joseph and Rolinda Schonwald

BEFORE AND NOT AFTER

And these are the ordinances that you shall place before them. (Sh'mos 21:1)

I WANT TO SHARE SOMETHING VERY IMPORTANT with you.

The laws of this world and the laws of the Torah are completely different laws. When the Torah says not to steal, it is not given in order to explain what happens when someone steals.

When you learn the Torah laws of stealing, they are so holy, that when you learn them – you simply can't steal anymore. But in the today's society, the laws of stealing only come once someone stole.

With the Torah it's the other way around – they come before it happened. This is what it means when the Torah says, *"Asher tasim lifneihem"* – "place the laws before them," not after they might have fallen. After you learn the laws of stealing, you don't steal anymore.

When you learn about what happens to you when you kill someone, it's not that, G-d forbid, you already killed somebody and then you learn the laws. In the Torah it says that when someone, G-d forbid, killed somebody – they should be killed. In the time of the Holy Temple – as long as we Jews were the way we should be – there was never any killing going on.

How come? Because our laws begin before, *"lifneihem."* Because when G-d says, "Thou shalt not kill" – it is so holy that we simply couldn't kill anymore.

I always think that the way we teach our children the laws of the Torah is *"achareihem,"* after they already fell.

A lot of people know all the laws, but they know it like it's in the back of their head. It's got to be *"lifneihem,"* before me. The Pshischer Rebbe says, *"lifneihem,"* it's got to be before their eyes all the time, it has to be in front of me, not behind me.

ENSLAVING OTHERS

If you buy a Jewish bondsman . . . (Sh'mos 21:2)

AFTER THE REVELATION ON MOUNT SINAI, EVERYbody went home and began to daven. At twelve o'clock they came back to the mountain and Moshe Rabbeinu began teaching the Torah they had just received.

Wouldn't it be beautiful if Moshe Rabbeinu would give a lecture on the existence of G-d, or on the importance of being Jewish immediately following Mount Sinai?

Instead Moshe Rabbeinu begins by teaching, *"Ki sikne eved Ivri,"* – "when you buy a Jewish slave." On the seventh year he has to be freed. And if this slave says, "I want to remain a slave," he must be freed on the fiftieth year.

Now I want you to know, some of our sages say that the holy court never sold someone into slavery. (*Tosfos Ri'd* on *Kiddushin* 18a, *Ne'os Deshe, Mishpatim, Ki Sikne*). If that's the case, who is the Torah talking to?

All the Rebbes say that the Torah is not talking to the slave, the Torah is talking to the slave master. You see what it is, we are so often masters over somebody else. You know how much parents are masters over their children?

Sometimes a husband is a master over his wife and sometimes the wife is a master over her husband. Sometimes my child did something wrong, and the way I let them know they did wrong is by "enslaving" this poor child.

This is what our holy Rabbis are saying. You have to know deep in your heart, if you can make somebody else into a slave, then you were not on Mount Sinai. If you can make somebody else into a slave, you didn't hear G-d's voice saying, "I am the Lord who took you out of slavery . . . there is only one G-d."

I want you to open your hearts to the deepest depths. We are not slaves to G-d, we are servants to G-d. What's the difference between being a slave to a human being and being a servant to G-d?

When I am a slave, how does someone show me that they are my master? They throw me down to the ground and put their dirty feet on my face. A master is someone who makes you small, reducing you to nothing. If I am a G-d person, how do I show you that I am your master? How should parents show their children that they are a little bit their masters? By lifting them up.

Being a master over someone means I have the power to lift you up. You know what a good teacher is? Not someone that knocks you down, gives you bad marks, calls you names, and you are ashamed to show your face. It is someone that raises you up to the highest heights.

Sometimes you walk into a house and the man has a yarmulke and a beard, the woman wears a *sheitel*. They eat glatt kosher meat but the way they yell at each other is absolutely the lowest. You know what their problem is? They were not at Mount Sinai, as simple as it is, because if you know that the only Master of the World is G-d . . . how can you make someone else small?

At Mount Sinai G-d says, "I am your master, and you know what I did? I lifted you out of Egypt." The way G-d is our master is by lifting us up to the highest level. Children are constantly asking us to pick them up because they know we are their master, and they know their master lifts them up.

I want you to know the deepest depths. What does it mean when I lift up the Torah after reading from it? The Torah was given to us but we can make the Torah even deeper and higher. You can drag the Torah down as well. When someone asks me a question, at that moment I am their master. I can drag the Torah down to the lowest, or I can *mamesh* lift up the Torah to the highest. The way you look at a person, you either drag them down or you lift them up.

So the holy Ba'al Shem Tov said that this was the test. Moshe Rabbeinu comes back and says, "Okay friends, you all stood on Mount Sinai, let me give you a test if your feet were there or if you were there. If anybody here thinks they should be master over anybody else, then they were not on Mount Sinai."

*

We Jewish people, children of Avraham Avinu, have a very deep sense of paganism. We have an absolute refined sense of what idol worship is. Idol worship doesn't just mean taking a piece of wood and bowing down to it. That is not idol worship, that's just simple stupidity. Idol worship is if a human being takes for himself more power than he should have. It's when I make myself bigger than I am. I'm just a human being, that's all.

You see what it is, a human being has a right to be a teacher, but if you make yourself more than you are, it's really a bad scene.

It might not matter to those who don't have this refined sense.

I'm not only referring to other religions. When I see a rabbi making himself bigger than he is, it's also idol worship. If a teacher takes more power than he has in the classroom, makes himself more a master over the children than he should be, it's terrible.

Imagine I will tell you, "I want you to know, I have divine powers. I want you to kiss my toes and bow down before me." What am I doing to you? In order to be more than I am – I have to take away from you.

You know something? It's so strong in my heart. I wouldn't bow down before the holiest man in the world. I would walk up to him, shake his hand and kiss him. I respect him, but bowing down? I only bow down before G-d, nobody else. I only bow down before G-d.

You can cut my throat, but I'm not bowing down before a human being. When you fall down on the floor, and kiss someone's toes, do you know what that means? I am nothing in their presence. Being nothing in someone's presence is only relevant to G-d, and even He doesn't like it too much.

When we spoke to G-d on Mount Sinai, do you think we were lying on the floor, licking the toes of Moshe Rabbeinu? When we stood on Mount Sinai, we stood straight up.

I'll tell you something very deep. The Ba'al Shem Tov says the difference between bowing down before a human being and bowing down before G-d is very simple. To bow down before a human being, the smaller you get, the more you bow down.

The way to bow down before G-d is to make yourself as tall as you possibly can. The fact is, we only bow down to G-d one time on Rosh Hashanah and three times on Yom Kippur. How come? Because even bowing down before G-d is a heavy scene.

*

There are moments when I have a chance to become a master over somebody else. If you stood on Mount Sinai, then you know that only G-d is the master. If you didn't stand on Mount Sinai, you make them into a slave and keep them as a slave.

This can happen between parents and children . . . between husband and wife.

The worst thing in the world is when we play G-d over somebody else. What is politics? People playing G-d over a country. If they would have one billionth of one ounce of Mount Sinai, they would be afraid to do it.

When someone wages war, they are basically declaring that they don't give a damn that thousands of people are about to be killed. But you know something? Only G-d has a right to decide over life and death, nobody else.

When I was working for the Lubavitcher Rebbe, at one time I did something really bad, so he called me in and he had to scold me a little bit. But the way he told me I did something wrong was so gentle, so not enslaving. He didn't, G-d forbid, tell me straight to my face that I did something wrong. He simply hinted that I made a mistake in such a soft way. After he softly spoke to me, I said, "I'm so sorry, I know I did wrong. I hope I can fix it."

As I was walking out he said to me, "I want you to know, I'm heartbroken that I had to tell you, but in order for you not to be angry at me, I want to give you a gift." He took one of the books off his shelf and gave it to me.

Can you imagine?

So afraid of becoming a master over somebody because this is taking away from G-d.

The worst thing about our school system is that a good teacher is someone whose students are afraid of them. It's the worst of the worst, it's school idol worship. Those teachers clearly did not hear G-d's word on Mount Sinai.

RECEIVING FACE-TO-FACE

Based on Mei Hashiloach II, Parshas Mishpatim

WHAT ARE WE BUSY DOING IN THIS WORLD? What is every soul, sent down to this world, trying to accomplish? Everyone and everything is about fixing the sin of the Tree of Knowledge.

G-d says to Adam, "You are my guest here in paradise. You can eat from all the trees – just don't eat from the Tree of Knowledge." (Bereishis 3:1) When Adam ate from the Tree of Knowledge, it's not that he ate from the wrong tree, it was that he was, so to speak, stealing. And this is cutting right through to the deepest depths.

I want you to open your hearts to the deepest depths.

Adam and Eve stole, and after they stole, they began to hide. As a result of this hiding, we are reduced to being slaves in this world. When someone steals, they don't want anyone to see them. What's the difference between stealing and receiving a gift?

When I steal, I want to make sure that the owner doesn't see me. When I receive a gift, I look at the person who is giving it to me. When it comes to everything G-d gives you, are you looking at G-d? One of the greatest blessings in the world is to have the privilege to receive face-to-face from G-d.

Now let's go one step deeper. When we received the Torah, G-d says don't have *"elokim acherim"* – "other gods" before me. We usually translate *"elokim acherim"* as "other gods."

Can this just mean that G-d is telling me not to take a piece of wood and bow down to it? It can't be. I am standing on Mount Sinai, I know there is one G-d, so it's got to be deeper than that.

The Zohar HaKadosh says (Tikkunei Zohar 56b) that *"elokim acherim"* comes from the word *"achor,"* my back. When G-d gives you something, you will be receiving it from G-d's front.

When you steal – G-d lets you have it, but it's from his back. He turns his face away from you. When I give something to someone I hate, I throw it from my back. Do you know what G-d says? *"Lo yehiyeh lecha elokim acherim"* – "You will not have other gods," don't have a relationship with me where the receiving is from the *"achor,"* from the back. I want that everything between us should be face to face.

I remember my brother and I were once invited to eat by someone. During the meal, my brother gave me a little push under the table. He was hinting to me that our hosts' eyes were glued to our spoon. They were following the spoon with their eyes, and you could see them following the soup as it was going into our *kishkes.*

You know what their problem was? They didn't want us to come for dinner in the first place, they had to pretend they wanted us to come. How much energy did we receive from that food? Nothing, because it was not given whole-heartedly, it was thrown to us from the back.

So here comes an amazing Torah from the *Heilige Mei Hashiloach.*

A thief is someone who doesn't want to receive from G-d face to face. The deepest question is: Are you receiving from G-d while He is looking? Or do you not want G-d to look?

Heartbreaking. Do you know why it's so heartbreaking? Because when we take something behind G-d's back, it has no taste. You can do favors for someone like this as well. What happens to that favor? It's behind their back. They are doing it, but they are throwing it from behind their back.

Do you know what Mount Sinai is all about? *"Panim b'panim diber"* – "G-d speaks to us face to face." (*D'varim* 5:4)

Everyone has to know, I have something to fix in this lifetime. What is the Tree of Knowledge and what is the Tree of Life? The Tree of Knowledge is that I receive everything when G-d isn't looking. And because I don't receive the real essence of what I seek, I can only receive it, so to speak, from behind G-d's back.

Between people, whenever someone gives you something, are you receiving it face-to-face? Are you face-to-face with people?

If you are not face-to-face with people, it means you are not face-to-face with G-d.

We notice it all the time. You can walk over to a person and say good Shabbos, and they barely answer you. You know what that means? Their Shabbos is not face-to-face with G-d. They keep Shabbos, they eat *lokshen kugel,* but they didn't receive Shabbos from G-d's face.

Sometimes you see a Shabbos *Yid.* I'll never forget the first time I was with the Bobover Rebbe, the first Rebbe who came to the US from Europe after the war. When he walked in, the way he said "Good Shabbos" still gives me shivers. My brother and I said to each other that from this one "Good Shabbos" you could be a Jew your whole life.

Do you know why? Because he receives Shabbos from G-d's face.

NON-COMPLICATED

And on the seventh day he shall go free. (Sh'mos 21:2)

WHEN A PERSON IS HOLY, HE IS NOT COMPLICATED.

The more a person is unholy, the more it's complicated.

Some people are so complicated, so confused, but it's only the outside. On the inside they are connected to something so untouched. On the inside they are connected to *"u-bashvi'is"* – "the Seventh Day."

G-d promises you that even if you fall down to the lowest slavery, one day G-d will bless you with *"shvi'is"* – the Seventh. You will feel something inside of you that is so simple, so non-complicated. On Shabbos I don't work, on Shabbos I don't drive my car. On Shabbos something is shining into me which is so deep, so holy, so uncomplicated. It is something that is so simple, but not simply out of stupidity, it is simple because it's so good.

How is it that the lowest slave never gives up hope that one day he will be free? Where does this hope come from?

Here G-d says, *"Shesh shanim ya'avod"* – "for six days he will work," but *"u-bashivi'is,"* – "on the Seventh Day" he will taste freedom.

This is what you and I are waiting for, this is what the whole world is waiting for.

CROWN KNOWLEDGE

Everything that HaShem has spoken we will do and we will obey (Sh'mos 24:7)

THE TALMUD SAYS (SHABBOS 68A) THAT WHEN WE were on Mount Sinai, and we said *"Na'ase v'nishma,"* – "we will do and we will obey" (Sh'mos 24:7), angels came and placed crowns on our heads. What are these crowns all about?

I want you to know, "Mount Sinai" knowledge is not book knowledge. Mount Sinai knowledge is "crown" knowledge.

I could go to a psychiatrist and share everything that ever happened to me in order that the doctor gets to know me. But with someone you love, everything that happened to me is on the level of the crown.

How do you know if it's "crown" knowledge or "mind" knowledge? It's very simple. When it comes to crown knowledge, even after you know what you just learned about, it becomes such a deep mystery. After you know something based on mind knowledge, nothing happens, nothing grows.

Whom do you truly honor? You give honor to those who you know are so much more than you'll ever know about them. I can be a great scientist and know exactly how human beings are created. What can I do with that knowledge? I can explain it to someone else, but that's it.

Mind knowledge will not bring peace to the world. Crown knowledge is the knowledge that will bring peace to the world because I only hate based on what I think I know.

When we Jews left Egypt, we became free again. The world thinks freedom is a mind thing. The world understands freedom to mean you don't have to do anything that someone is telling you to do. For us, freedom is expressed by the crowns we adorn.

And this is what G-d told us when he took us out of Egypt, "I want you to be a kingdom of kings, of priests." (Sh'mos 19:6) A king wears a crown, a priest wears a crown.

It's time to bring the crown knowledge back into the world.

BE WHERE YOU ARE

Ascend to the mountain and be there. (Sh'mos 24:12)

MOST OF THE TIME WE ARE NOT WHERE WE are, we are somewhere else.

In the portion of the week, G-d says to Moshe Rabbeinu *"Alei elay haharah"* – "Come up to the mountain," *"Ve'h'yeh shom,"* – "and be there." (Sh'mos 24:12)

Without even getting involved in interpreting this passage, the words themselves are very special. Can you imagine what level Moshe Rabbeinu is on that G-d tells him to come up to Mount Sinai?

But you see how deep this is, it is possible to be on the level of Moshe Rabbeinu where G-d is teaching you for forty days and you can be somewhere else. So therefore, G-d says, *"Ve'h'yeh shom,"* make sure you are spiritually there while you are physically there.

And here I want you to know the deepest depths.

What is the sign of a good doctor? If the doctor says, "I know all about the human body, all about medicine, I can cure any sickness," I wouldn't trust this doctor. If the doctor says, "I'll be honest with you, I know very little, but I'm learning more and more every day," this is my doctor.

A teacher who says, "I know all about teaching, I know all about kids," this teacher knows absolutely nothing. I would be afraid to let this teacher get close to kids. If the teacher says, "I'm just beginning, I'm just beginning to find out what teaching is all about, what children are all about," this teacher has a chance.

When do I really learn something? Not while I know what I know, but at that very moment that I know that I don't know. When this happens, I really am on top of things. The moment that I know I don't know; I understand things so much deeper. Then, and only then, do I grow.

If a person walks around thinking, "I know something," he automatically becomes finite because he only knows as much as he estimates. But the moment I know that I don't know, I wish I would know, I'm really infinite because I am yearning to know more, I am in touch with the infinite.

You see what it is, when I have this tremendous yearning for something, I have everything.

What was the holiness of King David? His holiness was that he was really yearning so much, in the most unbelievable way. Why didn't King David build the Holy Temple? Had he have built it, in a certain way it would have minimized his holiness, because his holiness was that he always "wanted" to.

In a certain way, if he would have really built it, he would have stopped his holiness. He would have been as holy as he was, but the strangest thing is that the Holy Temple is called the House of David. *"Mizmor Shir Chanukas haBayis l'David."* (*Tehillim* 30:1)

David HaMelech says, "I cannot sleep at night because I want so much to go to the Holy Temple." The stones were put together by his son, but he was the one who really built it.

There are some people you meet and they have this kind of holiness. They so want to do it, they want *Mashiach* to come, they want the whole world to be one. They want to love you so much; they want to do something for you. Maybe they didn't do anything yet, but there is something very holy about them.

Then you meet somebody who has many achievements and accomplishments but there is something so obnoxious about them. You see, when *Mashiach* is coming – the wanting and the doing will go together.

When do you get a taste of this today? On Shabbos. What is so beautiful about Shabbos? We are not doing anything. On Shabbos no one can say, "I did this, I did that." The holiness of Shabbos is that you don't do anything, but what you are saying is, "I would love to do something. I would like to do anything for you."

Now listen to this. When G-d calls Moshe up to the mountain, He says come up to me "*Haharah*" – "to the mountain." The Ishbitzer says (*Mei Hashiloach* I, *Parshas Mishpatim*) that "*Haharah*" means "to come to the end of the mountain." G-d is saying to Moshe Rabbeinu, "Before you come up to Mount Sinai, before I can talk to you, you have to go to the end of the mountain.

You have to go through everything there is to know in the world. You have to know that you only get a taste of something when you truly know you don't have it, but *gevalt* do you want it." How do you get there?

Let me ask you, friends, did you ever honestly stop for one moment and ask yourself, What do I really know about G-d? I know he created the world, and I know he is still around today, but what do I know? Nothing.

What do I know about the holiness of Israel? I know they went through Egypt, I know they were on Mount Sinai. I know about the two temples; I know about the Six Million. I know we came back to Israel after two thousand years, but what do I really know?

What do I know about my own soul, what do I know about my own holiness? What do I know about the world? What do I know about birds, about trees, about flies? So I begin to slowly get into the whole thing. I've got to know more about it, but I still know that I don't know anything. It's a long process of not knowing.

So the Ishbitzer says like this: What is the most pure thing in the world? The purest thing in the world is life itself. Is there anything purer that flows down from G-d than life itself? Not diluted, not colored, not sand, not dust . . . *mamesh* life itself. The holiest, deepest, purest thing in the world is life. The question is, how much life do you receive?

But even more so, the moment life reaches you, what are you doing with it?

The way life is flowing into me is the purest thing in the world; the question is what am I doing with it? You can take the purest thing in the world and pour it into a garbage pail and after one second it smells bad.

So G-d says to Moshe, until you reach that level of going from mountain to mountain to mountain, life can't reach you. Only after that, can you truly be there, "*Ve'h'yeh shom*."

What does it mean to truly be there? It means to truly be alive.

You see friends, we are not really living yet. We are only half alive. How could it be that one minute we are good, one minute we are bad. One minute we are holy, one minute we are unholy. One minute we love, one minute we hate.

We never have a place of our own. We never stand firmly in place; we just limp around from one place to another. Falling, rolling, even flying . . . but not gaining anything real from the experience.

So G-d is telling Moshe Rabbeinu, G-d is telling us, you have to get to the level of reaching for life itself, before its purity can flow into you.

תרומה

T'RUMAH

תרומה

בצפייה לבניית בית המקדש השלישי
ולחידוש העבודה בו במהרה בימינו

Yearning for the building of the Third Temple and reviving the sacrifices within it quickly in our days

פרשת שבוע זו הוצאה לאור בעזרת תרומתו של

דוב בער (סקוט) רוזנברג

לכבוד פרשת בר המצווה שלו.

שכל התורות על ענייני התרומה והנתינה תהיינה
חקוקות בליבנו ובליבות עם ישראל כולו לעד.

Publishing of this *parsha* has been made possible by the donation of

DOV BER (SCOTT) ROSENBERG

in honor of his bar mitzvah *parsha*.

May the Teachings of donating and giving
be enshrined in our hearts
and the hearts of all of *Am Yisrael* forever.

MAKING SOMETHING SPECIAL

Let them take a portion for Me. (Sh'mos 25:2)

IN *PARSHAS T'RUMAH* WE READ THAT G-D TOLD Moshe to tell the children of Israel to give gifts to build the Holy Temple. This gift is called *T'rumah.*

T'rumah means a gift, but it has two more meanings. *T'rumah* comes from the word *"L'romem"* – "to elevate." *T'rumah* also comes from the word *"L'havdil"* – "to separate."

On a simple level it means that if I have ten dollars and I give five dollars for the Holy Temple . . . I separate this five dollars from the other five dollars. As simple as it is, when I am giving for a high purpose, it means I am making it high.

Imagine I am very wealthy, and everyone knows all about my riches. I give money here, I pay that insurance there. While paying my bills, I send my donation for the Holy Temple. How does this type of giving sound to you? I might be giving two million dollars for the Holy Temple on a weekly basis, but with this kind of money you can't build a Holy Temple.

You can build an apartment somewhere, but not a Holy Temple because when it comes to the *Beis Hamikdash* it has to be separate. You don't pay off a telephone bill and credit card, and while you're at it, give some money for the Holy Temple.

Let's go one step further. Separate does not only have to do when it comes to money for the Holy Temple. Everything you do for G-d has to be separate. If you do it in the same sentence as you are doing something else, forget it. Forget it, don't waste your time, don't waste G-d's time.

You see what it is, we are in G-d's hands, and also humanly speaking, G-d is in our hands. That which happens to me is in G-d's hands, but you know what is in my hands? To make G-d high or low . . . that is in my hands. I can make G-d so high or I can, G-d forbid, drag G-d down so low, so meaningless, so empty. I can make G-d so unimportant in my life.

There are a lot of people who believe in G-d, but the G-d they believe in is not special. There are those who stay in the Hilton in Istanbul, sometimes in the Hilton in Tel-Aviv, and when they come home it's the same thing. Then there are some people that when they open the door to their house it is always so special.

So the Ishbitzer says (*Mei Hashiloach* I, *Parshas T'rumah*), everything I do for G-d has to be separate. It cannot be the same as something else. Everything I am doing for G-d has to be so high, so special. The most beautiful thing about it is that it's up to me, it's my choice.

Now I want you to open your hearts even wider.

G-d cursed the snake that the snake should eat dust, so everybody is asking the question, what is so terrible about it? In the meantime, the snake is never hungry, the snake has no trouble being full. The snake has everything it needs.

Let me ask you, friends, what does it mean that the snake is eating dust? It means that everything tastes like dust. You can place the most delicious food before the snake – it also tastes like dust. Sadly enough, we have met a lot of snake people in our lives. Everything is nothing, everything is dust. Everything is a joke.

These are the snake people, these are the "Tree of Knowledge" people. Then there are the "Tree of Life" people. These are the non-snake people who don't eat dust, they know the difference between dust and a *Shabbosdika challah.* Not only do they have special moments, they become special people. A special person is somebody who has something special in their life. If you have something special in your life, everything has the chance of becoming something special.

You see, friends, G-d wanted us to build the Holy Temple, but isn't the whole world G-d's Holy Temple? It is, but it begins by building a holy little tabernacle, and from there it expands all over the world.

If I have five minutes and I choose to use those five minutes to learn, I made those five minutes special. Do you know what happens after that? Whatever I do with the rest of the time becomes so holy as well, so special.

The destruction of the Holy Temple means there is nothing special in life anymore, everything is the same. Going to the synagogue, going to the office, writing out a check . . . it's all the same. Playing baseball, playing with my children . . . sadly enough, it's all the same.

MAKING YOU AWARE OF THE LITTLE THINGS

WHAT'S THE DIFFERENCE BETWEEN A HOLY light and an unholy light?

Very simple. Imagine here I have psychedelic lights, the biggest lights in the world flashing like crazy. Then one person comes with a little flashlight. I say to him, "Are you crazy? I don't need it."

Friends, if the great light is really holy, when someone comes with a little light, it adds so much, because the great light makes you aware of the little things.

What is the difference between holy money and unholy money? Imagine if one millionaire gives two million dollars, and then Moishele the thief gives one quarter, I'll say "You're crazy, we already have two million dollars," because it's not holy. But if it's holy, you say, "Unbelievable! Your quarter is the most precious thing we ever got."

When King Solomon built the Holy Temple, he sent out messengers to collect money and jewelry for the Holy Temple. The messengers came back with gold and silver. But then King Solomon asked, "Where are the pennies of the poor?" So the messengers said, "When the poor people saw we are collecting gold and silver, they were ashamed to give their pennies."

So king Solomon says, "Let's make another collection, a collection only of pennies, only pennies." Everybody knows, three walls of the holy temple were built with the gold and the jewelry, but one wall was built with pennies. The Western Wall, the wall which cannot be destroyed was built with pennies.

On Rosh Hashanah it says *"U'b'shofar gadol yitaka"* – "When the great trumpet will be blown," *"v'kol d'mama daka yishama"* – "you will hear the voice of the most inside," which can't even be recorded (*Mussaf* High Holiday Prayers).

Listen to how deep this is.

I would say it's the other way around. When the great trumpet is blowing, there is so much noise, you can't hear anything. The real holy trumpet is when you hear the sound of the great trumpet, suddenly you become aware of the sounds of the deepest voice inside you.

You see, friends, if your heart is really holy, I'm sure you can receive the little pennies, the little voices that make us most aware of what is truly important in life.

BUILDING OF MISFITS

THERE IS A PASSAGE IN PSALMS – *"EVEN MA'ASU habonim ha-y'sa l'rosh pinah"* – "The stone which was cast away by the builders," the stone which was a misfit, "became the crown of the building." (*Tehillim* 118:22)

One of the rules of the building of the Holy Temple was that you couldn't cut. You couldn't cut stones, you couldn't cut anything.

Sometimes I wish I could teach parents how not to cut down their children. Children are so holy, they are little Holy Temples. They are little holy stones in the *Beis Hamikdash.* You can't build a Holy Temple with cut up stones.

If you ever stand by the Holy Wall, it's the strangest sight in the world. One stone is big, one stone is small. One had four corners, one has eight corners. But the great miracle is that they all fit together.

So when the people were building the *Beis Hamikdash,* they used uncut stones, and it all went very well. But there was one stone that was an absolute misfit, so the builders threw that stone away.

Then they started building the Holy of Holiest, and the Holy of Holiest had a little roof. There was an opening in the roof, a strange kind of opening, and there was no stone which fit that opening. Suddenly, the builders remembered the misfit, the stone which was cast away. It was the only stone that fit the opening, the only stone which could be the crown on the building.

King David asked why this was so, and answered, *"Me'eis HaShem ha-y'sa zos he nifla'as b'eineinu"* (*Tehillim* 118:23) – because it's G-d's world, because G-d is working wonders. Only a real misfit, only someone who has been cast away by the world, can be the crown of G-d's building.

All the young people of the world today, all the holy beggars, are also so-called misfits. But on the great day when *Mashiach* comes, they will be the crown of the world.

Believe me, the Messiah will not surround himself with anybody else — only with castaway stones. Only with those holy castaway stones. Do you know why? Because *"Me'eis HaShem ha-y'sa zos"* – it's G-d's world.

CLEANSING THE SUBCONSCIOUS

In the previous portion of *Mishpatim,* we learn that if someone's ox, G-d forbid, kills a person, the owner has to pay full compensation.

Now listen to what the Ishbitzer says (*Mei Hashiloach* I, *Parshas T'rumah*).

When I walk into somebody's house and the dog jumps on me, do you know what the dog is letting me know? "Let me tell you, don't go in here, they don't want you to come in, they don't love you. They might smile at you and tell you that they are so glad you came, but they don't mean it."

Animals don't pick up the consciousness of people, they pick up the subconscious of people. That means that if a person is unconsciously a murderer, his ox will go out and kill somebody. Imagine I'll walk in here and really hurt somebody – G-d forbid. Even if I say that I didn't mean to do it, consciously you didn't mean it, but obviously you are not in touch with your subconscious.

If your unconsciousness is completely clean, you couldn't possibly hurt anyone. Sometimes you hurt somebody's feelings and you say "I didn't mean it." It's a poor excuse, because if you would be completely cleansed inside, it simply wouldn't happen.

So here the Ishbitzer comes and says that after we *Yiddilech* heard that a person must cleanse himself and be in touch with the essence of his subconscious, we began to cry. We couldn't imagine reaching such a high level.

So this *parshah* begins with *"V'yikchuli T'rumah."* Do you know what cleanses out your subconscious? Every time you give something with all your heart on a conscious level, it cleanses your subconscious.

So the Ishbitzer says that the whole building of the *Beis Hamikdash* was not to cleanse our consciousness; you can do that through the Torah and mitzvahs. When it comes to the Holy Temple, *"V'shachanti B'socham,"* – "and I dwelled within them," – inside, inside, inside, it's all about the inside.

Sometimes you meet people and you really see where their subconscious is at. How do you know where people are at the subconscious level? If in their presence you feel more pure – their consciousness is also more pure.

One of the biggest Rebbes I have had the privilege of being in the presence of is the Holy Amshinover Rebbe. When he talks to a person, nobody exists but this person. The way he speaks to people is out of this world. I once brought a couple from America who had no children for fifteen years.

When I told the Rebbe that they have been married for fifteen years and don't have children yet, he got white like a sheep. The pain of this couple hurt him so much, he felt their pain in the deepest depths of his heart.

But you see what it is, his conscious-self is so much at peace in oneness with his subconscious, he is so in tune with the *Beis Hamikdash* in his heart.

ANI, ATAH, HU

REB TZADOK HAKOHEN BRINGS DOWN (*TZIDKAS HaTzaddik* 247) that there are three ways of referring to G-d's revelation in this world:

There is "*Ani,*" there is "*Atah,*" and there is "*Hu.*"

Sometimes G-d is revealed to me on the level of "*Ani,*" which is "I," sometimes on the level of "*Atah,*" which is "You," and sometimes on the level of "*Hu,*" which is "Him."

There is a passage that says: "*Ani HaShem hashochen itam b'soch tum'asam.*" G-d says, "I, G-d, am dwelling with them in the midst of their impurity." (Vayikra 16:16) It means that even if we get to the lowest place, the *Ribbono shel Olam* is there.

This revelation of G-d in the lowest place is called "*Ani.*" It's the kind of revelation that doesn't disturb you. Obviously, if you can sit there and steal and kill while you are somewhat aware of the presence of G-d – it's a low revelation.

Then there is another revelation, which is called "*Atah.*" When we pray we say *Baruch Atah HaShem.* This is when I'm talking to G-d and I *mamesh* know He's there. This is higher than "*Ani.*" It's not just that He is here, but that I can't ignore Him!

Then there is the level of "*Hu.*" When we say "*Baruch Hu u-Varuch Sh'mo*" or "*asher kid'shanu b'mitzvosav v'tzivanu,*" both of these are on the level of "*Hu.*" This is when I know He exists and that He is running the world, and yet the whole thing is absolutely beyond me.

So Reb Tzadok says that the Holiness of the Holy Land, of *Eretz Yisrael,* is on the level of *"Atah."* When it comes to the Holiness of Moshe Rabbeinu, Moshe Rabbeinu is on the level of *"Hu."* Moshe Rabbeinu was so much aware of G-d that he realized that he didn't know anything.

Then there was the *Beis Hamikdash.* What's the holiness of the *Beis Hamikdash*? It is when the *"Atah"* and the *"Hu"* meet together.

And here I want you to open your hearts in the deepest depths.

Everybody knows the *Beis Hamikdash* has two names. The *Beis Hamikdash* is called a *"Mishkan,"* and the *Beis Hamikdash* is called a *"Mikdash." Mishkan* means dwelling. The *Mishkan* is that kind of holiness which is on the level of *"Atah,"* when you *mamesh* see it.

The moment I do a mitzvah, I make a vessel for G-d. It's an indwelling, I am bringing G-d right in. I address G-d in the present, as if He is *mamesh* here, face-to-face. Therefore, the blessing I say when I'm doing a mitzvah starts off with *"Baruch Atah."*

But you know something? The holiness of a *Yiddele* is that it's not just the holiness of doing a mitzvah. There is a kind of holiness that is inside of me. I know it's there. I just can't put my finger on it. This is the level of *"Hu."*

And here I want you to know something so strong.

It's not that kind of holiness that I can say, "G-d is within me even if I do wrong," which is the level of *"Ani."* It's not *"Ani."* There is something so holy inside of me, absolutely untouched. You cannot address it face-to-face, it doesn't show anywhere, and yet it's there.

Every moment that you shine into your heart that there is *mamesh* one G-d, all the darkness is expelled from your heart. Every ounce of darkness that is inside of us is only because it's not completely filled with that knowledge that there really is one G-d.

Our knowledge of G-d is on the level of "*Ani.*" There are moments when we reach "*Atah.*" Rarely, very rarely, do we get to the "*Hu.*"

In the Temple, we connected to G-d in all three ways in on place at the same time. In the Temple, G-d's presence was real, immediate, and full of awe.

תצוה

TETZAVEH

תצוה

This *parsha* is dedicated to:

The brave *chevre* of
MOSHAV MEOR MODIIM
& their families

May the teachings of *Tetzave* give them the insight and the strength to ensure that the bright light of the Moshav continues to shine, as they rebuild their lives, their homes and their community.

פרשה זאת מוקדשת ל:

החבר'ה האמיצים ממושב מאור מודיעים ומשפחותיהם

שיקבלו תובנות וחיזוק מהתורות של פרשת תצוה להמשיך את האור החזק של המושב תוך כדי בנייה מחדש של חייהם, בתיהם וקהילתם הקדושים.

DEEPER THAN PROPHECY

Now you shall command. (Sh'mos 27:20)

AFTER THE GOLDEN CALF, G-D TELLS MOSHE HE will wipe out all the *Yidden,* so Moshe Rabbeinu said to G-d, "If you want to wipe out the *Yidden* from the world, *"mecheni na m'sifrecha"* – "wipe me out from your book as well." Therefore, everybody knows that Moshe Rabbeinu's name is not mentioned in this week's portion.

We usually read the portion of *Tetzaveh* before Purim. In the reading of the Megillah Scroll of Esther, G-d's name is not mentioned, but *gevalt* is G-d's name felt in every word of the Megillah. Here, too, in *Tetzaveh,* Moshe Rabbeinu's name is not mentioned, but *gevalt* is Moshe Rabbeinu felt in this portion.

And here I want you to open your hearts.

Someone once asked me if he should go to a certain function or not. I said to him, "You should only go to a place where if you don't go, they will feel the absence of your presence every second you are not there. But if it really wouldn't make a difference if you are there or not – don't go." Moshe's absence is felt in every passage of *Tetzaveh.*

When G-d says to Moshe, "I'm going to wipe out the Jews, and you will be the only one left," would you have the *chutzpah* to contradict G-d? How could Moshe have said what he said?

Moshe Rabbeinu did everything on the level of prophecy; he was always in tune.

Here Moshe Rabbeinu was connecting with the inside of the inside. His inside of all insides said, "I'm sorry to tell you *Ribbono shel Olam,* but I can't be without *Yidden,* so if you wipe out the *Yidden,* you have to wipe me out, too." What level did Moshe Rabbeinu reach at that moment? Moshe Rabbeinu reached a level that is even deeper than prophecy.

So here G-d says to Moshe, "I'm not putting your name in this *parsha,* not because I am angry with you, but because you have tuned into the deepest secrets of the world. And since this is where you are – '*Ve'ata tetzaveh es b'nei Yisrael,*' I want you to tell your brother Aharon to kindle the light in the Holy Temple."

What kind of light was it?

Let me ask you, what kind of a light do we have to shine into the world? I have to shine a light of "*mecheni na,*" a light that is deeper than whatever the world is accustomed to.

This is the light of the Holy Temple. This is the light of Purim. This is the light of love between all *Yidden.*

OIL

They shall take for you pure olive oil. (Sh'mos 27:20)

OIL IS A SYMBOL OF JOY, A DEEP KIND OF PLEASURE.

One of the things we must refrain from during mourning is called "*sichah*" which is the use of oil for physical needs, which can bring one to *simcha,* to happiness.

Impure pleasure means that after I am finished doing something, I don't want to do it again. By the next day, I forget about it. I am consumed by that little flame of pleasure while I am doing it, but I don't want to do it again.

G-d gave us a very strong nose. Our soul is a strong nose. We know exactly what is right and what is wrong. After we do something wrong, deep down we don't want to do it again. It's only that the next day we forget that we promised not to do it again.

Holy oil means that while I am doing it, I am already kindling another light. I already want to do it again.

*

Our Sages teach us that oil is good for memory. What kind of memory are we talking about? Does it matter if I remember that George Washington was the first president of the United States? We are obviously talking about something else. When the Torah says, "Remember the Sabbath and keep it holy," (Sh'mos 20:8) this is a different kind of remembering.

What does it mean to remember someone I love? At the moment when

I remember them, everything else is forgotten. To remember somebody you love means that everything in the world reminds you of them.

How does a Jew remember Shabbos? Everything reminds him of Shabbos. I can stand in California, looking at the sky, and it reminds me of the holy city, *Yerushalayim*.

Whenever G-d blesses us with children, memory is mentioned. It says, "And G-d remembered Sarah." "And G-d remembered Rachel."

Children come from that high place which is called G-d's memory. To love children means that everything reminds you of them. What does it mean when children remember you? It means that everything reminds them of you.

WISDOM OF THE HEART

And you shall speak to all the wise-hearted people. (Sh'mos 28:3)

WHEN G-D SPEAKS TO MOSHE AND ASKS FOR the garments of the priests to be prepared, he calls for those who have "*chochmas halev*" – "wisdom of the heart." What is this wisdom that is in the heart? What's the difference between that and the wisdom of the mind?

There is a fire burning in the heart of each and every one of us. This fire is so infinitely passionate; it wants to know G-d in an infinite way.

If you come to somebody and say "Would you like to know G-d in an infinite way?" they are ready. If you ask them, "Would you like to know G-d in a finite way and start by putting on *tefillin* every morning?" they are not ready because our hearts yearn for the infinite.

There is wisdom of the mind and there is wisdom of the heart. As important as the wisdom of the mind is, you cannot know G-d with the wisdom of the mind alone. You have to know G-d with the wisdom of your heart. It is through all the emotions that G-d created in my heart that I should know that there is one G-d. But what is the wisdom of the heart?

As much as I'd like to know G-d in an infinite way, you have to realize one thing. You are living in this world and you will not know G-d unless you do the finite things as well. G-d promises you, in this finite thing I'll pour in the infinite. This is the vessel.

Here I want you to know the deepest depths.

Before G-d created the world, everything was infinite. In order for G-d to reveal his kingdom, G-d had, so to speak, to contract his infinity. When He created the world, He put aside all the great lights and left an empty space, and in that empty space He created the world.

What is this "empty space" all about?

There is a very strong passage in the psalms. King David says, *"v'libi chalal b'kirbi"* – "I made a little hole in my heart." (*Tehillim* 109:22) What does this mean? The same way G-d made space in His heart for me, I have to make space for G-d, to understand Him in my heart.

When I make a little space, G-d can shine my emotions into me, and then I begin to know how to serve Him. When I think evil thoughts, my heart closes up and I cannot use the same heart to understand G-d.

Therefore, Reb Nachman says something very deep. The moment you think you want to serve G-d, make a little space in your heart, and G-d can reveal Himself to you there.

So Reb Nachman says that the space I create in my heart means that for one minute I, so to speak, stop being infinite. Just like G-d did with the creation of the world. You see, everybody wants to know G-d in an infinite way alone, but you can't. You have to make yourself finite by creating a little space inside of your heart.

In that place is where G-d is really living. And this is the secret of creating the world. This is the secret of serving G-d more and more and more. This is the wisdom of the heart.

You see what it is, when you love somebody very much, you are ready to do the smallest finite favors for them with all your heart and soul. How come? Because if you are really with it, you understand that the finite is also infinite.

The same goes for prayer. When I pray it has to be in a completely infinite way, and yet it has to be finite. What's the holiness of a siddur? It's the most finite thing in the world. The words we pray were composed two thousand years ago. But the way I'm praying has to be in an infinite way.

You see what it is? As much as I'd like to know G-d in an infinite way, you have to realize you will not know G-d unless you do the finite things as well. Then G-d promises you; I will pour the infinite into the finite vessel you just created.

So Reb Nachman says this is what the wisdom of the heart is all about. Since my heart is the place where I fathom G-d the most, it must be infinite. If it wasn't infinite, how could G-d be there? But since I'm living in the world, G-d gave me finite vessels to understand His infinity. I connect my finite vessels with my infinite emotions through the wisdom of my heart.

כי תשא

KI SISA

כי תשא

This *parsha* is dedicated to:

MOSHE AHARON ben YEHUDA LEIB

In honor of his *parshas* Ki Sisa bar mitzvah anniversary. May he continue to be blessed with length of days, Torah, *mitzvot, maasim tovim* and *nachas* from the *kinderlach*.

פרשה זו מוקדשת ל:

משה אהרן בן יהודה לייב

לציון הבר מצווה שלו בפרשת כי תשא.
באיחול לשנים רבות של שובע, תורה,
מצוות ומעשים טובים – וכמובן
הרבה נחת מכל צאצאיו.

HALF SHEKEL

This shall they give – everyone who passes through the census – a half of the sacred shekel. (Sh'mos 30:13)

CONNECTING TO WHAT'S ALREADY THERE.

In the time of the Holy Temple, each person had to donate a *machatzis hashekel* – half a shekel. So everyone is asking, why only half?

Imagine I would have to create light. It would be a very heavy thing, but if the light is there and all I have to do is to connect it, it means I only have to do half. Something is already there, all I have to do is to plug it in.

Now listen to the deepest depths. Haman came to Achashverosh and said, "I'm giving you 10,000 shekels to wipe out the Jews." The *Medrash* says that G-d says to the *Yidden,* "You give half a shekel and I'll wipe out all the shekels of Haman."

You know what that means? Evil comes to you and says, "You can't bring any light into the world with half a shekel. You have to create the whole thing on your own, which is not simple at all. Don't kid yourself, you won't make it in your lifetime." So here I come and I say, "The world is filled with light. All I have to do is to connect to it, it's right here."

I want you to know, it's also so true between people. If I have to create love and the other person has to create love, it's very heavy, and we probably won't make it. The world filled us with love. All you need is this half a shekel, this little connection, this little bit of plugging-in.

Do you know what happened to us on Purim? *LaYehudim hayesa orah v'simcha v'sason v'yikar* – "The Jews had precious light, happiness and joy." (Esther 8:16).

On Purim we realized the whole world is filled with light. Every little good thing you are doing connects you to the highest light there is. Some people think I have to work like a dog and cut myself into pieces for two thousand years until I smell or feel a little bit of light.

The light is right here, you just have to connect.

HOLY BROKENNESS

G-D IS EVERYWHERE. SOMETIMES IT LOOKS LIKE He's nowhere. When you really understand something, it's clear to you that you don't understand it at all.

When are you really close to somebody? When you realize how far away you really are. When you love somebody very much, your heart is so full and yet it's so heart-breaking. When you are really happy, when you are smiling, you have tears in your eyes.

And if you are really crying, you are also laughing in the inside. When you love your children, your heart grows so large, but in the same moment it is also heart-breaking. When you stand by the Holy Wall, your heart becomes whole and also begins to crack open.

Take a husband and wife who really love each other. They make each other whole and they break each other's hearts. Not in a sad way, but in a deep way.

You know why the Holy Temple was destroyed? Because the Holy Temple only made us whole, it stopped breaking our hearts. There was no other way. So G-d says, "If your heart is not broken with joy, I'm sorry, I'll have to break it with something else."

You know why we Jewish people follow a lunar calendar? The sun is beautiful, but the sun is always whole. The real light is the moon. The moon's light is full and also broken.

The Talmud, the book of all books, begins with page two. Page one is a blank piece of paper. It's a broken page. Nothing is written on it. When you learn with the deepest depths of your heart and soul, you kiss the blank paper.

You see, the world wants peace that makes them whole. They don't want that kind of peace that breaks each other's hearts.

So once a year there was a collection for the sacrifices of the Holy Temple. Everybody was giving a half a shekel, a broken shekel. And this is how we kept the Holy Temple going. You know what we are telling each other? It breaks my heart to be a Jew.

It breaks my heart to be able to buy something for the Holy Temple.

GOLDEN CALF

Do I Believe in G-d?

I WANT YOU TO KNOW SOMETHING VERY DEEP. THE Golden Calf was not so simple, not that I am telling you stories to justify, I am just telling you what happened.

Before Moshe Rabbeinu went up to Mount Sinai, he told the Jewish people, "I'll be back on the fortieth day." Everyone knows we got confused with the timing. We didn't know if he meant forty days after, or including the the day we received the Torah.

Now listen to this. The first day the Brooklyn Bridge was built, thousands of people wanted to see the bridge so everyone started going onto it. Suddenly one person starts yelling that the bridge is falling in.

Only one person yelled and people started jumping off the bridge. Twelve people were killed and many were injured, and it was all because one person had yelled. (Note: The bridge opened on May 24, 1883, but the incident happened six days later, on May 30th. According to the New York Times, "a woman tripped on the bridge and screamed. Other pedestrians, terrified that something was wrong with the bridge, stampeded.")

So you see what it is, everyone was waiting for Moshe to come down and keep his promise, and he wasn't coming down. One person got up and said, "He will never come back because he went up to heaven and that's it."

You have to realize that a lot of people came out with us from Egypt who weren't part of our nation. When Moshe Rabbeinu proclaimed freedom to the world, any slave in Egypt who had a sense that they wanted to be free walked out with us, but they weren't really ready for it yet.

They might have not wanted to be a slave, but not wanting to be a slave doesn't mean you are ready for freedom. It takes a lot more than that. Once they saw Moshe wasn't coming down, these people started saying, "We have different ways, if this doesn't work, we'll just go back to our idols."

The question is why did G-d test them like this? Why didn't G-d make the timing clearer?

Here I want to share with you the deepest depths.

Do we believe in G-d because it works? Are we believers because someone who is a representative of G-d is keeping his promise?

If this is where I'm at, then I'm not even on the road yet. With all due holiness and respect to Moshe Rabbeinu, is my link to G-d broken if I see that he is not coming down from the mountain?

You see what it is, whoever says their religion works is simply involved in pagan worship. A religion that works is paganism; it means that I am utilizing G-d in my religion to do something with it.

Our religion doesn't work, maybe it does, maybe it doesn't.

My worship doesn't depend on whether it works or not. My serving G-d has nothing to do with whether I'm going to hell or heaven. If I would hear a voice from heaven that all pagans are going to heaven and all Jews are going to hell, I would still be a Jew.

Ultimately the Golden Calf is all about me needing something that works. If I need something of G-d that works, then G-d becomes the Golden Calf. Don't kid yourselves, friends, it doesn't last.

And here I want you to open your hearts. When I pray and G-d answers, there is a little sense of pagan worship there. The test is if you pray to G-d and He doesn't answer.

When did Moshe Rabbeinu teach us about prayer? Moshe Rabbeinu prayed to G-d many times to go into the Holy Land; it was one of the most powerful big prayers any man has ever prayed. And G-d says no. When Moshe Rabbeinu teaches *Yiddelach* how to pray, he says, "Look at me. I was praying to enter the holy land and G-d didn't answer, but even after G-d said that I won't go in, I still kept praying."

You have to pray. If G-d doesn't answer, it's between G-d and G-d. Moshe Rabbeinu is the one who teaches us that praying has nothing to do with being answered. The pagans of the world will always come and try to disprove the oneness of G-d by showing that it simply doesn't work.

The holy Rizhiner says something unbelievable. The holy Rizhiner says that before *Mashiach* comes, the whole world will be pagans, but there will still be some people who do not worship idols.

Then, finally, the whole world will meet somewhere, they will bring fire down from heaven, but we *Yiddelach* won't, do you know why? Because the ultimate test is: are you worshiping G-d because it works, or are you really worshiping G-d because you know there is one G-d? This means that there is nothing in the world that can take away my belief in G-d.

To believe in G-d means that I don't see anything and I have nothing to hold onto, nothing.

So therefore, on Succos, we say, *"Hosha na shalosh shaot hosha na,"* – "Please, G-d, help me for three hours." The Rizhiner says that everyone has to go through three hours. I don't know how long those three hours are, but this is ultimate test when even G-d doesn't work and everything is falling apart . . . everyone has to go through these three hours.

The Rizhiner says that during those three hours it will be so hard to believe in G-d, it will literally be like walking up a wall. How can you walk up a wall? There is nothing to hold onto; that's how hard it will be.

This was one of the last things the Rizhiner said before he passed away. So someone asked him, "Why are you telling us all this?" So the Rizhiner said, "I want you to tell your children, grandchildren, and great-grandchildren . . . please tell them I said so. Tell them to please hold onto each other."

How do you walk up a wall? You have to stand one person on top of the other, you have to get together because you can't climb it alone.

WHY

EVERYONE WANTS TO KNOW, WHY DID WE MAKE A Golden Calf?

We didn't want G-d; we wanted a god. It didn't really matter to us who, as long as we had something.

There is a classic story that happened many years ago in Hungary.

A man was engaged to a younger daughter in a certain family, but then, like Lavan, the father of our holy mothers Leah and Rachel, the same story happened. The father of the bride couldn't accept that the younger daughter is marrying before the older daughter, so he decided to put the veil over the older daughter. And so it ended up that the older daughter was under the *chuppah,* marrying this groom.

After the *chuppah,* they wrote to all the great rabbis to ask if their marriage was valid. You know what happened? The rabbis needed some information. They wanted to know how the groom felt about the switch. They wrote him and asked him, "Aren't you upset? Look what your father-in-law did to you!" But the response was, "Okay, she's also a woman, who cares."

He just wanted to marry a woman, he didn't really care which one.

*

When we made the Golden Calf, what is it that we were really saying?

We don't need Moshe Rabbeinu anymore, we can make a Golden Calf instead.

If someone, G-d forbid, says to his wife, "You are not working for me, I can get another woman that works for me," this is the Golden Calf.

But you know something so deep, a husband can get another wife, a wife can get another husband, but a father can never get himself other children.

A LEADER'S REFUSAL TO BELIEVE

HaShem spoke to Moshe, "Go descend – for your people that you brought up from the Land of Egypt have become corrupt." (Sh'mos 32:7)

EVERYONE KNOWS, THE DOWNFALL OF THE world began with *lashon hara* gossip and slander. The snake began speaking *lashon hara,* which led Chava to eat from the Tree of Knowledge. Until the great day comes, fixing this situation is what we need to work on.

I want you to know the deepest depths. G-d says to Moshe Rabbeinu, "*Lech red ki shiches amcha*" – "Go down because your people made a Golden Calf." (Sh'mos 32:7)

You know what Moshe Rabbeinu said? "*Im ayin m'chaynee nah m'sifr'cha*" – "If you don't forgive them, wipe me out from Your book." Do you know what he was really saying? "*Ribbono shel Olam,* if you want me to believe that Your *Yiddelach* made a Golden Calf, You have to take me out from Your book, too, because I'll stop believing in You." (Sh'mos 32:32)

You know what Moshe Rabbeinu did when he came down? G-d really showed to him that they really didn't do it. They did on the outside, but not on the inside. The greatest thing in the world is not only to be forgiven, but when G-d shows us that on the inside, we never did wrong at all.

THE BREAKING

He threw down the tablets from his hands. (Sh'mos 32:19)

REB NACHMAN TEACHES THAT THERE ARE TWO *nekudos*, there are two points in a person's life (*Likutei Moharan* 6:1). A *Nekudah Elyonah* and *Nekudah Tachtonah*, a high point and a low point. A *nekudah* is something that is the essence of everything.

If my high *nekudah* is shining into my low *nekudah*, everything I do is connected to the deepest depths of my soul. When my two points are connected – I know exactly what I am doing in this world. When these two points are, G-d forbid, disconnected, I'm in exile.

Each and every one of us has something very special which we have to do in this world. This special something is so deep and concealed, that it cannot be written down in a book. It can only be learned through crying for it. The question is, when I do everything the Torah says I should, am I doing what my soul is really here for?

Now imagine that the Torah was given to me on such a level, where I take the book, I understand everything it says, and I can't ever forget it. How precious would it be? Imagine not having even one shadow of a doubt in my head that there is one G-d.

If everything we learned would be so clear to us, we wouldn't feel the need to cry our eyes out, talking to G-d, asking him what it is we are supposed to be doing here. The beautiful thing about learning is that it's not clear. But the lack of clarity's purpose is to bring you to cry out to the Master of the World to have compassion on us.

So listen to the deepest depths. By breaking the tablets, Moshe Rabbeinu brought something down to the world that is much deeper than clarity. Moshe Rabbeinu realized one thing. If I want the *Yidden* to really know the Ten Commandments – I have to break the Ten Commandments, and by breaking the Ten Commandments I make them cry for it.

T'SHUVAH OF THE SOUL

WHAT IS THE DEEPEST LEVEL OF *T'SHUVAH*?

T'shuvah on the outside means I didn't keep Shabbos and now I will start keeping Shabbos. In the deepest depths, it's something else. The deepest level of *t'shuvah* is when my soul itself is doing *t'shuvah*. You can do *t'shuvah* for what you did with your life, or you can do *t'shuvah* for what you do with your soul.

Imagine if you love somebody very much and you have a fight. You can be sad that someone hurt your feelings and you are heartbroken over it, but there is something much deeper to be sad about. The question is, what happened to this great love between us?

Can you imagine how much we cried when Moshe Rabbeinu broke the tablets? We weren't crying over broken tablets, we were crying over the distance we suddenly felt from G-d.

I want you to know something very deep. When Moshe Rabbeinu came down from the mountain and saw what he saw, he couldn't believe it. It's not that he couldn't believe we could worship the Golden Calf; he couldn't believe that the great love between G-d and his people could be so broken.

"How can you even dream of serving G-d when you bow down to idols?"

MORE THAN KNOWING

THE ISHBITZER SAYS THE DEEPEST TORAH.

Anything you think you have, you already lost. If I think I'm *frum*, if I think I know the Torah, at that moment I already lost it. When we stood at the foot of Mount Sinai, sadly enough, we thought we knew everything.

Our sages teach us that before we made the Golden Calf, we really didn't forget anything. But it takes more than just remembering. What did Moshe Rabbeinu do when he broke the tablets? He put in our hearts that in order to know the Torah, you have to be a little bit broken-hearted.

You see, a *Yid* who is *mamesh* a big "*lamdan,*" not only does he know how to learn *Tosafos,* but every *Tosafos* breaks his heart. Every Rambam breaks his heart. It stops becoming a matter of knowing or not.

Today, *Baruch HaShem,* we have a lot of broken hearts. Especially after the Second World War, when we lost all the real "*gedolim.*" So right now is a good time to learn.

KNOWING WHAT'S ON THE INSIDE

IMAGINE THERE IS A BOX I'VE BEEN CARRYING around and I don't know what's inside. You know what happens when it breaks? Everything inside starts flowing out.

When Moshe Rabbeinu broke the tablets, the inside, the deepest depths of what the Torah is, the beauty of G-d's dreams for the world, began flowing out.

If someone were to ask who knows more about the Be*is Hamikdash* – we who are in exile or the people who lived before the *Beis Hamikdash* was destroyed?

Obviously, we know more because if they knew what we know, the Holy Temple would have not been destroyed. They saw a building that was holy, they saw a priest who walking around serving G-d. Even if they felt very high, they obviously didn't know what it's all about.

Moshe Rabbeinu realized that we stood on Mount Sinai and everything was clear to us, yet we were capable of making a Golden Calf. He knew that the only way we would be in tune with the depths of the Torah is only once it broke open.

How does a *Yiddele* know what the *Beis Hamikdash* is all about? Only because it's destroyed and broken open. *Gevalt,* do we know what the *Beis Hamikdash* is all about!

WIPE ME OUT

And now if You would but forgive their sin – but if not, erase me now from Your book that You have written. (Sh'mos 32:32)

CAN YOU IMAGINE THE LEVEL MOSHE RABBEINU reached when he came down from Mount Sinai? As high as he was, he climbed even higher.

When he said "*mecheni na misifrecha*" – "erase me from your book" – he was even higher. *Mecheini na mesifrecha* is not a cute little gesture.

Do you know what Moshe Rabbeinu taught us with these words? When he came down from mount Sinai he was only able to teach us that you have to keep Shabbos, put on *tefillin* and light Shabbos candles on time.

When Moshe Rabbeinu broke the tablets, he taught us that the Torah without *Yidden* is not a Torah.

*

What is the basic difference between Noach and Avraham?

Noach knew the whole Torah, but Noach did not believe that the Torah has the power to change people. If you keep Shabbos your whole life, you will be fine. If you ever started to be a sinner, there is no hope for you.

Why is the Torah given to the children of Avraham? Because Avraham believed that with Torah you can change people.

When it comes to the evil people of S'dom, Avraham Avinu says, "Give me fifty *tzaddikim* –righteous people – and I'm moving into S'dom and opening a yeshiva. In a few years you will have a *Heilige* Ba'al Shem Tov running around."

I want you to know something so special.

Why did the angel come to tell Avraham that S'dom will be destroyed, and at the same time he tells him you will have a son Yitzchak?

Because this was the whole thing. G-d says "I cannot trust you with Jewish children unless you believe that the Torah is stronger than the whole world." I can teach my children that the only way to be a Jew is to keep away from the world, because G-d forbid if you get involved with the world – you can't turn back." But I can teach my child that "*Gevalt*, the Torah is so holy, the Torah can change the whole world, I have dynamite in my pockets."

After the Golden Calf, G-d says to Moshe, "I have to wipe out the *Yidden* because they are worshipping idols." Moshe Rabbeinu says, "What kind of a Torah did you give me? Did you give me a Torah that can't change idol worshippers?

Do you mean to say the Torah is only good for someone who does good his whole life? You make a mistake and you are out? It's not a Torah I'm interested in, *m'chaynee nah m'sif-r'cha asher kasavta*. Please give me a Torah which can take a *Yid* who is worshipping idols and can still change."

I don't want to say anything bad – what's a little bit wrong with our *Yidden?* They are a little bit *B'nei Noach*. They look at a *Yid* who doesn't yet keep Shabbos and they don't believe that one awesome Shabbos can change him. They don't believe that one Torah of the *Heilige* Ishbitzer can turn over your *kishkes*.

One time I was going to play for the Israeli soldiers up in Lebanon, holy soldiers who are ready to die for Israel a thousand times.

I asked a chaplain, "Are you teaching them anything?" He says, "Most of them are not religious. They are not really interested."

I walked up to one non-religious soldier, you could swear he eats on Yom Kippur. He m*amesh* looked so rough, he looked so far from everything holy and real. I asked him, "Do you want to maybe learn something?" He says, "Why not, I have nothing else to do today." I took out *Oros Hakodesh* of Rav Kook. I want you to know, his tears were flowing from heaven, he was *mamesh* so touched.

*

The Kuzimer says something out of this world.

When Moshe Rabbeinu broke the tablets, what was he really saying? "Master of the World, do you want me to be the only *frum* religious Jew in the world, do you want me to be the only *tzaddik* – righteous person? I refuse. I want to be together with all the *Yidden*. If they do wrong, I want to do wrong along with them."

Imagine if all of us would learn this Torah, how much we would love each other.

So in the *Sh'monei Esrei* we say, "*Vesim chelkinu imahem le'olam velo neivosh*" – "And put our destiny together with theirs [all of Israel] and we will never be ashamed." *Ribbono shel Olam*, let me be together with all the *Yidden*. If they are holy – I want to be holy. If they are not so holy – I don't mind being not so holy. Do you know why? Because the holiest thing in the world is to be together with *Yidden* . . . there is nothing holier in the world.

Feeling the Pain.

Rav Kook says there were two highlights in Moshe Rabbeinu's life: One was when he brought the Torah down from Mount Sinai, and the other was after the Golden Calf, when he says, "If you don't forgive your people, wipe me out of your book."

The Zohar HaKadosh says that all the Rebbes in every generation have a little bit of Moshe Rabbeinu, and here Rav Kook says a *gevalt* Torah.

All of them are part of Moshe Rabbeinu's first highlight, coming down from Mount Sinai and teaching Torah, but not everyone is part of the second highlight, the part of Moshe Rabbeinu saying, *"m'chaynee nah m'sif-r'cha."* Only a few special people are connected to it.

We see *"gedolim"* – "Torah giants" – who are so much into the Torah, but not so much into *Yidden.* They are still connected to Moshe Rabbeinu, but only to one part of him.

There are very few leaders who can *mamesh* bring the Torah from Mount Sinai and are also willing to say *"mecheni ne misifrecha,"* – "wipe me out of your book," if you don't take care of every Jew.

AYEH

Make your ways known to me. (Sh'mos 33:13)

ACCORDING TO OUR HOLY TRADITION, IF WE hadn't made the Golden Calf we would have never had the tabernacle. That means that in a certain way, we brought G-d's holiness closer to the world through the Golden Calf.

It was only after the Golden Calf that we started asking, "Where are you, G-d?" The question is, why did we only start asking then?

Open your hearts. As much as G-d has been hidden since the creation of the world, it doesn't compare to the way He will be hidden before the Messiah comes. Before the Messiah comes, the hiddenness will be very strong.

The world will be filled with great intellectuals; people will give speeches and print books in all the languages of the world. They will fill the world with, so to speak, "conscious knowledge," but woe to them! Woe to their souls! A little boy who believes in G-d knows more than all of them.

If they would at least speak the lie in the name of lies it wouldn't be so bad, but they will speak their lie in the name of truth.

At that point, the only thing you can ask is, *"Ayeh M'kom K'vodo,"* Master of the World, "where is the place of Your honor?" Once you ask where He is, you will find that He is everywhere.

You see what it is, G-d revealed Himself to us in the desert, because in the desert you don't know where to go, you don't know where you came from. You don't know where your place is, and you don't know where G-d's place is – it is completely placeless.

In the desert you begin asking where G-d is. Once you realize you have absolutely no place in the world, then you really start asking G-d where He is. And only then does G-d talk to you.

Before the great day, seeking G-d's place will be so strong that He, so to speak, will have no choice but to build the Holy Temple – may it happen soon in our day.

AFTER THE GOLDEN CALF

SOMEONE ONCE ASKED THE S'FAS EMES, "WHO DO you consider to be a real Jew?" So he says like this: "I'll tell you something; I saw a real Jew – the Kotzker Rebbe."

The S'fas Emes was only seven years old when his grandfather took him to Kotzk. From all the Rebbes, the Kotzker Rebbe had the poorest followers because his *chassidim* were completely out of this world.

As an example, someone once told the Kotzker that a rich man is coming and he wants to contribute some money for the *chassidim* , so that they should have something to eat. Everyone thought the Kotzker Rebbe would be so happy for this. "Money?!!!" the Kotzker screamed and spat to the ground. For years later, when someone said the word "money," this *chassid* who told the Kotzker Rebbe about this rich man had to vomit. Money had become so ugly to him.

So the S'fas Emes says, "I was there in Kotzk one Friday afternoon. Suddenly there was a big tumult and the *Rebbetsin* the Rabbi's wife began crying. She said, "I already bought everything for Shabbos and a thief came and stole everything out from the house."

So one of the *chassidim* says to the Rebbetsin, "Holy Rebbetsin, don't be angry with me, but you don't lock any doors and you don't close any windows. You leave everything open. No wonder everybody is stealing everything here."

The Kotzker overheard this and said. "What do you mean? How can anyone steal? G-d says don't steal." So the S'fas Emes says, "It suddenly hit me so strong; I realized that when you hear G-d saying, "You know that you simply can't steal," it's not that you shouldn't, it's that you *mamesh* can't."

So the S'fas Emes says that a real Jew is for whom G-d's word is not a piece of advice. When G-d says you can't do something, you can't.

I want you to know the deepest depths. Do you know what the downfall of the Golden Calf is all about?

G-d's word started sounding different to us. Before the Golden Calf we heard G-d saying, "Don't steal," and it was not that we felt we shouldn't steal, we simply couldn't. After the Golden Calf, sadly enough, we fell and G-d's word reaches us on the level of "You shouldn't."

RECEIVING

THERE ARE TWO MAIN FUNCTIONS IN THE world, giving and receiving. There is such a thing as doing something, taking action and making light shine in the world. And then there is something else – to receive light.

"Moshe kibel Torah m'Sinai" – "Moshe received the Torah at Sinai." (Mishnah *Avos* 1:1) Moshe is the one who literally received the Torah completely. Why was Moshe Rabbeinu chosen to go up to Mount Sinai? Because the most important thing is knowing how to receive. *Gevalt,* do you have to empty out your insides to have room to receive.

When it comes to actively doing something, you have to believe in yourself that you can do it. I was once in a car with a driver who didn't have one ounce of self-confidence. It was so dangerous. He didn't know when to step on the brakes or when to step on the gas. No self-confidence.

On the one hand I have to know that I am something, that I am doing something in the world. However, when it comes to receiving, I have to completely annihilate myself. The more I annihilate myself, the more I can receive.

There are so many conversations where people just don't hear each other. Why didn't you listen? Because you are so involved in being yourself that you misunderstood the other person. What makes someone a good listener? A person who can stop being himself for five minutes. Forget about yourself; someone is talking to you. Listen to that person. Receive from them.

Why is it that most parents never hear their own children? Because they are so busy telling them what to do or what not to do. I've met a few rabbis who might be good teachers, but they are only good for giving, not for receiving. They never know what their students are really asking because they are so busy teaching.

Most people don't need advice, they just need someone to listen to them. When someone says, "I need your advice," most of the time they mean "Have *rachmanus*, have compassion, listen to me a little bit." We need good ears: "*Sh'ma Yisrael*." A *Yiddele* doesn't have to say so much, but he definitely has to be a good listener.

The greatest secret in life is being absolutely balanced. Having self-confidence, knowing what you are doing in this world is awesome, and on the other hand, be willing to completely annihilate myself. "I just want to hear what you have to say; I'm not even thinking about what I want to tell you."

After we made the Golden Calf it was clear to us that we did not receive the Torah in the right way. G-d's word didn't get into our bones one hundred percent. There was still something left inside which didn't hear there was one G-d.

Sometimes you think you are *mamesh* a Jew. You are a servant of G-d, you believe in G-d, and then something happens to you and you realize maybe it wasn't true.

There is a very deep Ramban. When it comes to all the trials and tests G-d is giving us, the Ramban asks, why is G-d testing us? Is G-d a schoolteacher who wants to test us?

The tests are there to give me a taste of where I am standing.

Imagine I'm keeping Shabbos my whole life. One Friday night, at two in the morning, I see two million dollars in cash lying on the street. Do you know what I could do with two million dollars? When nobody was looking, I said to myself, "Who cares, G-d understands," and I picked up the two million dollars.

What does that mean? That means I kept Shabbos my whole life on the outside. On the inside, Shabbos hasn't reached my heart because if I was a real *Shabbosdik* person I'd understand that this whole incident was G-d saying to me, "Hey brother, let's see how *Shabbosdik* you really are."

Now listen to the other side. Again, here there are two million dollars on the floor. I could use all this money for G-d. Do you know what it means to walk away from the two million dollars now?

But now listen to the deepest depths. Do you know how *Shabbosdik* I feel when I walk away? *Gevalt,* do I feel Shabbos. *Gevalt,* do I know what Shabbos is. "*Ribbono shel Olam,* for your Shabbos, I'll do anything in the world."

At that very moment that I don't pick up that money, I *mamesh* receive the Torah from the deepest depths there is.

THE ORCHARD

EVERYBODY KNOWS THAT THERE IS SUCH A THING as *"pardes,"* an orchard.

"Pardes" stands for *P'shat, Remez, Drosh,* and *Sod,* the simple meaning, the hints, the derived meanings and the secrets.

Our holy Rabbis teach us that in everything there is such a thing as *pardes.* Every word in the Torah, everything I'm doing; everything I'm feeling between me and those around me; there are always those four letters.

What are these four levels?

I'll tell you something very simple. Imagine I walk on the street and a *Yiddele* says to me, "Good morning!"

So the *P'shat* is – good morning.

The *Remez* is – how did it strike me when he said good morning to me? Maybe the *Remez* was that he was *mamesh a Heilige Yid,* or, G-d forbid, what a creep!

A *Remez* is something which is so deep, you say it without saying it; you're saying it when you say something else. I can walk up to someone and say, "Listen, I love you," so the *P'shat* is I love you, but the *Remez* is I can't stand you. It's possible.

But *D'rash* is something else. *D'rash* is what is G-d telling you at this moment. Let's put it this way. Here I'm asking someone for a cup of coffee. The *P'shat* is he gave me the coffee, and the *Remez* is, "I think he is my friend." But now comes the *D'rash*; the *D'rash* is what am I learning from it? What is G-d telling me; what's happening? Something is happening; every second something is happening and this happening is called *D'rash*.

Now there is a passage that says, "*Sod HaShem l'yereiav*" – "G-d is a secret to those who fear him." (*Tehillim* 25:14)

Can I tell somebody what G-d truly means to me? It's a secret. If you tell someone you loved the soup you just had, can you explain the taste to them? Taste is something which is absolutely secret.

If you read a bestseller that explains about knowing G-d, you may get a taste of G-d. It might taste sweet, but there is something so much deeper. I want you to know the deepest depth there is.

Now listen to this. A lot of people know the *P'shat* of the Torah; they know the actual words of the Torah. Some people get the *Remez* of it, and some people get the *Drash*. But when it comes to the *Sod* it's something else. Connecting to the *Sod* of the words means actually tasting the inside of the Torah.

Between people it's so deep. Some people love you, some people understand what you mean without saying it, but how many people taste your soul? Do you know what it means to have a taste of someone else's *neshama*? This is the deepest connection two people can have.

I can keep Shabbos and know what Shabbos means, I can write a book on Shabbos, but I might have never tasted Shabbos in my whole life. You know how many people come to *Yerushalayim*, but never taste *Yerushalayim*? How many people stand by the Holy Wall and never taste the Holy Wall?

I'll tell you something very deep. A lot of people know everything that is going on in our generation, but very few people have tasted our generation. Very few know what's really going on.

We are living in a very deep generation. We need more people to give us courage, to tell us how special we are. If people would tell us how special we are, then maybe we would eventually make it.

The specialness of our generation is that we absolutely want to taste it; we *mamesh* want to taste what G-d is all about. It's not enough for us to know and feel. We want to taste it, we want to have a secret between G-d and ourselves.

I'm sure my grandfather was very holy, but for him it might have been enough to know and understand what Shabbos is. Today we are living in a generation that *mamesh* wants to taste Shabbos.

If you offer someone to put on *tefillin,* and they say, "I want to know the reason first," do you know what they really mean to say? "Please give me a taste of *tefillin.*" They just don't know how to say it. If you ask someone, "Why don't you keep Shabbos?" And they say, "It doesn't turn me on," they are simply trying to say that they want to taste Shabbos and they haven't tasted it yet.

Everybody knows that when *Mashiach* comes, he will reveal *ta'amei hamitzvos* – the reasons for all the Torah's commandments.

What does this mean? *Ta'am* can either mean reason or taste. The sad translation is that he will give us a reason for every mitzvah. Who needs a reason? The reason is that G-d told you. This is not what's bugging us. The deeper translation is that when *Mashiach* is coming he will give us a taste of the mitzvahs. We are so close, we can feel it already, so we are just begging G-d to give us a little taste.

And here I want you to open your hearts in the deepest way.

One way of knowing G-d is by looking at the world and realizing there is a G-d.

Thank G-d! In that respect, our generation is really far advanced. There is hardly anybody left in our generation who would say, "I see the world and I don't believe in G-d." Whoever says this doesn't belong in our generation.

Not everybody who lives today is really part of our generation. Some people are here for unfinished business. They're sweet, they're cute, I love them, but I don't bother with them. They don't turn me on or off because they are really not part of the scene. Anybody today who is part of the scene, really believes in G-d.

There are two ways of knowing about G-d. One way is when I see the world and I see such a beautiful world. The second knowing of G-d is called "*Ma'aseh Merkava*" – "The Workings of the Chariot." *Ma'aseh Merkava* is the way G-d runs the world. The way the "*ba'al ha'agala*" – "wagon driver" controls his horses.

It's a *gevalt,* the way G-d leads the world; the way G-d is leading my own life is the deepest depths there is.

What is the difference between these two ways? Very simple. To know G-d from looking at the world means I'll open my eyes and I see it. I'll sit on the beach and I'll see the sun is going down.

But the way G-d is leading the world is not on the level of seeing; it's on the level of knowing. It's not anything I can point at and show you, it's just on the level of knowing.

This is the difference between knowing G-d by Avraham, Yitzchak, and Ya'akov and Moshe Rabbeinu. Avraham Avinu discovered G-d because he saw the world. He took a look at everything around him and asked, "*Efshar bira be'lo manhig?*" – "Can there be a world without a leader?" (*Bereishis Rabbah* 39:1)

There's got to be somebody who made this world. He saw the world. Moshe Rabbeinu is something else. The way you know G-d from the Torah is much deeper than that.

And here I want you to know something very beautiful. There is a difference between an "Av" and a "Rav." Moshe Rabbeinu is called Rabbeinu, our teacher. Avraham Avinu is called Avinu, our father.

A father is showing his child. A teacher is giving him knowledge.

Avraham Avinu is the one who is showing us. Avraham Avinu is taking every *Yiddele* by the hand and saying, "Look, what a world, what a world, *Ribbono shel Olam*'s world." Every Jewish father and mother should show their children the world.

The *Heilige* Rizhiner said that when he was three years old, his father was still carrying him. "One time, my father took me to the top of a mountain, and we looked down and suddenly it looked to me like it's the end of the world. You look down and you see that heaven goes down to earth, and the land reaches the sky.

So I asked my father if this is the end of the world. My father says to me, "Yisroel'ke, it's not the end of the world because the world is so big, the earth is so big, and heaven is even bigger." But then he says to me, "Yisroel'ke, there's one G-d who created all this."

The Rizhiner says, "I still shiver when I remember the way my father told me there is one G-d who created all this." This is the level of a father showing you, showing you the world.

Learning Torah is knowing G-d on a different level; it's not because I saw something. I know there is one G-d; I know it on a much deeper level. It's like a revelation from heaven.

Between people, it's also very deep. You can look at somebody and love them very much; they are very beautiful, they are very special. So I know them on the level of Avraham. Sometimes I meet somebody and I see something that can't be seen – and it's much deeper than all this.

Somehow, I know. This is on the level of Torah, on the level of revelation. Don't kid yourself, Avraham is also a revelation, no one else saw what he saw.

So you see, both are revelations, but they are different revelations. Avraham Avinu's revelation is on the level of seeing, and Moshe Rabbeinu's is on the level of knowing.

I want you to know something very deep. When it comes to learning

Torah, you can have a Rebbe who shows you the words and translates the words, and then you see the words and you learn them. It's a very high revelation very similar to a father's relationship to his children.

Then there's a Rebbe who shows you the words, but you know something you didn't know before. It's strange, it has to do with the words and it doesn't; it's much deeper than all this . . . so much deeper.

Some people went through something and they saw G-d – it's very beautiful. And some people are privileged in their little life to have a *Toirahdike* revelation, and they *mamesh* know.

So here Moshe Rabbeinu was asking G-d, *"hodieini nah es d'rachecha"* – "please let me know your ways." (Sh'mos 33:13) Don't just show me, let me know. Do you know how deep this is?

Now listen to this. HaShem reveals himself on the highest level to Moshe Rabbeinu, it says, *"u-Sh'mi HaShem lo nodati la-hem."* – "And My name *Yud Keh Vav Keh* is on a level that I did not reveal to them – Avraham, Yitzchak, and Ya'akov." (Sh'mos 6:3)

What *Yud Keh Vav Keh* means is *"Haya Hoveh v'Y'hiyeh"* – "He was, He is and He will be." (*Adon Olam*) *"Mehaveh kol Havayos,"* – "the ultimate cause of all existence." The same G-d who created the world, has always and is still creating the world.

I want you to know something very deep.

There is a level of seeing G-d like Avraham Avinu where I see G-d created the world. But seeing that G-d created the world doesn't necessarily mean that I know how much G-d wants the world to exist. The name *Yud Keh Vav Keh* means that G-d desperately wants the world to be amazing.

I'll tell you something very deep. I can walk up to somebody and tell them, "I love you"; this is like seeing; I see the words, I hear the words. But then there is a person who is *mamesh* desperate to love me or is desperate for me to love them. Knowing this is beyond seeing, it's just a revelation.

This kind of knowing is so deep. This kind of *Yiddishkeit,* knowing G-d on the level of *Yud Keh Vav Keh,* G-d created the world and he wants the world to exist forever: "*Baruch She'amar v'Haya haOlam.*" – "Blessed is He Who spoke and the world came into being." (Daily Siddur: *Pesukei d'Zimra*)

What's the major difference between us *Yidden* and the whole world? The world knows that G-d created the world, but they are not part of this revelation of how desperately G-d wants the world to succeed; how much G-d cares.

What is the reason that we *Yiddelach* can't kill someone? Because when we heard G-d saying to us, "Don't kill," what we really heard was G-d saying, "I want this person to live."

How come some people can kill a cockroach without even thinking about it and some can't?

Because G-d created this little cockroach, and if I know *Yud Keh Vav Keh,* then I know that G-d is desperate for this cockroach to exist; otherwise it wouldn't exist in this world. Can you imagine on G-d's level wanting it to be?

When somebody tells you something, do you know how much they care for what they say? To know how much they care is what "*hodi'eini nah es d'rachecha*" is all about – "Please G-d, let me know your ways." Do you have one person in the world who ever asked you, "Please, reveal to me how much what you just said really means to you."

Imagine I know all the laws of Shabbos, but imagine if I know how much Shabbos means to G-d – not to me, to G-d. Then I wind up celebrating Shabbos because G-d celebrates Shabbos. Imagine if I could have a taste of what G-d felt when he kept Shabbos. *Gevalt,* what a Shabbos!

The Ishbitzer says that on Mount Sinai, when G-d says, "*Zachor es Yom haShabbos l'kadsho*" – "Remember the day of Shabbos to keep it Holy,"

(Sh'mos 20:7) he gave us a taste of how it felt for G-d to keep Shabbos.

The Ten Commandments is to have a taste, a G-d taste, a G-d moment; a different kind of moment. This G-d taste, this PARDES taste, is also knowledge. A different kind of knowledge, not word knowledge.

Why was Moshe Rabbeinu stammering? The answer is so deep. When it came to anything else that didn't have to do with this G-d taste, he couldn't say it. When Moshe Rabbeinu came down from Mount Sinai, he didn't stammer anymore because every word was G-d's word, a different kind of word, a different kind of knowing.

To taste is a gift from G-d. It comes from such a high place – not because you deserve it or because you did something: "*Sod HaShem l'yireiav*" – "The secret of G-d is for those who see." It's a gift from G-d.

ויקהל

VAYAKHEL

ויקהל

This *parsha* is dedicated to:

Rabbi Shlomo Katz,
Nachman Futterman,
Shema Yisrael Witt,
and their families

May they be eternally blessed for their endless efforts in archiving, selecting and publishing Reb Shlomo's Torahs. May they ascend and have success in all their endeavors along with all their holy brothers, sisters and friends.

פרשה זאת מוקדשת ל:

הרב שלמה כ"ץ, נחמן פוטרמן,
שמע ישראל וויט,
ומשפחותיהם

שיזכו לשפע ברכות על מאמציהם הכבירים בשמירה, בחירה והפצה של התורות של ר' שלמה. שיעלו ויצליחו בכל מעשה ידיהם עם כל ישראל אחיהם ואחיותיהם הקדושים.

LET'S TRY AGAIN

And Moses gathered the entire assembly of the children of Israel. (Sh'mos 35:1)

SOME OF US THINK WE CAN GO TO SHUL AND PRAY without feeling close to G-d, but praying without feeling close doesn't work.

The Holy Temple is the headquarters of prayer. Before you build the *Beis HaMikdash,* before you build a house of prayer, you have to be close to G-d.

That's why, when Moshe Rabbeinu gathers the *Yidden,* he first tells them about Shabbos and then about the building of the *Beis Hamikdash. Yidden,* let's have Shabbos, let's get close to G-d again, close to each other, and then we can start davening.

If you pray just for yourself – it's meaningless. Praying has to be *"b'shem kol Yisrael"* – "in the name of all of Israel." The Arizal brought down that before you daven you have to say, *"Hareini mekabel alai es mitzvas haboreh v'ahavta lerei-acha kamocha"* – "I *mamesh* accept upon myself to love every person like myself."

When I go to a grocery store, I don't have to buy groceries for somebody else. When I go shopping in G-d's grocery store, and I only order for myself, G-d says, "I'm sorry, I'm sold out." By G-d, it's only when you shop for somebody else as well.

So here it says *"Vayakhel Moshe es Kol Adas B'nei Yisrael"* – "And Moses gathered the entire assembly of the children of Israel." You must make sure everybody should be close to one another. How could you walk into the *Beis HaMikdash* without praying for somebody else?

SHABBOS AFTER THE GOLDEN CALF

And Moses gathered the tribes of Israel. . . . Six days work may be done, and the seventh day shall be holy for you . . . (Sh'mos 35:1–2)

WHEN MOSHE RABBEINU GATHERS TOGETHER all the *Yidden*, the first thing he tells us about is the mitzvah of Shabbos.

Everyone is asking why didn't Moshe Rabbeinu just tell us about Shabbos in parshas *Ki Sisa*, before the Golden Calf? Why does he have to tell us about Shabbos again in *Vayak-hel*?

The answer cuts right through everything.

Before the Golden Calf, it was enough to have a cute little Shabbos, and make sure you keep all the laws. It was enough to have chicken soup, read the *Jewish Press* and go for a Shabbos walk.

After the Golden Calf, after you fall so low, you need more than that, you need much more than that. After the Golden Calf you need Shabbos beyond this world. You need a Shabbos that can blow your mind.

Let me ask you the deepest depths. When are we longing to have more of something?

Sadly enough, when things are good and I feel established, I don't have vessels to ask for anything more than what I currently think I have. Sometimes we go into orthodox shuls and it's cute and sweet, but what is missing? We are not longing for "more" anymore. We are fine with the way it is, with what we think we have.

When do you long for everything? When you are at the end and there is nothing left.

When did we have vessels for the Holy of Holies? I want you to open your hearts. If we would have not made the Golden Calf, and would have just had the *Beis HaMikdash,* it would have been a sweet *Beis HaMikdash,* but it would not have been a *Kodesh Kodashim*. But because we made the Golden Calf, and years later we built the Holy Temple, there is a Holy of Holies.

You know what it is, after a husband and wife have a little fight, they better become closer, much closer. Only after I made the Golden Calf do I realize, "*Ribbono shel Olam,* holy is not enough for me, I need the holy of holiest." When we are in exile we are praying, "*Ribbono shel Olam,* don't just take me back to *Yerushalayim. U-l'Kodesh Kodashim,* I need to be so much closer, I need to taste the Holy of Holies."

So here Moshe Rabbeinu is gathering all the *Yidden* and saying, "I want you to know, it's time to be so much closer to each other, it's time to be closer to Shabbos, it's time to be much closer to the *Ribbono shel Olam*."

*

Imagine my child is learning piano and I say to them, "You play piano beautifully but I don't know if you will be playing for long, you will be tired of practicing." If you tell this to a child three times, they will never try playing the piano again.

This is what Amalek did to us. As much as we conquered Amalek, the fact that we met him impacted us with such darkness – so much so that when we stood on Mount Sinai we didn't even believe in ourselves anymore. We stood there wondering how long this feeling is going to last.

Here we are coming out of Egypt, feeling so close to G-d, and Amalek says to us, "Hey folks, don't kid yourselves, this high won't last." And sadly enough, it really didn't last; we ended up making the Golden Calf.

Amalek comes and cools you off and says, "Listen to me, you really think you can live beyond the world within this world? You are crazy.

You can have a little Red Sea attack, and then on Yom Kippur you feel really close to G-d. From time to time you can do this, but you cannot live this way for real."

But on Purim I'm wiping out Amalek. I stop wondering how long the deep, real, and exalted me will last. Something changes in me. How does this happen? When is it that Amalek can't touch me?

In the Megillah, Esther says to Mordechai, "Bring all the *Yidden* together" (Esther 4:16) and the Shabbos after Purim we usually read, "*Vayakhel Moshe*" – "Moshe gathered all the *Yidden* together." (Sh'mos 35:1)

Why is Moshe Rabbeinu gathering everyone? Because now is the time to wipe out Amalek; on account of Amalek we made the Golden Calf and the tablets broke.

Amalek says to you, "You have no friends. You are all alone in the world. Nobody cares for you. Your parents don't care for you. Your friends don't care for you. Nobody cares for you. Just you." Cools me off. How do I wipe out Amalek? "*Vayakhel Moshe es kol adas Yisrael*" – "And Moshe gathered the tribes of Israel." You do have friends, you do have people who feel close to you and who believe in you. Just come together again.

WHEN EVERYTHING FITS

The Mishkan, its tent, and its cover. (Sh'mos 35:11)

WHEN YOU LOVE SOMEONE IN PROPORTION, you are constantly measuring if you are good or bad. When I love someone beyond proportion, I blow my mind over every little thing you do.

You might be the worst Jew in the world, but if you tell me that one time in your life you fasted on Yom Kippur . . . I can't believe it, I blow my mind over it.

When a child makes a little drawing, it's sweet but I don't blow my mind over it. When you hear your child making a *b'racha,* is it in proportion or beyond proportion? It blows your mind.

The Holy Temple was destroyed because we only loved each other in proportion. Nothing blew our minds. Do you know why? We forgot how we built the *Mishkan* – our Tabernacle – in the desert.

Why is it that when they built the *Mishkan* everything fit? Hundreds of people were working on the *Mishkan* and suddenly it all got together.

How so? So the Ishbitzer says that the *Yiddele* who was building the *Kodesh Kodashim,* the Holy of Holies, was thinking "*Gevalt,* I wish I would be as holy as the *Yiddele* who was putting nails in the *chatzer,* the courtyard."

The *Yiddele* who was putting nails in the *chatzer* was saying "*Ribbono shel Olam,* I know I don't even deserve the *chatzer,* but *gevalt,* I wish I was as holy as the *Yiddele* who is building the *Kodesh Kodashim.*" Every *Yiddele* was blowing his mind over what the other *Yiddele* was doing.

I want you to open your hearts in the deepest way.

Everyone has something very holy about them, but it's covered, it's hidden. Reb Nosson says that when it came to the building of the *Mishkan,* every *Yiddele* brought this one *nekudah tovah* – good point – that they had. Moshe Rabbeinu took all the *nekudos tovos* – good points – and built the *Mishkan* with it.

How do you put two people together? You don't match up what's wrong with them because what's wrong with me and what's wrong with you will never get together. What needs to happens is that my good part and your good part should connect.

So you see, the *Mishkan* was built from those little things.

*

What's the holy temple all about, what's a house all about? A house means permanent. When I stay in a hotel my feet are there, my hands are there and my head is there but something is missing.

My house is completely mine whether I am there or not. When it comes to my house . . . I can take a trip for five years and come back, it's still my house. The house is the deepest connection, the deepest.

When we made the Golden Calf, the problem was obviously we weren't connected to G-d anymore. We stood on Mount Sinai, received the Torah, but the connection was still not so good. This Shabbos we are building the Holy Temple – the Holy Temple is absolutely the most permanent connection.

So here comes the story. The Rebbe Reb Elimelech dreamt that the Third Temple was being built, and he saw millions of people running around like crazy. So he stopped one of the angels, and said, "You are wasting so much time. If you had fewer people then you wouldn't fall over each other and finish the job faster." So the angel laughed at him and said, "You don't understand Reb Elimelech, G-d wants everybody to take part in rebuilding the *Beis haMikdash.*"

The *Medrash* (*Kohelet Rabbah* I) says that Reb Chanina Ben Dosa wanted to bring something to the Holy Temple. He was very poor, so he took a stone and *mamesh* put a beautiful *tallis* on it, and then he realized that he can't even carry this stone. He was so heartbroken that the Master of the World sent angels to carry the stone for him.

Sometimes we have dreams to do so much, to rebuild the Holy Temple, and we realize that we can't even carry it, but it's not a problem. There will always be some angels to help us.

פקודי

PEKUDEI

פקודי

This *parsha* is dedicated
to the loving memory of:

ISAAC DJEMAL

יצחק ג'מאל בן לאה

May his memory serve as a blessing
for his children,
grandchildren
and great grandchildren.

A VORKER ACCOUNT

These are the reckonings of the Tabernacle. (Sh'mos 38:21)

HERE WE ARE READING *"EILEH PEKUDEI haMishkan"* – "This is the account of the Tabernacle." (Sh'mos 38:21) Moshe Rabbeinu gives us an account. What kind of an account is Moshe Rabbeinu giving?

In the grocery store, I have an account. At the butcher I have an account, in the bank I have an account. With my own wife, my own children, with most people, I don't have an account. For some reason, everything goes. Who cares what they do? I can yell at my children. I can yell at my wife because there is no account. Who cares? They are living with me in the same house.

It is very beautiful to be very close to G-d, but, on the other hand, if you feel so close, you lose the *cheshbon*. Listen, I'm so close to G-d, everything goes, but you know what? It doesn't work like this. The secret of life is to have an account and yet to know that it is much deeper than that.

My connection to the grocery store is just the account. My bank, it's just an account. My wife and children, with G-d, it's not the account, but we should feel as if we do have an account as well.

You know, friends, between husband and wife you see it all the time. They would never talk to a stranger the way they talk to each other. You know why they talk like that to each other? Because they don't have an account. Maybe they should open an account. You wouldn't dare yell at someone else's children. Why do you yell at yours?

Only Moshe Rabbeinu can do this. He opens an account and yet he lets us know, *"b'chol ma'a-seihem"* – "in all their deeds," wherever you travel, whatever you do, G-d is with you.

But here I want to share with you another type of an account, a Vorker account.

One of the greatest *chassidim* of the Holy Vorker was Reb Yankele. This Reb Yankele was very rich in his heart and in his mind, but *nebech*, not so much in his pockets. And another one of his greatest *chassidim* was Reb Moishele; he was not rich and not poor; he had a few rubles.

Reb Yankele has to marry off his daughter. He needs two hundred rubles to make a little wedding for his daughter. He goes to his neighbor, Reb Moishele, and asks a loan for two hundred rubles. "Will you give it back to me?" Reb Moishele asks. "I promise I'll give it back."

Five years later and he hasn't given back the money. He doesn't have it. But Moishele, he's a straight guy, he is big on accounts. Whenever he sees Reb Yankele, he asks, "When are you paying me back?"

Once, late at night, Reb Moishele hears that the Vorker is coming to see Yankele. This is a good time to ask for the two hundred rubles. He knocks on the door and the *Heilige* Vorker opens the door.

"Reb Moishele, so late at night. What brings you here?" Reb Moishele says, "I don't want to say anything bad, I don't want to put anyone to shame, it's just you and me and Reb Yankele. Reb Yankele owes me two hundred rubles for five years and he hasn't paid me back."

The Vorker says, "You are one hundred percent right. He has to pay you back. Reb Yankele, bring me here all the money you have in the house. Every penny you have. Put it on the table." *Nebech*, it was like *"bedikas chametz"* – "searching for bread on the eve of Passover." He's looking for money and he comes back with fifty-seven pennies.

The holy Vorker begins to count. One two, three, four, five. He counts to fifty-seven and then he keeps on counting the same pennies, fifty-eight, fifty-nine, he counted all the way to ten thousand rubles. He took the fifty-seven pennies and he gave them to Moishele. Here, this is yours for giving Yankele two hundred rubles. After a few weeks, Yankele was a multi-millionaire.

You see what this deepest depths is? When you love somebody very much, you take the same penny and count it a thousand times. If you love somebody very much, maybe once in their life they did you a favor, but you count that one good thing they did ten thousand times.

Gevalt, do we need a Vorker account.

KEEPING IT TOGETHER

"It was in the first month of the second year on the first of the month that the Tabernacle was erected." (Sh'mos 40:17)

THE *MEDRASH* (*MIDRASH TANCHUMA* 39:11) SAYS that Moshe Rabbeinu put the tabernacle together and it fell apart every day for a week. Each time it fell apart, the crying was to high heaven. Only at the end of the week did it stay together. Friends, keeping it together is no simple thing, on any level.

How do you know if you *mamesh* have it together? Very simple. If you don't have it together you give up when it falls apart. If you really have it together inside, there is no such thing as giving up.

Take a look at us *Yidden*. How is it that we were away for two thousand years from the Holy Land and we never gave up? Because there is one thing we have together. Maybe we don't have Shabbos together, but the Holy Land is something that nobody can take away from us.

What happens to you when you stand by the Holy Wall in *Yerushalayim*? Maybe you will still eat a hamburger next Yom Kippur, but something inside of you has it together.

But you see what it is, only Moshe Rabbeinu can put it together. Do you know why Moshe Rabbeinu can put the *Mishkan* together? Because "together" is the teaching from heaven, not from this world. It's not from the Tree of Knowledge; it's from the Tree of Life.

Moshe Rabbeinu brought down the *mahn* – "manna," Moshe gave us the Torah, but what is Moshe Rabbeinu really teaching us at the end of the book of redemption? He brings down the Torah of how to get it together.

This is the end of the book of Exodus, because if you don't have it together you are still in exile, you are still a slave.

MAGNETISM

And the Honor of G-d filled the Tabernacle. (Sh'mos 40:35)

THERE ARE TWO TREMENDOUS POWERS IN THE world. There is a power that pulls and brings me closer, and then there is a tremendous power that pushes me away. According to Reb Nachman, the whole world is based on these two forces: pulling towards or pushing away.

The secret of life is to know exactly when to get close and to know exactly when to pull away from something. If you know the secret of magnetism, you are in touch with the deepest core of your soul. But when you know this, you also know exactly when to cut away.

When you do a mitzvah, you are drawing G-d's light into the world. What is it that Moshe Rabbeinu did? *"Ba Moshe Vehoridan La'aretz"* – "Moshe came and lowered them down to the earth." (*Bereishis Rabbah* 19:7)

He went up to Mount Sinai and was drawing G-d's light down into the world. You see what it is, after the experience of Mount Sinai it's not only a question of doing good or doing bad.

When you do good, you are bringing G-d's light into the world, you are adding to the magnetism. Moshe Rabbeinu gave over to us this holy secret of drawing closer to G-d. He also taught us what happens when you do wrong and you are, G-d forbid, pushed away.

Let's go step by step.

When I do somebody wrong and I then apologize, I might be forgiven but I haven't even begun the fixing. In the meantime, the pushing away took place. When you do *t'shuvah,* you apologize to G-d for leading a rotten life.

As much as this is important, do you know what really happened to you? You got away from G-d's magnetism, you got away from G-d's gravity. G-d can forgive you, but the most important thing is to figure out how to get back into the cycle of holy magnetism, into the cycle of drawing G-d back into the world, of being drawn to G-d.

When you really love someone, a tremendous magnetism takes place. Now imagine you still love this person but you don't know what happened, and suddenly there is no magnetism. It's heartbreaking.

Between children and parents – it's so strong. When children are little, a tremendous magnetism is taking place. When they grow older, something changes. It's not that they don't love their parents; they still do, but there is no more magnetism. One way or another there must have been so much pushing going on, and this pushing away took over the relationship.

Now listen to the deepest depths. It is possible to be a servant of G-d and do everything right while never tasting G-d's drawing close to you. It's also possible to not do so much good, but with the few good things I did, I taste this unbelievable closeness.

And here I want you to open your hearts like mad. When somebody calls you by your name, they can call you and it has no effect on you. Or they can call you by your name and your whole soul is turning over and suddenly you're drawn close. It's the deepest depth there is.

This is what the High Priest would do when he pronounced G-d's name on Yom Kippur. He brought down G-d's light into the world again.

When I stand before G-d on Yom Kippur, I admit that "I pushed you off with this, I pushed you off with that." But you see what it is, the High Priest didn't bring down forgiveness; forgiveness is something you can do on your own.

It's this magnetism, this being drawn to each other that Aharon HaKohen reestablishes. Therefore, by Succos I'm so drawn to G-d, I leave my house and I'm building a little tabernacle on the street because I'm just so drawn to G-d. Nothing else matters.

The headquarters for this drawing close is *Yerushalayim,* the Holy City. After two thousand years of not being there, *Yerushalayim* drew us back, which is not to be believed.

Now open your hearts like mad, and let this really sink in.

Reb Nachman says like this: The laws of gravity are so powerful. When you throw something up in the air, for a few moments you are defying gravity, but the moment this power of defying gravity ends, it comes right back to the earth, which is the utmost of G-d's gravity.

So Reb Nachman explains that this happens because the earth is so humble. You can walk on the earth because of its humility.

Take it on a very simple level. Who are the most un-magnetic people? Arrogant people.

The more arrogant a person is, the more he's pushing you off, because arrogance is absolutely the opposite of G-d's gravity. The more humble you are, the more you are like the earth and the earth is a vessel for G-d's gravity. Therefore, Reb Nachman says, the real holy people of the world, the *tzaddikim,* they are the earth people, they are G-d's gravity people.

So you see what it is, when a person feels himself pushed away from G-d, eventually he will come back because the pushing away is always temporary, like throwing something up into the air. The pushing off is just for a little bit, but the eternity of all eternities is G-d's gravity. So therefore, all those people who are pushed away eventually have got to come back.

Now the tabernacle is called a "*Mishkan.*" Reb Nachman explains that *Mishkan* comes from the world "*mashcheini*" – "to draw near."

Do you know what Moshe Rabbeinu realized? Even though he had gone up to receive the Torah, we *Yidden* were still capable of making a Golden Calf. He realized we had not entered yet into G-d's gravity.

If you can love somebody, and the next day walk away from them, that doesn't mean you don't love them; it just means you are not that close yet. The closer you get – the stronger the magnetism gets. Therefore, Reb Nachman says, only Moshe Rabbeinu could put up the holy tabernacle because the tabernacle is the headquarters for G-d's gravity, for this holy drawing which takes place in this world.

Moshe Rabbeinu, who was on the level of earth, and was the most humble person of all, he is the one who is able to draw G-d into the world.

At the end of the book of Exodus it says, *"u-ch'vod HaShem milei es haMishkan"* – "G-d's glory filled the tabernacle." (Sh'mos 40:35)

You know what that means? Honoring G-d is by being absolutely drawn to G-d. What does it mean to honor someone? It means to tell this person, "I'm drawn to you."

How do you know if you are really honoring someone? Very simple. Honor is something which must grow. The more you honor someone, the more you are drawn to them.

How do I honor G-d? If I am drawn to G-d today the way I was drawn yesterday it's dead, simply because magnetism is something which always grows.

Rabbi Shlomo Carlebach was born in Berlin, Germany in 1925. He grew up with his twin brother, Eli Chaim and his sister, Shulamith near Vienna where his father, Rabbi Naftali was Chief Rabbi. In 1939, as the war began to escalate and the Nazis' grip tightened, Shlomo and his family miraculously escaped to New York where he spent time learning by some of the greatest Torah scholars of the last century, such as Rabbi Ahron Kotler, Rabbi Shlomo Heiman and the Lubavitcher Rebbe. Even as a young boy, Shlomo's vision and clarity of thought always set him apart from his peers as being amongst the most brilliant of the scholars around him. Through that vision, courage, and a deep love of all people, Shlomo took on a mission and set off on a path that many didn't believe in.

Reb Shlomo believed that to uplift, inspire, and bring joy to every human being was truly his reason for existing. Through his words of Torah, his music and his stories, Reb Shlomo touched the hearts and souls of all who were blessed to hear him. He sought to remind people that they are never alone, that there is one God who loves them, and that every person has a unique and important mission to discover for themselves. He was able to mend the spirits and lives of the most broken, distraught people worldwide – people of all faiths and cultures. Much of Reb Shlomo's life was spent traveling the world where he would sing with the poor, the lost and the lonely, and always swear he learned from them.

Even now, since his passing in 1994, hundreds of thousands of lives are changed by Reb Shlomo's teachings, messages and melodies.